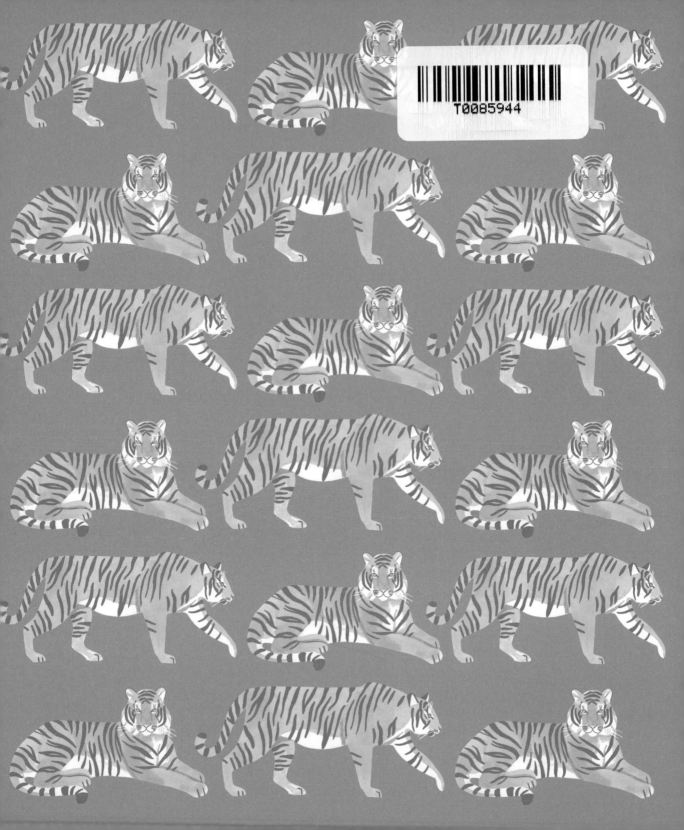

# YOUNG ZOOLOGIST
# TIGER

## A FIRST FIELD GUIDE TO THE
## BIG CAT WITH THE STRIPES

NEON  SQUID

# CONTENTS

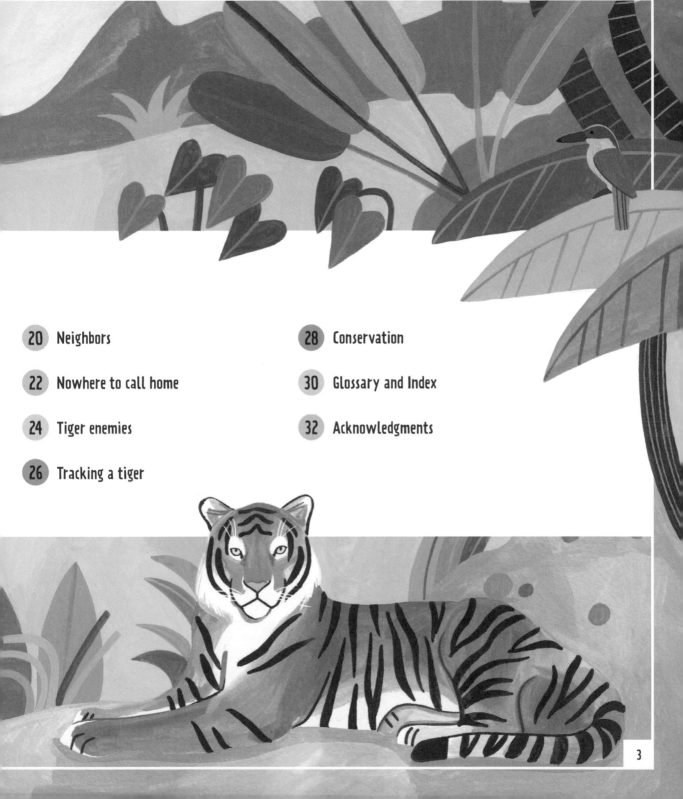

# HELLO, YOUNG ZOOLOGIST!

My name is Samantha Helle and I'm a conservation biologist who studies the biggest of the big cats: the tiger! This iconic striped cat is a favorite for many, and I'm thrilled that I get to be your guide in this book. Despite being so well-loved, there are less than 4,000 wild tigers left in the world. Tigers play a key role in managing and keeping balance in the ecosystems they live in. That means that losing them would be devastating. So come take a prowl with me in the jungles of Asia to learn more about tigers and what we can do to save them from extinction!

SAMANTHA HELLE

# FACT FILE

## SCIENTIFIC NAME
*Panthera tigris*

## CLASS
Mammal

## FAMILY
Felidae (cats)

## SUBFAMILY
Pantherinae (which includes jaguars, leopards, lions, tigers, snow leopards, and clouded leopards)

## EATS
Tigers are carnivores, which means they only eat meat. They primarily hunt large deer called chital, sambar, gaur, and wild boar.

Sambar

Gaur

Chital

Wild boar

## WEIGHT
Males: 440–600 lb (200–270 kg)
Females: 240–400 lb (110–180 kg)

Male

Female

## STATUS
Endangered

## WHERE THEY LIVE
Thailand, Nepal, India, Indonesia, Russia, China, Bhutan, Bangladesh, Cambodia, Laos, Vietnam, Malaysia, and Myanmar

## LIFESPAN
Average is 8–10 years, but they can live to 15.

## NAME
In Hindi and Nepali, the word *bagh* means tiger. *Bagh* is derived from the ancient Sanskrit word *vyaghra*, meaning "the one who tracks by smell."

# BEFORE YOU GET STARTED

Scientists do a "tiger test walk" in front of cameras to make sure they are placed at the right height on a tree.

**① CAMERA TRAP**

Camera traps are one of the most widely used tools in wildlife conservation work. They allow us to monitor tigers through photos and videos without ever having to touch or disturb them.

**② RADIO COLLAR**

If you are interested in where tigers move or which habitat they prefer, you can put a radio collar on a tiger. These collars have a GPS unit in them that allows us to track tigers using satellites in space.

**③ GPS UNIT**

As well as using GPS to help us track tigers, scientists can carry a GPS unit with them. They use this tool to navigate the thick jungle and mark on a digital map where they find tiger tracks and scat (poop).

Before we head into the wild, you'll need to pack a few things. Conditions in the field are often hot, rainy, and muddy—and you'll have to watch out for biting insects! Here are a few things we'll take with us on our adventure studying our big furry friends.

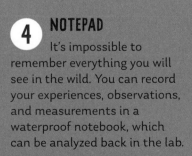

6

5

You can collect tiger DNA from scat, blood, skin, and hair samples.

**4  NOTEPAD**

It's impossible to remember everything you will see in the wild. You can record your experiences, observations, and measurements in a waterproof notebook, which can be analyzed back in the lab.

**5  JUNGLE CLOTHING**

A hat, long-sleeved shirt, pants, and some sturdy boots are necessary to protect you from thorny bushes, the hot sun, and bloodsucking leeches!

**6  SCAT COLLECTION KIT**

Get your test tubes and gloves ready, it's time to collect some poop! You can analyze a tiger scat sample to learn more about tiger population health, as well as individual tigers and their diet.

# MEET THE TIGER

## STRIPED FUR

Why do tigers have stripes? This type of camouflage is called disruptive coloration. It breaks up the outline of a tiger's body, making it difficult for prey to see where the tiger's body starts and ends!

**Tigers are the biggest wildcat in the world.**

## EXCELLENT EYESIGHT

Large, golden eyes at the front of a tiger's head are used for stalking (sneaking up on) prey. Tigers also have excellent night vision and can see six times better than humans in the dark.

## SENSITIVE WHISKERS

Ultra-sensitive whiskers help tigers to hunt, navigate in the dark, and detect other animals.

## LARGE PAWS

Big, furry paws have retractable claws 4 in (10 cm) long. These paws are used to grab prey, tear flesh, mark territory, and battle other tigers.

What do you think of when you think of a tiger? Maybe orange fur and black stripes? You'd be right, but that's just the tip of the iceberg. Tigers have loads of amazing features that they use to hunt large prey. Let's take a look!

## FAKE EYES

Tigers have white spots on the back of their ears. These look like eyes to spook any animals brave enough to approach them from behind!

## LONG TAIL

A tiger's tail is up to 3 ft (1 m) long. It is used to help the tiger keep balance when it is prowling through the jungle.

## SHARP TEETH

Razor-sharp teeth help these carnivores tear flesh with ease. Tigers have longer canine teeth than any other big cat.

## SPRING-LOADED LEGS

Long back legs allow tigers to leap 33 ft (10 m) in one jump!

# THE FAMILY

### SOUTH CHINA TIGER

Compared to the famous Bengal tiger (see below), South China tigers have a lighter, more yellow coat with narrow black stripes. Believed to be extinct in the wild, a few individuals remain in conservation facilities.

### BENGAL TIGER

Bengal tigers are the largest of the tiger subspecies. They live in India, Nepal, Bangladesh, and Bhutan, and are occasionally sighted in Tibet.

### SUMATRAN TIGER

Sumatran tigers are the only remaining island species of tiger left in the world and are the smallest subspecies. They have a large beard called a ruff.

Fossil records show that the first tigers started evolving more than two million years ago. Some tigers have gone extinct, but there are six living subspecies of tigers that vary in size and color. Let's say hello to the family!

## MALAYAN TIGER

Critically endangered, there are only an estimated 80–120 Malayan tigers left in the wild.

## INDOCHINESE TIGER

These tigers have narrow faces and dark orange fur. They roam Southeast Asia, and more than half of them live in Thailand's Western Forest Complex.

## SIBERIAN TIGER

Many people mistakenly think Siberian tigers are white, but they are orange and black like other tigers! They have long, fluffy fur to keep them warm in eastern Russia.

# DIFFERENT HABITATS

## GRASSLANDS

Tigers love grasslands, especially when they're hunting. Their dark stripes blend in with tall grass and their reddish-orange fur is nearly impossible to see during sunrise and sunset.

## MANGROVES

Did you know tigers are great swimmers? In these coastal wetlands, tigers have to navigate river systems and mudflats that change with the tide.

A habitat is an area an animal lives in that has all of the resources—like food and water—that it needs to survive. Tigers have adapted to thrive in an amazing range of different habitats across Asia. Some of them might surprise you...

## SNOWY FORESTS

Tigers in the snow? You better believe it! Siberian tigers live in the birch and pine forests of eastern Russia and parts of northern China.

**Most of the world's tigers are found in the forests and grasslands of South Asia.**

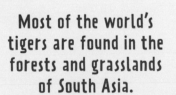

## TROPICAL FORESTS

Tigers can often be found in lush tropical forests. A variety of ferns, shrubs, and trees provide shade and cover for tigers and other wildlife.

## MOUNTAINS

Studies in the mountains of Bhutan have recorded tigers dwelling at altitudes over 13,000 ft (4,000 m).

# APEX PREDATORS

## A WORLD WITH TIGERS

Tigers are top of the food pyramid. Below them sit herbivores—animals that only eat plants. Tigers help to keep herbivore populations balanced by hunting and eating them.

Deer and other herbivores feed on grasses, shrubs, leaves, and buds.

Herbivores help to control the growth of plants and trees, keeping forests healthy. Healthy forests are important for providing habitat for other wildlife, and keeping rivers and lakes clean.

Every habitat has what is called a food pyramid. At the top of the food pyramid sits the apex predator, who isn't hunted by other animals. Tigers are apex predators, and this means they play a really important role in their ecosystem.

## A WORLD WITHOUT TIGERS

Without tigers, entire ecosystems collapse from the top down. The loss of an apex predator leads to large herbivore populations.

With no tigers hunting them, herbivore populations grow and grow. But, this also means they will eat and eat, destroying the forests around them. It just shows how important tigers are!

# GROWING UP

## 1 PREGNANCY

Females start breeding at three to four years of age and are pregnant for about 100 days. Before giving birth to up to five cubs, the mother tiger will find a sheltered spot to create a den.

**Tigers learn everything from their mums—from hunting to territory marking!**

## 2 NEWBORNS

Cubs are born blind, with woolly striped fur that helps them to hide among thick vegetation. They remain in the den and drink milk from their mother.

## 3 YOUNG CUBS

After two months, cubs start making short trips outside the den with their mother to explore her territory. They do a lot of playing! The mother will sometimes carry them by the scruff of their necks.

Like many big cats, tigers spend most of their life alone. Males and females only come together to breed, and females raise their cubs alone. The young will stay with their mother for up to two years, and there's never a dull moment!

**4** ### DINNER IS SERVED
Mum does all the hunting until her cubs are big enough to hunt for themselves.

**5** ### GETTING BRAVER
As they grow bigger, the cubs will make short trips away from their mum to hunt and explore. Once they start outgrowing their mother, she will slowly encourage them to leave her territory.

**6** ### TIME TO LEAVE
At the age of two it's finally time for the young tigers to leave and establish their own territories! They reach full maturity when they are three or four years old.

# THAT'S MY TERRITORY!

## MALES AND FEMALES

Male territories are a lot bigger than female territories, and often contain the territories of two or three females. The male will breed with all of the females in his territory.

**Special glands between a tiger's toes leave behind their scent when they're scratching trees.**

## SCENT MARKING

Tigers leave chemical scents around their territory to communicate with other tigers. They do this using special scent glands or by spraying pee. You might have seen house cats doing something similar!

Tigers are very territorial animals. They spend a good part of their day marking the boundaries of their territory to let other tigers know: *this area is mine!* A tiger's territory can stretch over an area bigger than New York City!

Tigers mark the boundaries of their territory by making long scrapes on the ground.

Tiger pee is really sticky, which enables it to stay on trees.

## SCENT READING

To read a scent, a tiger will scrunch up their face and open their mouth. This exposes a scent-reading organ that can tell if the marking was from a male or female tiger, and if that tiger is ready to breed!

Your turn: scrunch your face and stick out your tongue like a tiger!

## GREAT HORNBILL

This large, colorful bird's scientific name (*Buceros bicornis*) means "two-horned." These birds get all of the water they need from the fruit they eat.

# NEIGHBORS

Tigers have quite a few neighbors, both big and small. By protecting tiger habitats, we're also protecting many other animal species. Let's meet some of them!

## SLOTH BEAR

Named for their slow-moving habits, these black bears use their thick claws to feed on fruits, ants, and termites.

## LEOPARD

Leopards can adapt to many habitats and are expert tree climbers. After a hunt, they will drag their kill up a tree to hide it from other predators.

## DHOLE

These endangered wild-dogs travel in family packs and are fierce hunters. They can take down prey five times their size!

Many animals rely on a chital's alarm call to alert them when a tiger is present.

## CHITAL

These deer are an important prey species for tigers, making up 45 percent of their diet. Chitals live in large herds of up to 100 individuals.

## ONE-HORNED RHINOCEROS

This endangered rhino is an "ecosystem engineer"—its grazing habits shape grasslands and benefit many other wildlife species.

# NOWHERE TO CALL HOME

## HABITAT LOSS

Tiger habitat continues to be destroyed or fragmented (broken up into small pieces). This is due to growing human populations, road-building, farming, and demand for resources such as timber and palm oil.

In the last 100 years, tigers have disappeared from 95 percent of their historic range. The main reason? The loss of their habitat due to human behavior. This means that tigers are increasingly coming into contact with humans, which isn't good for tigers or humans.

## COMING INTO CONFLICT

As tiger habitat shrinks and their natural prey disappears, sometimes out of desperation tigers kill farm animals. This creates conflict with farmers, who lose money as a result.

## A DANGEROUS ANIMAL?

Living near a large carnivore like a tiger is not always easy for people. Tigers are normally shy and secretive animals, but they sometimes attack people if they get too close.

# TIGER ENEMIES

## POACHERS

Large, international crime groups work together to hire local people to poach tigers. A reported 150 tigers are poached each year.

## ILLEGAL MARKETS

Every part of a tiger has been found in illegal wildlife markets, including skin, bones, teeth, claws, and whiskers. Tiger skins sell for more than $100,000 on the black market.

Teeth

Tiger skin

Claws

The illegal hunting of wild animals is called poaching, and it presents a huge threat to tigers. Some people have the false belief that eating tiger parts can cure illnesses, while others think tiger furs make them look rich and impressive.

Poachers often use snares, poison, and guns to hunt tigers.

## TIGER FARMS

There are more tigers in captivity than in the wild. Tiger farms and illegal zoos breed tigers. These animals are kept in horrible conditions, often just so that people can take photos with them. Such places encourage the demand for tiger parts, and as a result wild tigers continue to get poached.

# TRACKING A TIGER

The stripes on one side of a tiger aren't always the same as on the other side.

## TIGER TRAILS

The best places to look for tigers are along forest paths, or near ponds, rivers, or streams. Like a human fingerprint, each tiger has their own unique stripe pattern. To photograph the pattern from both sides, scientists place two camera traps on trees across from one another.

While some people want to do tigers harm, tiger scientists are working hard to learn more about this species so we can better protect them. But how easy is it to find a tiger? And how can you identify an individual tiger once you've found it?

Camera traps take photos or videos when they detect movement.

Tigers like to take easy walking paths, just like humans do!

## PAWS FOR THOUGHT

Scientists can also use tiger tracks, or "pugmarks," to find tigers. You can tell the sex of a tiger from the shape of their tracks.

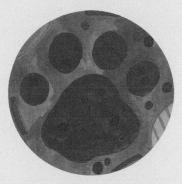

Male pugmarks are large and wide, with lots of space between very round toes. You will not see any claw marks, because tigers have retractable claws.

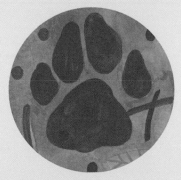

Female pugmarks are smaller than male pugmarks, and have little space between long, teardrop-shaped toes.

# CONSERVATION

## WE'RE ALL IN THIS TOGETHER

Including local communities in tiger conservation is the key to reducing poaching, restoring habitats, and creating local support for conservation projects. Increasingly people are keen to pay money to see tigers in the wild. The money made from this ecotourism must benefit the people who live near the big cats, too.

Forest management by local people has helped to maintain and increase tiger habitat. Both local people and tigers benefit from this practice.

## TELL THE WORLD!

We must continue to urge governments to stop the sale of tiger parts. You can help, too! Tell your friends and family about the threats wild tigers face.

**SAVE THE TIGERS!**

We've learned a lot about tigers and the threats they face as an endangered species. But there is hope! There are many people around the world working hard to save these majestic cats from extinction. Will you join them?

## WILDLIFE RANGERS

Every day wildlife rangers face very difficult working conditions and risk their lives to protect tigers from poachers. Supporting rangers helps to save tigers and their habitat.

## CAMERA TRAPS

Scientists will continue using cameras to identify tigers and keep track of their population numbers. This is crucial to help us understand if our conservation efforts are working.

## RADIO COLLARS

Placing radio collars on tigers that live close to people can help prevent conflict. It's also useful for scientists to research how tigers are moving and adapting to changing landscapes. This way, we can adapt our conservation efforts so they work more effectively.

# GLOSSARY

**Breeding**
The reproduction process of animals or plants to produce offspring (babies).

**Camouflage**
Colors or patterns that make an animal difficult to see.

**Carnivore**
An animal that only eats meat.

**Conservation**
The protection of wildlife species, their habitats, and ecosystems.

**Ecosystem**
An area where animals, plants, and the physical environment are linked and interact with one another.

**Ecosystem engineer**
A species that significantly impacts other species in the same ecosystem by changing, maintaining, or creating habitat.

**Endangered species**
A species of animal or plant that is at high risk of extinction (dying out).

**Extinction**
The complete loss of a species.

**Food pyramid**
A way of organizing food relationships in an ecosystem where predators are at the top and plants are at the bottom.

**Habitat**
A place that has all of the necessities (food, water, shelter) an animal needs to make its home.

**Herbivore**
An animal that only eats plants.

**Poaching**
The illegal hunting of wildlife.

**Predator**
An animal that hunts other animals.

**Prey**
An animal that is hunted by a predator.

**Pugmark**
A special name for a tiger paw print. "Pug" means foot in Hindi.

**Retractable claws**
Claws that can be extended and then drawn back into a special sheath in the toes.

**Subspecies**
Members of the same species that may look alike but are genetically different from one another.

**Territory**
An area that is defended by an animal for the purpose of mating, raising young, and feeding or hunting.

# INDEX

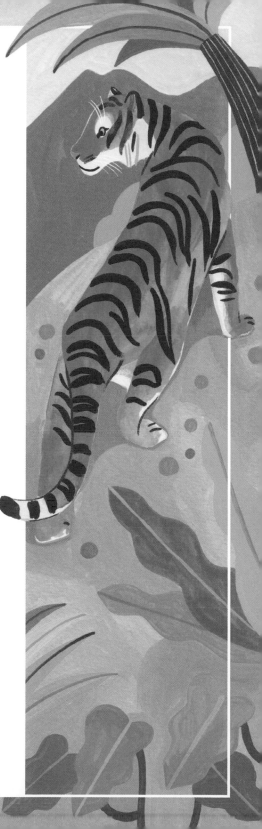

This has been a

# NEON SQUID

## production

*For my nieces, Poppy and Olive. May you never stop exploring and experiencing the limitless adventures of our big beautiful planet.*

**Author:** Samantha Helle
**Illustrator:** Sally Agar

**Designer:** Amy Child
**Editorial Assistant:** Malu Rocha
**US Editor:** Jill Freshney
**Proofreader:** Laura Gilbert

Copyright © 2024
St. Martin's Press
120 Broadway, New York,
NY 10271

Created for St. Martin's Press
by Neon Squid
The Stables, 4 Crinan Street,
London, N1 9XW

EU representative: Macmillan
Publishers Ireland Ltd,
1st Floor, The Liffey Trust Centre,
117–126 Sheriff Street Upper,
Dublin 1, D01 YC43

10 9 8 7 6 5 4 3 2 1

Library of Congress Cataloging-in-Publication Data is available.

Printed and bound in Guangdong, China by Leo Paper Products Ltd.

ISBN: 978-1-684-49359-3

Published in January 2024.

www.neonsquidbooks.com

**From David:** I dedicate this book to our beautiful daughter, Kristy Schooler Matheson, who has picked up the mantle of compassionate care through her work with hospice and her preparation to become a clinical counselor.

**From Jayne:** I dedicate this book to a dear friend and mentor, Judy Rycus. No words can adequately describe Judy's worldwide impact on child welfare through writing, training, and equipping. She has spoken into my life in many ways—challenging, encouraging, and believing in me. Thank you, Judy.

# THE GENDER IDENTITY GUIDE
## FOR PARENTS

# THE
# GENDER IDENTITY GUIDE
## FOR PARENTS

Compassionate Advice
to Help Your Child Be
Their Most Authentic Self

Tavi Hawn, LCSW

ROCKRIDGE
PRESS

Copyright © 2021 by Rockridge Press

All rights reserved. No part of this publication may be reproduced, stored in a retrieval system, or transmitted in any form or by any means, electronic, mechanical, photocopying, recording, scanning, or otherwise, without the prior written permission of the Publisher. Requests to the Publisher for permission should be addressed to the Permissions Department, Rockridge Press, 1955 Broadway, Suite 400, Oakland, CA 94612.

First Rockridge Press trade paperback edition 2021

Rockridge Press and the Rockridge Press logo are trademarks or registered trademarks of Callisto Media Inc. and/or its affiliates in the United States and other countries and may not be used without written permission.

For general information on our other products and services, please contact our Customer Care Department within the United States at (866) 744-2665, or outside the United States at (510) 253-0500.

Paperback ISBN: 978-1-63807-002-3 | eBook ISBN: 978-1-63807-140-2

Manufactured in the United States of America

Interior and Cover Designer: Alan Carr
Art Producer: Megan Baggott
Editor: Nora Spiegel
Production Editor: Matthew Burnett
Production Manager: Eric Pier-Hocking

Illustrations © 2021 Shutterstock.
Author photograph courtesy of Chris Jay Photography.

10 9 8 7 6 5 4 3 2 1

*To Waya Lekan Zinnia Hawn:*
*May you always be free*
*to be you, little wolf!*

# CONTENTS

## PART III: GENDER-AFFIRMING PARENTING STRATEGIES                 61

## PART IV: FREQUENTLY ASKED QUESTIONS, ANSWERED                  107

# INTRODUCTION

Hello, and thank you for picking up *The Gender Identity Guide for Parents*! Maybe you're reading this book because you want to provide a nurturing place for your child to grow into their own gender identity. Maybe you chose this book because you have a kid who might be gender expansive and you want support as you learn what that means and how to navigate social situations. Maybe you know your child is transgender and you want to be affirming. Or maybe you're a therapist, healer, or educator who's reading this to be better able to support the families you work with or to ensure that you have a vetted resource to share with them.

This topic might seem overwhelming and even scary at times. That's okay. This book was written with the goal of meeting people where they are and taking things at a manageable and digestible pace. The book is for all parents and caregivers, whether your child is cisgender, gender expansive, or transgender, or if you're not sure of their gender identity right now.

While some of the concepts in the book will be helpful to people raising kids of any age, most of the content focuses on children who haven't hit puberty yet. You can find some resources for teens in the Resources section on page 135.

Gender identity is a person's true, felt sense of their own gender. This is independent of body parts or any outward presentation. Our gender identity is one aspect of what makes us our full, whole selves. It's important to honor and affirm someone's gender identity, since it is a piece of what makes them who they are. It can cause hurt and a range of problems when a person's gender identity isn't honored, respected, and affirmed. I know none of us wants anybody to feel that way, which is why you picked up this book!

I'm a therapist and national consultant who has worked with many families and kids, as well as other providers and educators who are serving kids and families. I've been able to bring my lived experience to the work, as a Native person who uses the words "transgender," "nonbinary," and "Two Spirit" to describe my gender identity. In the past, I've used the term "genderqueer" to describe my gender identity. I give this example to show that the ways we understand or talk about our gender can grow and change over time. For me, that term wasn't the "wrong" word for my gender, but I use others now that are a better fit. It's been an honor and a joy to support families and gender-expansive children and youth on the journey of gender identity development that's unique to each person. In this book, I'll share concepts, viewpoints, strategies, and practice exercises that have helped the folks I've worked with over the years. As a parent myself, it's become even more clear to me how needed this information is for caregivers who are striving to parent in supportive ways.

This book is written in a way that builds on each chapter, but also in a way that allows you to skip around to parts you're interested in and revisit sections you've already read. In chapter 1, I'll cover some foundational concepts and terms, such as "gender expansiveness." You may already be familiar with the content (although it's always good to have a refresher) or it may be new to you. I'll introduce several gender identities, and discuss gender roles and gender dysphoria. Chapter 2 covers gender identity

development and the difference between identity and expression. You'll gain some ideas for embracing your child's authentic self and being a gender-affirming parent. Part II of the book introduces broad parenting concepts, approaches, and strategies. It invites us to identify what beliefs and experiences we might bring to the table. This section will help us think about the kind of parent or caregiver we want to be and practical ways to practice those behaviors. Part III delves into strategies related to affirming gender identity and expression, such as what questions to ask and how to follow your child's lead. You'll get tips on how to create an affirming home environment, suggestions on how to prepare for puberty, and instruction on what to consider if your child is going to socially transition. Part IV reviews frequently asked questions by parents of kids and teens. Those questions address some topics that might not have been covered or discussed in depth in the book up to that point, including some things regarding older youth. Part IV also provides resources and references.

There are different opinions on capitalizing "trans," "intersex," and related terms, and I acknowledge and understand the various views. I've decided for this book to use lower case in accordance with current recommendations of the Radical Copyeditor because transgender/trans is not always an identity, and not usually a specific gender.

My hope is that this book encourages you, builds your confidence, gives you new ideas, and supports your commitment to affirm whoever your child says that they are, because these things benefit our kids. It might not answer all your questions or meet everybody's needs, but it will be a stepping-stone for further reading, conversations, and research for you in the future. Enjoy the journey!

# PART I

# Covering the Basics

In this first part of the book, we'll be reviewing gender identity, gender roles, terminology, gender identity development, gender expression, and how to embrace authenticity. Just a few little things, right?! Don't worry, we'll take things slow and build onto the concepts as we go.

You may already be familiar with the foundational content; that's okay. I believe that even if we're gender expansive or transgender ourselves, it's good to make sure we're really rooted in these ideas and continuing our own path of "unlearning" (releasing mainstream dominant cultural ideas or values that have been placed on us).

# 1

# Gender Identity 101

Tis chapter provides an overview of foundational concepts related to gender identity. We'll review the difference between gender identity and assigned sex or gender, take a look at gender roles, go over a few gender identities, and define gender dysphoria. The history of multiple genders around the world is rich, and I encourage you to do further research on your own about these histories.

# Understanding Gender Identity

Not everyone has had equal exposure to certain terms or ideas, and because we are all in the process of recognizing predominant social messaging about gender and sex, it can take several exposures of reading or hearing these concepts to really absorb them. You might want to reread this section a few times, and that's okay!

*Gender identity* is a person's true, internal, felt sense of gender. This is independent of any body parts or outward appearance. *Gender expression* is the many ways that a person might outwardly or socially express their gender identity. This may or may not include things like one's name, pronouns, hairstyle, use of makeup, accessories, clothing style, and mannerisms. The *gender spectrum* refers to the myriad of gender identities that exist. In separating these out, it can help to start with yourself. What's your gender identity? What are the ways you express your gender?

In our current mainstream society, babies are assigned a gender based on whatever their perceived "sex" is (i.e., the appearance of their genitals). Because of this, gender and sex are conflated based on this assignment, and mainstream society is organized around the sex and gender being either male or female. But there are not just two "sexes" in terms of what we consider "sex." This societal binary ignores the existence and recognition of people with intersex traits. There are more than 24 known intersex traits at the time of this writing, some involving chromosomal or hormonal makeup, some involving reproductive organs, and some involving genitals. These are naturally occurring traits that are also found in animals and plants. Rather than being an anomaly, we accept that there are more than two categories of sex characteristics. To be clear, trans identities do not come from being intersex. But if you can accept that we have evidence that binarism isn't the rule in physical biology, then we

can accept that gender identity isn't binary or dependent on physical appearance or characteristics, either. Because mainstream society also tends to equate sex and gender, babies are usually assumed to have a gender that is associated with their assigned sex. One of the main things this book asks of us is to question these very concepts: that there are only two sexes and only two genders *and* that we can assume what a child's gender will be based on an ultrasound anatomy scan (before birth) or a visual scan by an ob-gyn or midwife at birth. If this is the first time you're being introduced to this information, go ahead and let yourself breathe. Put the book down and give yourself time to take this in.

We also know that, historically, many cultures around the world did not, or do not, view gender as connected to genitals or body parts. Instead, gender is connected to essence or energy, or a child embodies the spirit of an ancestor and carries that gender, or the child is understood to be the one to share their gender identity when they are aware of it. Most of these cultures also had, or have, a recognition of multiple genders, and sometimes those who were of a third or fourth gender held sacred roles or highly valued positions with the community.

Sexual orientation relates to romantic or sexual attraction. It's important to know that a person of any gender identity can have any sexual orientation. For example, a trans woman could be lesbian, straight, pansexual, asexual, or any other sexual orientation. What's your sexual orientation? When did you know what your sexual orientation was?

## The Role of Gender Roles

Gender roles are the ways that a society expects a person of an assigned sex or gender to look, act, and show interest in certain things. Gender roles are not universal; they are connected to culture, place, and time.

From the 1800s to the 1950s, in the United States and Europe there was strong messaging in the media and from public figures and scholars promoting an increased distinction in appearance between men and women. This was also tied to an effort to further differentiate white people from Black, Indigenous, and other people of color. This effort included attempts to impose gender roles that originated with European Puritan beliefs. Prior to this time period, these roles and gender beliefs had been imposed on enslaved African and Indigenous peoples in often violent ways. It's important to recognize that some cultural and ethnic groups in the United States were able to maintain their traditional views of gender and gender roles in spite of this and everyone in the same country does not experience gender roles in the same way.

These stereotypes were expanded in the 1940s when toy manufacturers realized that they could get families to purchase two different sets of toys if they marketed them specifically for "boys" or "girls." They did this using the colors of blue and pink. They also designated certain toys for boys associated with traits that were stereotypically associated with boys: physical activity, competition, aggression, engineering, building cognitive ability, etc. This resulted in toys like sports equipment, cars, trucks, rescue vehicles, action figures, toy guns, blocks, and science kits marketed as "boy" toys. Girls were expected to spend childhood learning to care for children and other adults, learning beauty techniques, and practicing being pretty. This led to toys such as dolls (Barbies, princesses, baby dolls, paper dolls); stuffed animals; dress-up clothes featuring nurse's uniforms, tutus, and fairy wands; and crafting kits marketed as "girl" toys.

Current research shows that, since the 1950s, women have greatly increased entry into higher education and the labor force, but this increase has not led to wages equal to men or positions of authority in many cases, especially for women of color. And there is still an inequity in division of labor inside the home. This means that the stereotype that girls and women are "naturally

better at" or "more responsible for" childcare and housework remains today. The stereotype that men should not be interested in childcare or specific types of household chores might also remain.

What examples of these things that you've experienced come to mind?

The degree to which these stereotypes are reinforced in most facets of mainstream society is staggering. You just have to go down a toy aisle or children's clothing aisle, visit a preschool or elementary school, or watch children's television programming (and most adult TV for that matter) to be exposed to messages about what a boy is, what a girl is, how they look, and the things they like. With all this messaging, it's not hard to understand how very difficult it is for children to go against the grain. If children are not regularly exposed to a variety of gender roles, gender expressions, and gender identities, how will they really know what options might exist for them?

Socialization doesn't determine a person's gender identity (remember, that is internal); it just might make it harder or easier to realize and understand your own gender identity.

## What Does It Mean to Be "Gender Expansive"?

Gender expansive is an umbrella term for people who expand understandings of gender expression, roles, and identities outside of stereotypical or social norms. Gender-expansive people are not necessarily transgender. Transgender (or trans) is an umbrella term for a person whose assigned sex at birth does not match their gender identity (i.e., deeply held sense of gender). Some people underneath the trans umbrella may not use the word "transgender" to describe their gender identity. For example, they might instead use "genderfluid," "genderqueer," or "nonbinary." Some people may use culturally specific terms instead of "transgender" to

acknowledge that their identities cannot be separated—for example, "winkte" (Lakota), "mahu" (Native Hawaiian and Tahitian), "Two Spirit" (Native American), "kothi" (Indian), "tchinda" (Cape Verde). People should be able to use culturally relevant words for themselves, and culturally specific terms are not for use by people outside of that culture. Other people may use the phrase "woman of trans experience" or "man of trans experience" to express that "woman" or "man" is their primary identity and they happen to have the experience of being transgender.

## *Different Gender Identities*

Language is ever changing and is created and influenced by communities. There's no single authority or source on correct language because there are different communities and contexts that prioritize certain terms. All of us can be open to continuing to learn new terms and concepts, even if we are gender expansive ourselves. Although I'm definitely not the authority on language, it will be useful to review some terms that might be used often in the book and that you may encounter in your daily life.

### AGENDER

Somebody who is agender has no gender identity, may describe themself as "genderfree," or may be gender neutral. Agender people can use any number of pronouns and may or may not have a social or medical transition.

### BIGENDER

A person who identifies as having two genders can identify as bigender. A bigender person might express two identities at once or fluctuate between two genders.

### CISGENDER

A cisgender person is someone whose gender identity matches the sex they were assigned at birth. This word was introduced in the late 1990s and became more widely used in the 2000s.

The intent was to make language fairer and more inclusive and create awareness related to discrimination against trans people.

### GENDER NONCONFORMING

This is an umbrella term that refers to those whose gender identity or expression does not conform to stereotypical gender norms. Although more people are using the term "gender expansive" now, some people may still refer to themselves as gender nonconforming.

### GENDERQUEER

This is a gender identity that is outside of the concept of "male" or "female," or is a blend of male and female. The "queer" part of the word is often used to signify rejecting social norms, in this case related to gender.

### INTERSEX

Intersex means you're born with any one of normal variations of biological traits that are outside the strict male/female gender binary, whether it's your anatomy, chromosomes, or hormones. Intersex people may be assigned male or female at birth and historically often had medical interventions imposed during infancy or childhood to change their body to stereotypical male/female traits or appearance. Intersex advocates challenged this practice, and today more people realize that being intersex is not a medical problem. Some intersex people also identify as transgender, while others do not.

### NONBINARY

This can be an umbrella term for a range of gender identities other than "male" or "female." For example, some nonbinary identities are "demi-girl" (part girl or mostly girl), "genderqueer" (neither male nor female, or a mix of genders), and "polygender" (having three or more genders, at the same time or varying times). "Nonbinary" can also be a specific gender identity. When used to describe a specific gender identity, it can mean that a person's gender is something other than male or female, or

a combination of masculine and feminine genders. Nonbinary people can have any type of gender expression, and some use the term "enby" as short for nonbinary.

### OMNIGENDER

A person who is omnigender identifies as a mix of several genders, or as having all gender identities. "Pangender" is a similar term to "omnigender."

### TRANSGENDER

"Transgender" (or "trans") is an umbrella term for a person whose assigned sex at birth does not match their gender identity. Some people underneath the trans umbrella may not use the word "transgender" to describe their gender identity.

### TWO SPIRIT

"Two Spirit" is a term used by some Indigenous people to describe their identity within the context of their Indigenous or Native American identity. It can refer to gender and/or sexual identity and, as mentioned earlier, does not equate to Western or European understandings of gender and sexuality.

## WHAT IS GENDER DYSPHORIA?

Gender dysphoria is distress or discomfort that can occur when there's a mismatch between your assigned sex at birth and your gender identity. The unease or distress can be related to physical characteristics, but can also be connected to the ways that you're addressed and related to in public based on your perceived gender. Not all transgender people experience dysphoria. Many trans advocates don't like the term or the fact that it's included in the *Diagnostic and Statistical Manual of Mental Health Disorders* (DSM-V), but as long as it's necessary to be diagnosed for insurance coverage for transition-related healthcare, it remains in the manual.

Some children can experience gender dysphoria as early as ages two to four. It should also be noted that many won't experience dysphoria until puberty. In order to be diagnosed, an individual has to meet six of the following criteria (which themselves are contested for being highly gendered, including stereotypes, and not applying broadly—but at the time of this writing, this is the literal definition):

- An insistence that they aren't the gender they are told they are

- A strong desire to be a different gender

- A strong preference for activities, games, and toys typically associated with a gender other than the one they were assigned

- A strong preference for wearing clothing associated with a gender other than the one they were assigned

- A strong rejection of activities, games, or clothes typically associated with the gender they were assigned

- A strong dislike for their own anatomy

- A strong desire for physical sex characteristics that are more aligned with their felt gender

- A strong preference for playmates of a gender other than the one they were assigned

Gender dysphoria may never completely go away for many people who experience it, but there are options for managing it:

- Pubertal suppression is an option for children, and so is social transition (a process by which a person changes their name, pronouns, and/or gender expression to align with their gender identity).

- Gender-affirming hormone therapy (sometimes called hormone replacement therapy, or HRT) is an option for older adolescents and adults.

- Gender-affirming surgeries are another option for teens and adults.

- Therapy can also be a support for someone who's experiencing gender dysphoria.

  We'll discuss these options in more depth later in the book.

# Common Misconceptions about Gender Identity

There are a lot of misconceptions about gender identity. These misconceptions are likely to persist if we don't create spaces in schools, neighborhoods, families, and communities where children are around people of various gender identities and expressions and this variety is talked about openly and normalized. This will require active and intentional efforts on the part of all of us. Are you ready to change this? I think you are, if you've made it this far along in this book.

## *"Not Everyone Has a Gender Identity"*

This misconception is the one I most often hear from cisgender (cis) people. This happens when somebody confuses gender identity as being related only to transgender people and doesn't recognize that they, too, have a gender identity. A lot of cis people tell me that they haven't thought much about their gender identity since it always felt aligned with the sex (and gender) they were assigned at birth. But just because attention hasn't been drawn to one's gender identity or there hasn't been any discomfort doesn't mean that there is no gender identity. Sometimes people may also get confused when hearing terms like "agender" or "gender neutral" and think that means an absence of gender identity.

## "Parents Can Influence Their Children's Gender Identity"

This misconception overlooks the fact that gender identity is an internal, deeply felt sense of gender. It cannot be created or determined by external factors. Parents and caregivers can affect how long it may take a child to realize their gender identity or can intensify feelings of dysphoria by not validating a child's felt identity, but that is different from leading to the identity itself. I've worked with parents or family members who sometimes ask, "Did I do something wrong?" when their child comes out as trans. This means that (a) there may still be a belief that being trans is atypical and (b) there may be a misunderstanding that a parent or guardian can influence the child's gender identity. This can also be rooted in past transphobic theories that were promoted about the reasons for gender diversity being caused by "a lack of male/female role models," etc. No one person can cause another person's gender identity to change. A parent can only make the decision to actively support and affirm their child in whoever they are.

## "Children Change Their Gender Identity Because of What They're Exposed to Online"

This misconception stems from an idea that being transgender is now a trend and that if your child seems to have come out as transgender suddenly it may be because of something they were exposed to on social media. This idea is promoted in an article published in 2018 on the so-called phenomenon of "Rapid Onset Gender Dysphoria." The journal had to publish a correction later notifying readers of the poor quality and misleading findings of the study. This misconception again ignores the existence of transgender and gender-expansive people throughout history and around the world. It also ignores what I mentioned earlier in the chapter about how difficult it is for a child or adolescent to

act or express themself outside of stereotypical norms because of the negative comments and reactions they receive from peers and others. The Internet has made it easier to learn about multiple genders in a way that was more difficult in times past, and youth may read about things that they relate to. Having more positive trans visibility in media and entertainment has made it easier for some people to come out as well. This doesn't mean that learning about gender identity causes a gender change, but rather that children may feel more comfortable expressing their true selves when various identities are modeled and explained in a positive way. It's also the case that whereas parents or relatives may feel like a child or youth's coming out is "sudden," it may not be new at all for the young person but rather something they've known about themself in some way over time. Some young people do feel like they have a "lightbulb" moment where they suddenly put together several pieces in the puzzle of self-awareness, but these realizations are a valid part of the process.

## *"Changes in Gender Identity Mean That a Child is 'Confused'"*

A person's understanding and awareness of their gender identity can change over time as the person grows. A child or adolescent may use different words or terms to describe their gender identity and may have shifts in the ways they express their gender over time. This doesn't mean that any of these understandings are invalid. Part of our unlearning of our socialization around gender is in getting comfortable with change and fluctuation.

## *"Children Are Too Young to Know"*

This is a common statement I hear from parents and family members. I have never had someone say this to me about a cisgender child, only gender-expansive children. Where does

this misconception come from? It's a subconsciously biased view of gender-expansive people or transgender people. I say "subconscious" because I know the family members who have this misconception don't mean harm. It's important to understand that if we do not have a problem with cisgender children knowing their gender identity at a young age, then we cannot have a concern with gender-expansive or trans kids knowing their gender identity as well.

## *"This Is a Phase"*

I often hear parents worry that this is a phase, similar to their child trying a new hobby, being entranced with a new type of music for a few weeks, or being really into a new TV series that's a genre they normally don't like. It's understandable that parents want to understand whether something is a passing interest or not. Of the hundreds of children and youth I've worked with, I've never known one of them to revert to their assigned gender at birth after socially or medically transitioning. When I've seen people, either children or adults, discontinue their own path of transition, feeling an inability to move forward had a negative impact on their mental health. I have had young adult or older adult clients who sometimes decide to stop hormone therapy, not because they regretted starting it, but rather because their needs have changed or the way they want to express their gender identity had shifted. Phases in youth usually last only a few weeks or months, while gender dysphoria and new awareness of gender identity lasts longer than that.

## *"I Don't Want Them Doing Anything Permanent"*

Parents and family members want to take care of their children out of love and have been taught that children aren't able to make long-term decisions. There's a desire to protect kids from

doing things they may not understand. The gender dysphoria treatment options for children are not permanent. Puberty blockers are temporary, and when they're stopped, puberty picks up where it left off. Children can use a new name and pronouns and change their dress and hairstyle if desired to better align with their gender identity. You can be actively supportive and affirming by honoring these things as your child takes the opportunity to figure out what terms best describe themself, and what name and pronouns sound good when they hear them. If your child tries out a couple of different names, what is the harm in that? If pubertal suppression buys more time to learn about what your child is feeling and experiencing, then that could be a really great thing for your family.

## KEEP IN MIND

- Multiple genders have always existed. Variations of sex characteristics are naturally occurring throughout humans, animals, and plants.

- There are a lot of terms to describe one's gender identity. There can be nuances or slight differences in what the same term means to two different people.

- Most of us have been heavily socialized regarding gender identity, expressions, and roles, and it takes commitment and practice to unlearn these messages.

- People can experience gender dysphoria in different ways, and every person's gender transition is unique.

- Cisgender and gender-expansive children are able to know themselves, their gender identities, and the ways they like to express their gender.

- Gender identity is deeply felt and internal and can't be created or influenced by another person outside of oneself.

# 2

# You, Your Child, and Gender Identity

I n this chapter, we'll consider gender identity as it relates to children and parenting. We'll think about gender identity development, gender-expansive behavior, and ways to be a gender-affirming parent. We'll explore how to celebrate your child as their full, whole self. This will give us a foundation to use in implementing the strategies in parts II and III.

# When Children Develop
# Their Gender Identity

When do children begin to understand concepts of gender and solidify their own gender identity?

Children are not born knowing what "boy" or "girl" means. The Gender Affirmative Model (GAM), developed by Diane Ehrensaft, helps us understand how children develop a gender identity and to recognize that the process of becoming your true self leads to overall well-being. The GAM states that no gender identity is pathological or abnormal; gender identities and expressions can be culturally specific and vary around the world. Current research suggests that gender involves factors of biology, personal development, and socialization within a cultural context. Gender can be fluid and can change over time, and any distress that's present in gender-expansive children is usually related to society's misunderstanding of the child or negative reactions to their gender identity. How a child comes to have a gender identity can be a combination of genetics, internal awareness/ process, and observing social messaging; it is an interweaving of nature, nurture, and culture. Most children can communicate something of their gender identity at 2, 3, 4, or 5 years of age. A child's clarity about their gender identity can occur at any age. If pubertal changes are happening, they can prompt a young person to realize that they have an incongruence in their gender identity and assigned sex. This is one reason that we see an increase in young people coming out as trans or nonbinary around the time of experiencing puberty changes.

The Tanner stages were created by Dr. James Tanner, a pediatrician and child development researcher, to describe phases of physical pubertal development. Tanner stage 2 is when hormones start to send signals to the body for changes like pubic hair growth, beginning of breast development or menstruation,

testicle growth, etc. Tanner stage 3 is when these physical changes become more pronounced. Pubic hair thickens, height increases, fat can increase in areas such as the hips and thighs, voice changes occur, acne and increase in perspiration might happen, etc. These physical changes can start to cause gender dysphoria, or awareness of it, in gender-expansive kids. They may first start communicating their gender identity at Tanner stage 2 or 3, rather than earlier. Therapist Aydin Olson-Kennedy calls this the "clueing in" that happens before "coming out." (Researchers Colt Keo-Meier and Diane Ehrensaft also explore this concept in *The Gender Affirmative Model*.) As with any developmental milestone, not all children will develop a gender identity at the same age, and this is normal!

## *From Birth to Age 4*

Between ages 1 and 2, children are aware of physical differences in those labeled as "boy" or "girl." This awareness is influenced by the types of gender presentations, expressions, and language used to describe these that the child is regularly exposed to.

At age 3, a child may often label themself as "girl" or "boy." If a child has not been assigned a gender by their parents from birth, they may continue to say something like *I'm just me* or *I'm not a girl or a boy*. If they haven't been assigned a gender from birth, they may also identify themself as "girl," "boy," "nonbinary," or something else at this age, too. If a child has not been taught about multiple genders and known people of various genders, it will be difficult at this age to label themself as anything other than "girl" or "boy," although some children still find ways to try to communicate a nonbinary identity to the adults around them.

By age 4, a child becomes aware that for many people they are around, gender is a constant. The child's gender may be stable at this point as well, whether they are cisgender or gender expansive.

When given the option and positive messages about all options, most young children will play with all types of clothing, toys, and roles of various genders, regardless of gender identity. Playing is different from a child wanting to "be" another gender.

Children whose gender identity is incongruent with their designated sex present differently from children engaging in play that is typical in young children exploring their gender. For example, children assigned female at birth may describe themselves as boys or not girls, refuse stereotypical clothing, or attempt to stand to pee. Children assigned male at birth may describe themselves as girls, or not boys, express an interest in growing up to be a girl, refuse stereotypical clothing, or express wanting their penis gone.

## *From Age 4 to 6*

Children at these ages pick up on both verbalized and intentionally modeled adult thoughts and behaviors, as well as unspoken messages, facial expressions, feelings, and subconscious modeling. They want to do what the important adults in their life find acceptable and good, and are sensitive to what types of actions and words are rewarded. Children at this age are often more aware of things that are going on than adults think they are. They start to understand the gender "boxes" that exist and don't want to be seen as "bad" by moving outside the boxes that they've witnessed. Cisgender children may realize that there are expectations on how they'll express their gender. Gender-expansive children and cisgender children can be more comfortable expressing their gender in the ways that feel good to them with active support and affirmation by the adults and peers in their lives.

## *From Age 6 to 10*

Children of these ages start to lose magical thinking about the possibilities for the bodies they have, and gender identity can become more constant. They may move to more private thoughts, feelings, and behaviors, especially if their gender identity or expression is not affirmed. Stopping outward expression or communication of previously shown gender identity or fluidity does not mean the feelings went away, but may mean that the young person received some negative repercussions or criticism and is now trying to hide or repress them. Some children will start early stages of puberty at these ages. This is an age that may be appropriate for some children to begin puberty blockers. Puberty blockers are medicines that are used once puberty has begun to prevent further pubertal development. They've always been used with children for delaying early puberty and have gone on to be used with gender-expansive children to give the child and family time to figure out the child's gender identity and any needed transition steps to avoid potentially enduring a puberty that doesn't fit their gender identity. They are temporary, so when a young person stops taking the medication, puberty will resume. Alternatively, the young person can start gender-affirming hormone therapy if that's been determined to be the appropriate next step.

## *Early Adolescence and Beyond*

Children in early adolescence are experiencing the interaction between social pressure from parents/caregivers, peers, and self. They may be carrying on values and beliefs taught by their families, or more peer-oriented adolescents may adopt the values and beliefs of friends without much in-depth consideration. If young people spend a majority of their time in stereotypically gendered environments, they are more likely to display stereotypically gendered behaviors. However, these more

exaggerated behaviors decrease for most as they move into later adolescence.

A 2011 study showed that puberty, budding sexuality, and whether a young person is respected in their gender identity or not are all factors in the degree of gender dysphoria they might experience between the ages of 10 and 13 (Steensma et al., 2011).

Throughout adolescence, self-affirmation of one's own gender identity can grow and strengthen and rely less on external validation. In recent years, the later period of adolescence has expanded into "emerging adulthood." Becoming financially independent takes longer than in previous generations, and young people may find they have more time to consider all their identities and find what feels best to them. This may be one reason that in the largest US transgender study to date, 58 percent of emerging adults said that they disclosed their gender identity between the ages of sixteen and twenty-five, before starting a career or a family (James et al., 2016). Not having access to supportive environments or opportunities, such as college, can disrupt a young adult's path to self-awareness and affirmation. This can disproportionately affect Black, Indigenous, and other youth of color, as well as poor and working-class white youth.

## GENDER IDENTITY VS. GENDER EXPRESSION

*Gender identity* is a person's internal, felt sense of gender. *Gender expression* is the way someone expresses their gender through things like clothing, hairstyle, accessories, mannerisms, movements, voice, etc. These two things are separate and sometimes overlap or align.

A person's gender expression can change and fluctuate even when their gender identity is stable. For example, a transmasculine person might have a gender expression that is sometimes femme (feminine), sometimes highly masculine,

and other times a blend. That doesn't mean their gender identity as transmasculine is changing—only their gender expression. Another example is a cisgender girl who might have a "butch" or "tomboy" (i.e., masculine or boyish) gender expression. A trans woman could also have a "butch" gender expression. A cisgender boy may have an androgynous gender expression or enjoy things like polished fingernails or wearing a skirt.

Individuals may want a sense of freedom in being able to express themselves in a number of ways and not feel constrained by societal expectations of a certain gender identity.

# How Children Express Their Gender Identity

Kids can express their gender identity in a lot of ways. They may use hairstyle or clothing choices, nicknames or preferred names, mannerisms, nonverbal gestures and ways of moving their bodies, ways of relating in social relationships, etc. As I mentioned before, we can't assume a child's gender identity based on their gender expression or experimentation. We can create dialogue about gender in general, making sure kids know there are many genders and that cisgender boys or girls can express their gender in a lot of ways, too. We can understand that our child may not be cisgender, and this is normal and okay.

## *Gender-Expansive Behavior*

Gender-expansive behaviors can take many forms, such as taking on the role of another gender during play, choosing another name, identifying as another gender, or wearing clothes or accessories associated with a gender other than the one assigned at birth. It could look like talking about growing breasts

as an adult (if a male-assigned child), explaining that sometimes one is a girl and other times a boy, becoming outwardly upset (or quiet and isolating) when being asked or made to do something associated with the gender assigned at birth, doing activities or playing in ways that are usually associated with another gender, etc.

If your child shows gender-expansive behavior, you can respond in a supportive, respectful, and encouraging way. "I like that dress you chose from the dress-up station!" "You don't want me to call you Ericka today and you want to go by Rick? Okay, Rick." "You're taking good care of that baby doll, aren't you?" "Oh, you're practicing shaving your face, the way you see Uncle Devon do it." You can use some of those moments to normalize and validate all genders and gender expressions. "Girls, nonbinary people, boys—anybody can wear what they want to wear and do what they want to do."

## Embracing Your Child's Authentic Self

Most parents that I know and talk with—and I understand this even more deeply now that I'm a parent myself—want their kids to grow, learn, thrive, and be supported in who they are. Parents and guardians spend a lot of time and energy ensuring that their children have what they need to become people who are loving, caring community members who can live life to the fullest. Children need parents and caregivers to include all aspects of their whole selves in this active support. Even more, kids need to feel all parts of their beings actively celebrated, to receive the message that "you are special, unique, and wonderful in *all* the ways that you're you." This is not the same as giving the message that your child is *more* unique and special than other children, but instead that they are excellent just as they are. Sharing this

message with your child as they grow is crucial in their development of a strong and confident sense of self.

As a therapist, so much of my work centers on adults who are addressing wounds of rejection from childhood, or negative beliefs about some aspect of themselves that they absorbed from parents or family members growing up. As a parent or guardian, you can consciously strive to give attention to the words, actions, and behaviors you use with your child, as well as noticing urges you might have to avoid certain topics. You can intentionally choose to let go of any expectation of who your child is going to be and choose to practice joyful acceptance of who they are moment by moment. There is a lot of fear to manage as parents, especially for parents of color, and yet we can work hard to respond to situations with curiosity about who our child might be and how they might be different from us or who we imagined them to be. We can choose to practice letting go of fear as much as possible, parenting from a place of resilience, and finding joy in our child's development into their own unique person.

To actively embrace our child's authentic self, we must go beyond just allowing our child to try out different activities or appearances, and actively encourage a range of options. That's where the nurturing piece comes in. We want to nurture growth and development of self-awareness, so we want our children to be introduced to a broad range of choices in hairstyle, clothing, hobbies, interests, and the knowledge that they can also choose the pronouns they are called by. If we hear other children make comments about things "girls do" or things "boys like," we can pose questions that cause the children to think about other possibilities or that gently challenge those assumptions. While peer influence does exist in early childhood, at young ages, the worldview that parents and guardians share with their child holds the most importance. Sometimes as adults we assume that our kids will just know what we know or understand our values, but

we do need to make a point of both verbalizing those things and modeling them.

## Becoming a Gender-Affirming Parent

The term "Gender Affirmative Model (GAM)" began to be more widely used in the 2000s, to differentiate from previous terms that referenced sex "change" or "reassignment," as well as to contrast the beliefs of reparative and conversion therapies. The GAM reiterates that one's gender is not changing with any medical intervention; rather, the true, felt gender is simply being affirmed by aligning the body more with that gender. The GAM is rooted in the belief that all humans have a basic right to express their gender identity in any way and that gender expansiveness is not a problem that needs to be "fixed." The GAM creates an environment in which all people—cisgender, transgender, and gender-expansive—can freely be themselves without being boxed in by stereotypes and expectations. This approach is good for us all!

Like I mentioned earlier, children pick up on nonverbal cues, emotional energy, and parental behaviors and draw conclusions from them. Therefore, it's so important for parents to model gender-affirming behaviors and celebration of all identities. If a child picks up an absence of this belief, or any negative feelings about various gender expressions from a parent, it can be so much harder for that child to be themself. In the same vein, a cisgender child can absorb negative feelings or messages about trans or gender-expansive people and can develop biases against them that could lead to hurtful behaviors toward others. Let your child hear you compliment a gender-expansive person's makeup, sharp fade, or fabulous nails. Let your child see you express your gender in different ways. Listen to your language and try to modify it to be more inclusive. For example, instead of, "Hello, boys and girls," try, "Hello, friends." Instead of, "Look at that

girl over there roller skating," try, "Look at that person over there roller-skating." From situations like this, your child can learn that we do not know any stranger's gender just by looking at them. Ask your child, "Would you like for me to introduce you as my daughter, or as my kid/child?" This models that they can choose how they want to be referred to. Teach your child early on that people can use different pronouns for themselves. Introduce yourself to a new person by saying, "Hello, my name is _____ and my pronouns are _____." These changes in habits of language go a long way toward creating a gender-affirming environment for your child to grow up in.

## DOS

- Consider your own gender identity and messages about gender that you received growing up. What are the steps you can take to make sure your child is able to consider their own gender? What messages about gender identity and expression do you want to pass on to your child?

- Assess your own social circle. Does it include people of all gender identities and expressions? If not, what steps can you take to expand your circle so that your child is able to get to know people of all genders and various expressions?

- Practice using gender-open language with your family. Let everyone know what you're practicing and why. Family members can help each other out by suggesting new, inclusive ways of saying things or new ways to practice.

- Provide a range of options for clothing, toys, and activities for all your children, whether you think they are cisgender or not. For example, have skirts, clip-on earrings, shirts with rainbows, hearts, or floral patterns, spaghetti-strap tank tops,

and sparkles available to wear for assigned-male children, as well as your other children, and let them know it's okay to wear whatever they want. Do teach your assigned-female child how to throw a football, cut the grass, use a wrench, or build a fire if those are things you would also teach assigned-male children.

- Prepare your child for ways to respond to criticism or teasing they might encounter from other kids when they express themself or engage in activities that are outside of gender stereotypes.

- Watch TV shows and movies together with your child and talk about the ways they do or don't promote gender stereotypes, and whether multiple genders are represented or not.

### DON'TS

- Don't assume that your child is just trying to get attention by expressing their gender outside of cultural norms or by communicating another gender identity.

- Don't think that simply telling your child that they can be whoever they want or express themself however they want is enough on its own to balance the heavily gendered and stereotypical societal norms that exist.

- Don't believe that peers or parents can "make" someone's gender identity change.

- Don't try to dissuade your child from exploring various looks, mannerisms, or activities. This can create a deep and long-lasting shame that can be carried into adulthood.

- Don't fall for the misconception that children and early teens are too young to have a gender identity.

- Don't forget that as children grow and learn, their understanding of all aspects of their identities can also develop in new ways. Expressions, labels, and names might shift or change as a result.

- Don't confuse gender dysphoria with typical cisgender feelings about puberty and tell a young person they "just need to accept and love" a changing body. For example, a cisgender girl entering puberty may feel both excited about choosing a bra and uncomfortable thinking about new breasts drawing attention. A transmasculine youth entering puberty may feel disgusted or horrified by newly growing breasts or the thought that they may grow. These are different feelings based on very different experiences of puberty. One is connected to gender incongruence and the other is not.

## KEEP IN MIND

- Gender identity development is a process, and there's no exact timeline that applies to all children.

- Gender identity and gender expression are two different things. Cisgender and transgender children might have a spectrum of gender expression.

- Research studies are clear that celebrating a child's authentic self, including gender identity and expression, creates better mental health outcomes for kids, youth, and the adults they become.

- Parents and guardians can work to actively unlearn societal "rules" and "norms" about gender identity and expression to create the most affirming environment possible for their child.

- Most parents have some concern about their child's safety if they present their gender in a way that is broader than current cultural norms. This is especially true for youth presenting in more feminine ways. Families of color may have reason to be even more concerned about safety. There are ways to both affirm your child and consider risks, have conversations about safety, and engage in safety planning. Connecting with other families whose children want to express their gender in expansive ways can provide support around this, as well as ideas and suggestions from people who have had more experience with navigating those factors.

# PART II

# Foundational Parenting Strategies

In my work and personal life, I've met lots of parents who want to be gender affirming but admit that they aren't too sure how to go about doing that. In this section, we'll review some general parenting strategies as you seek to become more affirming of all genders and gender expressions. These strategies are for parents of all children, whether cisgender, gender-expansive, or transgender. There will be examples and suggestions for actions you can take or behaviors you can work on changing.

# 3

## Being Your Own Authentic Self

Esther is the mother of four-year-old twins, Michael and Malcolm. Growing up, Esther was instructed on what it meant to be a woman and a "lady." The role models in her life wore makeup every day, dressed in carefully curated outfits, and usually took on caregiving roles for children, elder family members, and people in the neighborhood or community in need of help. Esther carried these values with her through late adolescence and early adulthood. She took a lot of care with her appearance and grooming every day, and at times, put her own wellness and interests aside to care for other people in her life.

Over the past couple of years, Esther has come to the realization that she performs her gender identity and expression in ways that were automatic based on observations in childhood, or in ways that felt like obligations in order to do things the so-called right way. In a pivotal moment, Malcolm said to her one day, "Mama, I like your face before you put on that makeup." Her own growing self-awareness informed her that although she did like wearing makeup sometimes, she did not want to wear it every day. She also did not want to feel obligated to remove armpit, leg, and the light facial hair that society says is "unattractive" on women. In addition, Esther recognized that she missed developing a relationship with herself that allowed her to have her own hobbies and interests. She wanted to be herself outside of the responsibility of taking care of others. Esther rekindled her interest in photography that she'd nurtured in her early teens. She found her natural talent was still there and photography added fun and meaning to her days. She also knew that she'd been good at science classes in her youth but hadn't been encouraged to consider a scientific career path. Esther enrolled in a few courses at the community college to see how she felt about it now. She was able to ask for help with childcare from some of the neighbors and family members she'd been helping over the years.

As time went on, Esther felt freer and more able to be fully herself. She grew more comfortable on the days without makeup, more comfortable wearing casual clothes, and she fluctuated between growing out body hair and waxing it based on how she felt in a given month or season. Esther talked to Michael and Malcolm about how body hair and facial hair grows on people of all genders and everyone of any gender can choose whether to remove it. She felt more confident talking about all bodies being beautiful and believing it herself. Giving herself permission to spend time doing things she loved, even if other people didn't see the value in them or didn't understand her interests, added joy to her life and enabled her to better support her kids in whatever they were showing interest in at any point in time.

# Put It into Practice

We can model self-reflection, freedom in gender expression, and open, authentic selves with our children. It can be hard to encourage our kids in their gender identity development without doing that work ourselves. Being thoughtful about our gender identity, the ways we want to express it, and whether it's changed or not in our lives can enrich our sense of well-being. Things that lead to more contentment and joy for us as caregivers in turn benefit our child, as we parent from a fuller and more whole place.

**Reflect on your own gender identity and expression.** Think about your own gender identity development process. What has it been like? What were you taught about your gender? Were you treated in ways you liked or didn't like because of your assigned sex? Were there experiences or practices you were discouraged from participating in because of your assigned sex? What do you know about your own racial/ethnic background and the cultural views of gender, past and present, such as views and teachings on gender before colonization or imperialism? These questions can be food for thought to inform a deeper under-standing of your own process and identity formation. You can think about how you feel about your gender now and whether there are new things you might learn about yourself.

**If you've felt constraints, take steps to be freer in your gender expression, whatever your gender identity.** Are there ways you want to express yourself—ways you want to act, sound, move, or dress—that you've held yourself back from? Consider trying these out in stages, starting at the place that feels the safest to experiment and moving outward from that space as you gain confidence and security.

**Have open and honest conversations with your kids. Let them see the real, true you.** Know that children can often understand more concepts than we adults give them credit for. Let your kids see beyond the parent/grandparent/foster parent version of you. Watching you being authentic can give your children the knowledge that they can do the same.

## *Takeaways*

- Being yourself, in all aspects of your life, is a powerful example to give your children.

- It's never too late to evaluate your life and decide if you're living in ways that are true to you. We can engage in self-discovery throughout our lifespan. In the big picture, life is short, and it can be fuller when we embrace all parts of ourselves.

- We've all been socialized to exist in certain ways, and we all know what it feels like to have expectations placed on us that we can't meet. Let's practice letting go of unwanted expectations and commit to not placing the same burdens on our children.

# 4

# Unraveling Your Personal Biases

L uis and Paulina have two children, Gael (age 2) and Xavier (age 5), who as far as they know are boys. Their 17-year-old nephew, Alejandro, takes care of the children when Luis and Paulina are working. Alejandro likes taking the kids to the library to check out books every week, and the kids love reading a variety of books. Recently, while making dinner, Luis saw the latest library books on the kitchen table and started browsing through them. He noticed a book called *Julián Is a Mermaid* (Jessica Love, 2018) and another one called *Pink Is for Boys* (Robb Pearlman, 2021). He thought to himself, "I wonder why they picked those books," and then continued with dinner preparation.

The following week, Luis saw Xavier wearing a pink towel wrapped tightly around his waist and jumping around the living room. Luis asked, "What are you doing?" and Xavier answered, "I'm a mermaid! I'm swimming around with my fin!" Luis thought, *"Huh, okay."* He noticed that he felt uncomfortable but wasn't sure exactly why. He also noticed he felt a little worried, too.

The next day he talked with Alejandro about it and said, "I want you to make the kids space out how often they read books like those. They're young and I don't want them to be influenced to do things they don't really understand."

Alejandro asked, "What do you mean? What don't they understand?"

Luis wasn't sure, but noticed he still felt uncomfortable.

Alejandro said, "I think it's good for them to learn that boys, girls, and other genders can like whatever colors and styles and images they want. Don't you want them to know that?"

Luis didn't answer.

Later that evening, he brought it up to Paulina. "I'm a little worried that Alejandro's letting the kids read books they're too young for. And that they're getting exposed to things, putting ideas in their heads they're not ready for."

Paulina asked, "What are you worried is going to happen if they read the books?"

Luis thought about it and replied, "Well, think about what our parents and grandparents will say if they see them dancing around in pink towels. They aren't going to have a good reaction."

Paulina said, "We can start talking to our family members now to try to explain that we're letting our kids be themselves and like whatever they like."

Luis pondered this for a moment and replied, "What if reading these books makes them want to be like whatever the characters are? I mean, Alejandro mentioned 'all genders.' What if they start thinking they're another one of those genders the young people are talking about these days?"

Paulina thought for a minute and answered, "We've always said that we would love our children no matter what. I don't know if reading these kids' books can cause them to be any certain way, but even if it did, wouldn't we still try to show them we love them? I don't know exactly what that will mean if someday they say they're another gender, or if they're a boy who loves pink and wants to be a mermaid, but I want us to be proud of them and support them in their dreams and goals, even if it's not what we imagined. There were ways our own parents were hard on us, thinking it would help us and save us from trouble down the road, but that's not how it really felt to us in the end, right? I think we have a chance to do some things a little differently. What's really making you hesitate about this when you're usually so supportive?"

Luis thought for a while. He recognized that even though he considered himself an accepting and nonjudgmental person, he was having a reaction to the idea of boys being associated with stereotypically feminine things. He realized that he'd internalized messages about masculinity and his negative feelings revealed that some part of him believed Xavier's interest in mermaids and pink was abnormal. There was a piece about the physical and emotional safety of his child in there, but mostly it was bias. Through more conversations with Paulina and Alejandro, Luis came to a place where he could truly, fully embrace whoever his child was going to be and whatever ways his child wanted to express himself.

# Put It into Practice

Because almost all of us have been socialized and educated under a binary (two-gender, stereotyped) system, we have internalized and absorbed biased messages about many things, including gender identity, roles, and expressions. It takes effort, willingness, commitment, and practice to unlearn those things.

Questions to ask yourself about Luis's scenario:

- If I'm being fiercely honest with myself, have I had a moment where I reacted inwardly or outwardly like Luis, whether with my children or others? What fears come up in those moments?

- How do I know for myself when implicit bias is coming up?

- Who do I have in my life who holds me accountable for recognizing bias and unlearning? If nobody, do I need to work with a therapist who will help me with this or join an affinity group who is supporting one another in unlearning bias? What intentional actions do I need to take to continue identifying and letting go of bias related to gender identity and expression?

- What philosophies of parenting were passed on to me that I might want to let go of?

## *Takeaways*

- **We all have biases—every single one of us. We first have to recognize what they are, and then we can shift our beliefs and actions.**

- **We will pass our biases on to our children if we're not trying to identify and let go of them. Usually, we need people in our lives who can hold us accountable for this to work.**

- **Our children give us opportunities to change and to release old ideas and behaviors. This can be freeing!**

- **Clinging to our biases and judgments can at some point interfere in our relationship with our child.**

# 5

# Learning to Really Listen

L eilana, Ashley, and Will are co-parents of Luisa, who is 10 years old and autistic. She spends one week with Leilana and Ashley and the next week with Will, rotating households. Luisa identifies as bisexual, autistic, mixed race, and trans. One year ago, Luisa started using she/her pronouns and going by Luisa. She has made no other outward changes. All of Luisa's parents have expressed concern that Luisa didn't "show any signs" of being transgender before and that she hasn't made any attempts to change her hairstyle and clothing to be more feminine, yet becomes angry when she's misgendered in public. They also worry she may just be confused and not realize she doesn't "have to change genders to be attracted to men and women."

Leilana and Ashley are active in local cisgender lesbian groups and have received mixed messages and information about their child's gender identity and expression within LGBTQ+ circles. Will has heard that there are statistical correlations between trans people and autism but isn't sure what that means for Luisa, and is wondering if Luisa's belief that she's trans is just a manifestation of a symptom of autism. All parents say that they are trying to use Luisa's name and pronouns but are still slipping up about 50 percent of the time. Luisa has been getting into heated arguments with all three parents when they don't use the correct pronoun or refer to her as "son." When Leilana brought home a wig, suggesting that if Luisa wore it, it would make it easier for them and strangers to call her the right thing, Luisa said, "No, I don't want it." Recently after an argument Luisa hurt her hand when she punched a wall in anger. The family doesn't know what to do from here.

# Put It into Practice

As a therapist, one of the most common things I hear from children and youth is that their parents "never listen." They don't feel heard enough to be understood. I know most parents are trying and believe they *are* listening. But something's happening where the child doesn't feel that way.

Many of us may have grown up in a time when the parenting view was that children should "be seen and not heard," meaning the adults' opinion was law and nobody much cared what a child thought about something if their opinion differed from adults'. If we're parenting that way on purpose, or accidentally, of course our kids will not feel heard, right?

In thinking about my own parenting style, I've been marinating on the work of Akilah S. Richards in *Raising Free People*. I'll share some of what Akilah talks about in the way of really listening to our children.

*"I respond with questions so I can learn more, not so
I can bring the conversation back to my point of view."*

Ooh! Does anybody else feel read by that? Sometimes our kids know we're not really listening because we're using their words to further make our own point, instead of trying to really understand theirs. I wonder if Luisa had that experience with Leilana, Ashley, or Will.

*"I am learning to listen with a Disruptor's Ear, which
means I am practicing listening beyond my own biases,
so I can help foster trust and understanding."*

Listening beyond our own biases and opinions as parents is *hard*, but it's necessary if we want to build mutually trusting relationships with our kids. What biases did you notice Will, Ashley, and Leilana had? What might have helped them be more aware of those? What might the parents be missing that is important to Luisa?

*"I am learning how to just listen, rather
than trying to fix anything."*

As parents, we want to fix problems for our children much of the time. And we think we have the answers to so many of their problems if they would just listen to us. But if we're focused on fixing things, we might miss hearing what's most important to our individual child. We might miss that sometimes they just want to feel listened to and have our undivided attention. We might miss out on a chance to collaboratively problem solve, instead of making our own suggestions or giving unwanted advice. Where did you see a chance for the adults to partner with Luisa in collaboration instead of "fixing" and assuming solutions?

*"Sometimes the discussion calls for me to do nothing, besides offer context if I am asked."*

Here's a tool I try to use when I feel the urge to say something: WAIT (Why Am I Talking?). This is a chance to ask myself if it's necessary for me to speak in that moment if I haven't been asked for my opinion. (I don't always remember to do it, but you get the idea.) Can you imagine moments when Luisa's parents didn't need to speak, but needed to listen?

*"In conversations with children/teens I am mindful not to give verbal versions of long, persuasive essays."*

How many of us have memories of being sat down for a monologue from a parent? And it felt like you were sitting there for hours and eventually the parent's voice started to sound like that teacher from Charlie Brown? Nobody wants to be doing that! And yet many of us have the urge to give our child *all* the reasons why what they're doing doesn't make sense/is questionable/is not the best thing for them. And we don't want to be interrupted, either! What could Luisa's parents have done instead of giving long monologues about the reasons it's hard for people to gender her correctly or what she should do differently?

Another important thing to point out in this scenario is that Luisa's parents were receiving advice from people in the community who did not have the lived experiences Luisa had. To deepen their understanding of Luisa's experience, they could have talked to other trans, autistic, bisexual, mixed-race young people to hear their experiences and feelings, as well as seek out professionals who also shared several of these identities to consult. I've had numerous friends wonderfully model this by requesting "listening sessions" with people who had specific experiences or identities they wanted to understand better when trying to make an important decision. They usually gifted the person a meal, treat, or gift card to show appreciation for their time and vulnerability.

Can you think of times when you weren't really listening to your child? What got in the way? What was the outcome?

Are you ready to practice asking more questions, listening past biases, letting go of fixing, and being concise or not talking at all? Changing our habits is not easy, but a solid relationship with our child is worth the struggle.

## *Takeaways*

- The goal of active listening is to increase understanding, not to prove a point or make your case.

- We can challenge ourselves to listen at least 60 percent of the time and talk 40 percent of the time or less.

- Regardless of whether I hold any marginalized identities, I will still need to work to unlearn other "isms" that I've absorbed from society to be able to be fully open and understanding of what someone is communicating to me.

- As parents and caregivers, we take the position that we can learn from our children. They teach us new things and give us new perspectives, and this can happen only when we listen.

- Our kids don't always need us to fix a problem. Sometimes we see a problem where there isn't one. Other times our kid just wants us to listen and validate. If there truly is a problem, we can take a collaborative approach.

# 6

# Maintaining Open Communication

Joelle's noticed lately that her eight-year-old child, Promise, who identifies as "not a girl nor a boy" has seemed "sassy" and has started to cry if they're asked to clean up their room, feed the cat, or do their homework. Joelle commented to her child recently, "What's going on with you these days? I don't like the sass." Promise just shrugged, looked down, and answered, "Nothing." Joelle sighed, rolled her eyes, and kept putting away the groceries. She figures Promise is just going through an angsty phase and hopes the attitude goes away soon.

After several weeks of this pattern, Joelle is at her wits' end. She can't tell if Promise is being manipulative to try to get out of doing chores and homework or if there's something wrong that Promise doesn't want to talk about. When Joelle mentioned it to her mother and a parent friend, the feedback she received was to ignore the tears and just give consequences when chores or homework aren't done, or to laugh it off as a normal thing that preteens do where they act more grown than they really are and think they're above the rules. Joelle tries both options, hoping that one of them will work, but several weeks later, there's still no change and she doesn't know what to do. Joelle decides to look for a child counselor to see if somebody else can get through to Promise and find out what the problem is.

## Put It into Practice

Sometimes families come to me for help because their child has "shut down" or "withdrawn" and just doesn't seem like their usual self. Parents and caregivers have usually tried to get the child to open up with little success. By the time they come in for therapy, the situation has just gotten uncomfortable and frustrating for everybody.

As parents, we often have a million things on our minds and our plates on any given day. A lot of times we might be rushing around, trying to juggle our responsibilities and just praying that everybody in the family is alive at the end of the day. That doesn't set us up for using our best communication skills. Combine that with the reality that a lot of us didn't have those communication skills modeled for us growing up, and we might have developed some habits that make it harder for our children to open up to us and say how they're really feeling.

Here are some tips to creating open pathways of communication with your child.

## *Do:*

- State your needs and boundaries clearly. Your child can't read your mind.

- Model talking openly about emotions. Name when you're feeling sad, discouraged, afraid, or embarrassed.

- Look for common ground or things that you and your child agree on, even during a disagreement.

- Allow your child to have their own opinions, even if they're different from yours. Recognize that they need space to develop their own ideas and viewpoints.

- Choose your words carefully when you want to give guidance or share an opinion. Ask yourself, "If I sound confrontational or authoritarian right now, what's the likely outcome? How will that affect my relationship with my child?"

- Pay attention to how your child reacts when you bring up a touchy subject. Are there signs that they don't feel comfortable opening up to you? If so, what can you change about your opening or overall tone?

- Create an environment where it's okay to address hard things. Show that there is a safe container for difficult topics and feelings.

- Consider setting up weekly or monthly check-ins where anybody can bring up anything that they're feeling or thinking and the other person just listens and reflects back without needing to solve the problem; for example, "So this happened the other day and it was really hard," or, "It hurt your feelings when Travis said that." This means that you share, too! It doesn't have to be tense. Have favorite snacks and cozy blankets around and wrap it up with a board game or a movie.

## Don't:

- Don't argue with emotions. If your child is sad because it's time to stop playing and wash hands for dinner, don't say, *"You've been playing all afternoon. You need to eat while the food's hot and there's nothing to be sad about."* Say, *"It seems like you're sad. I hear that it's more fun to play than to come to dinner right now. It's okay to feel sad when we have to stop what we love and do something we don't want to."*

- Don't focus on obedience, even when external pressure tells us to exert control and have obedient, quiet children. You want to teach and model empathy, respect, and consent so your children can learn how to treat others. Work *with* your children to develop healthy communication and relationships.

- Don't neglect your own self-care, emotional awareness, and emotional processing and management. If you do, you'll take out your emotions on your children, which won't lead to the type of trust needed to have open communication.

- Don't expect your child to have the same ability to manage emotions that (some) adults do, and also don't underestimate your child's ability to communicate and learn emotional coping skills.

## Takeaways

- **The degree to which your child is open and honest with you can depend on your own communication style, delivery, and willingness to listen, even if what is being said is hard to hear.**

- Normalize feeling and naming emotions. Talk about emotions instead of just thoughts and opinions. Talk about where you feel certain emotions starting in your body and ask your child where they feel that emotion in their body (understanding that it may be different).

- Remember when you were young. What made it easier for you to open up to an adult, if you were able to? How can you use that information to make it easier for your child?

- Other people may judge you for your parenting style and choices. Your relationship with your child is more important than their opinions, so they can MTOB (Mind Their Own Business).

- Ask for help and take time for yourself and your needs. When you do that, you'll be in a better space to effectively communicate with your child.

- Get to know your child and what ways of communicating work best when they're having a hard time opening up. Do they prefer to text? Write in a journal that you trade back and forth? Use a chalkboard or dry-erase board hanging up on a wall? Talk while doing an activity so there's less eye contact and some distraction?

- Notice when you're ascribing something negative to your child's behavior and take a position of curiosity instead. Are there any alternative explanations to the behavior you haven't considered yet? Is something really wrong? Does this behavior trigger your own trauma response or remind you of something from your past?

# 7

# Practicing Patience

Aki and Ren are aunt and uncle to six-year-old Kaede. They've been raising Kaede since age three. Over the past year, Kaede has communicated several different gender identities, first telling Aki and Ren, "I'm not a boy, call me Kaley." Then a few months later, Kaede said, "I'm more like a girl-boy, you can call me Kaede again until I find my new name." Kaede recently watched a cartoon where a character was nonbinary and said, "I think nonbinary fits me. I'm 'they' like in the cartoon."

In *Parable of the Sower*, Octavia Butler writes, "God is Change." While I know change is constant and sometimes very much wanted, it can feel disorienting, scary, and unpleasant. To quote Butler in *Parable of the Talents*, "Kindness eases Change." That's what patience feels like to me sometimes—kindness. I can especially feel that when someone is being patient with me. If I know that it feels good to receive that kindness when another person has patience for my challenges, then wouldn't I want to offer that feeling to my child? Now let's go back to the example and notice how Aki and Ren practice patience with Kaede, and how Kaede also has patience with Aki and Ren. As you think about their story, notice where the adults could have been more patient.

Ren and Aki were supportive initially but have been expressing concern that Kaede's process is difficult because of the mental and verbal changes they have to make each time. They want a therapist to help Kaede "just pick something and stick with it." Aki and Ren are also concerned that Kaede is not yet clear on the term for their gender or the name they want to go by. They feel like it should be obvious to Kaede at this point. They don't like that Kaede gets frustrated when they don't remember the current name or pronouns Kaede is using. Sometimes Kaede even throws a fit if they slip up. They're also concerned because their extended family does not understand the changing names or terms at all. They're worried that if they continue to let Kaede try different names or gender identity labels, the rest of the family will judge them negatively; refuse to use the current name, pronouns, or label; and will even start to think Ren and Aki are doing something harmful in supporting this.

The stress of this has led to both of them being more short-tempered than they want to be, with Kaede and each other. They believe they need a resolution soon and plan to let the therapist know that they have a short timeline for getting this all figured out so they can move forward.

# Put It into Practice

As parents and guardians, our patience can run low for many reasons. Yet if we want to maintain a trusting, strong relationship with the children in our lives, we'll need to have a steady practice of increasing our patience. Here are some questions to consider as a starting point for your own reflection.

Where do you think Ren and Aki's feelings of impatience are coming from?

What are some situations in general with your own child that bring up impatience in you?

How do you tend to act when feeling impatient? What kind of outcome does this have, both short-term and long-term?

Here are some tips for practicing patience:

- Notice feelings of tension and take a deep breath. Think about relaxing your jaw and the muscles in your face. Think the words "let go" or "soften" as you exhale. Sometimes just signaling a sense of calm or release lets your mind know it can do the same.

- Consider whether the impatience is coming from your own expectations. (Notice any "shoulds" or "shouldn'ts" popping into your mind?) How can you adjust your expectations?

- Ask yourself, "*How can I slow down so I can respond to the moment more intentionally? Do I need to respond right now?*"

- Give yourself a break and step away if you need to.

- Try to find something positive about the situation. Brainstorm as many possible positives as you can.

- Allow your child to have their own process at their own pace.

- Remind yourself that practicing patience is being kind both to yourself and to your child.

- Remind yourself that the other person is doing the best they can with what they have in that moment . . . and so are you.

## *Takeaways*

- Flex your patience muscle by practicing accepting a delay in getting something you want, by accepting your inability to control the future, and by increasing your comfort level with uncertainty. Those things are hard, but it's possible to feel like it gets easier and easier to do the more you practice.

- Although it can be uncomfortable to try to be patient sometimes, there can be benefits in the moment. Let yourself enjoy something else instead. You could be surprised by something beautiful along the detour. You could compliment a stranger, help someone who's struggling more in that moment, appreciate the time to breathe, feel at peace, and lower your blood pressure. You could remind yourself that being patient creates harmony in your relationships.

- Remind yourself of the harm or downsides that can come when you're impatient.

- Ask yourself, "Will this moment matter 5 years from now? Or 15 years from now?" If the answer is "No," or "I'm not sure," you can probably let it go. "This too shall pass" is an old phrase that reminds us that most things are temporary and not everything has the same level of importance.

- When struggling to be patient, remind yourself of what kind of parent you want to be and ask yourself how you want to respond to the situation.

- Think about the most patient person you know. How would they react in this situation, and can you try to do something similar?

# 8

# Establishing Mutual Respect

Ande (he/him) is Mommy to Willo, age three. Ande wants to parent from a place of recognizing that Willo is a person, deserving of respect, no matter how young. Part of how he has done this is by teaching Willo about bodily autonomy. Willo is not asked to hug or kiss relatives or anyone that Willo doesn't feel like hugging or kissing. Ande models this by asking Willo, "Would you like a hug right now? Or maybe a high five?" This is to show Willo that she has autonomy over when she engages in physical connection, even with people she loves and is close with. When Willo has a doctor's appointment, Ande explains ahead of time what types of things will happen at the appointment.

While Ande had wanted to be called "Papa" by his future child, Willo started calling Ande "Mommy" early on and Ande allowed this. He wanted his child to be part of deciding his parental name, and he felt that to some degree it created a layer of safety for their Afro-Indigenous family to have some perception of heteronormativity to outsiders, since he is read as female sometimes by strangers.

Another aspect of this parenting approach from Ande was to not assign Willo a gender at birth. Ande felt, especially as someone who came to understand his own trans identity later in life, that he wanted to give Willo a chance to figure out what her gender identity was, without all the expectations and social cues that can be there when told from birth who you are. Willo has recently been saying that she is a girl and Ande fully supports this, using she/her pronouns for Willo as asked. Willo chooses her own clothing, even at age three.

Ande was raised in a family with the message that adults and elders were the ones to be respected and that they didn't necessarily have to show respect to children. He's trying to flip the script by teaching and modeling mutual respect. When his child pulls on his hair or grabs his glasses, he explains, "*I didn't give permission for my hair to be pulled,*" or, "*I need you to be mindful of being gentle with my glasses because I need them to see.*" Depending on how rough the behavior is he might start with "*Ouch,*" or "*Careful!*" When Willo is told she can't use the big butcher knife to cut her food by herself and tells Ande, "You're mean, Mommy, not to let me use the knife!" Ande answers, "You're mad because you can't use the knife right now. It's okay to be mad at me."

When Willo seems to be having a hard time with anger and is moving toward a tantrum, Ande suggests that she go to her calming space where she has activities like play dough, squishy toys to squeeze, stuffed animals to hug, paper to rip up, a soft blanket to wrap up in, and other sensory and soothing things to do. Sometimes Ande tells Willo, "*I'm feeling frustrated right*

*now so I'm going to take a break by myself for a few minutes to do some breathing. I'll come out when I feel less frustrated."* Occasionally Ande doesn't have it in him to respond that way and snaps, *"Willo, stop it! You're getting on my last nerve!"* When he's calmer, he apologizes to Willo for snapping and commits to working on managing his feelings in the moment. This models apologizing and commitment to changing a hurtful behavior.

# Put It into Practice

Think back to when you were a young child. Did you feel respected by the adults in your life? What types of things led you to feel disrespected? Respected?

How can those memories inform the ways you want to parent your child? What does mutual respect mean to you? How would you know if there is mutual respect between you and your child? This acrostic can be a fun way to remember some of these concepts as you're working on implementing them:

**M:** Model asking consent before touching.

**U:** Unlearn the idea that children are too young to deserve respect.

**T:** Talk to your child like they can understand a lot of what you're saying.

**U:** Use your best emotion regulation skills and teach them to your child.

**A:** Apologize when you say or do something hurtful and share what you're going to do to work on the behavior.

**L:** Let your child tell you when they're mad at you, or feeling like they don't like you much in a moment, or disappointed in you, even if it's uncomfortable and even if you don't agree

with the reason they're having the feelings. Have another adult in your life with whom you can process how it feels when your kid is angry or upset with you.

**R:** React from the same place of grace you would with a friend or a colleague as often as possible.

**E:** Empathize with your child about the things that are hard, frustrating, or sad. Model empathy and teach your child how to consider another person's perspective or experience.

**S:** Say what you mean and don't expect your child to be able to read your mind.

**P:** Practice patience.

**E:** Express respect through tone of voice, facial expressions, giving appropriate choices, and recognition that your child is their own person, not a miniature of you. That last part is one I don't think we talk much about in the parenting world, but if we're being honest, most of us have some dreams about how our kids will act like us, or enjoy some of the same activities or the same music, or look like us in their style of dress or features and hair. I think we can struggle emotionally sometimes, even if we believe our kids are their own person, to accept when they are different from us or from how we envisioned them being. Acknowledging this to ourselves can help us open up to who they're showing us they are, in a way that lets us truly celebrate their uniqueness.

**C:** Consider what you need, in order to be able to parent from your best place. Even though you won't be able to do that 100 percent of the time, you can have a sense of what it means to you. Brainstorm ways you could get those needs met, because when we're good as parents, that's better for our kids. We're more able to bring our best selves to that parent role.

T: Treat your child the way you want to be treated. How do you like to be talked to? Looked at? Asked to do something? Do your best to extend those same things to your child. Your relationship will be all the stronger for it.

## *Takeaways*

- It's never too late to start establishing a mutually respectful relationship with your child.

- Creating mutual respect with your child might mean doing things differently from the ways that you were raised or that people around you are relating to their kids, and that's okay.

- You can support your child's bodily autonomy, reinforcing the message that they are in charge of their body.

- You can talk to your kids and teach them things without assuming they are too young to understand.

- You can practice patience and empathy and model relationship repair when you fall short of these goals.

- You can communicate your needs to your child and recognize which needs will be met on your own or by another adult instead of your child.

# PART III

# Gender-Affirming Parenting Strategies

In this section, we'll go over some strategies specifically related to gender identity. These strategies will be useful to families with cisgender, gender-expansive, and trans children. Remember, knowing about our full selves and having freedom in the ways we express ourselves is good for us all!

# 9

# Talking to Your Child about Gender Identity

Lonnie is the foster parent to Justice, age four, and Marina, age seven. Justice is showing signs of being gender expansive, while Marina identifies with the gender she was assigned at birth. Lonnie reads books to the kids about children and adults of various genders. Lonnie initiates conversation after they read books and explains what different gender identities are represented. He asks them what they think their gender identity might be and listens to the response. He lets them know that there is no pressure for them to know right now, but if they do, he respects their identity. He also lets them know it's okay to learn new things about themselves, and this might mean at some point their word for their gender identity changes.

When the family watches cartoons or movies together, Lonnie sometimes makes comments like, *"Why do so many shows think 'long eyelashes' means 'female'?"*; *"Why are girls who like to play sports called tomboys in this movie?"*; or, *"The trans guy in the movie has a boyfriend. What do you think about that?"*

Lonnie teaches both children that they can express themselves by choosing their clothing styles and their hairstyles and provides a variety of options. Sometimes Lonnie lets the kids paint his nails. He plays dolls with them both and has them watch and "help" when he works on cars. When Marina was scolded by her teacher at school for arguing with a classmate about whether boys could wear dresses, Lonnie went to the school to explain why those sorts of dialogues are harmful to gender-expansive children, transgender people, and cisgender people who want freedom in self-expression.

When out in public, if Marina or Justice comment, *"Hey, look at that man on the big motorcycle,"* Lonnie reminds them that they don't know the person's gender identity without being told and models an alternative comment by saying, *"Look at that person on the motorcycle."* Lonnie is teaching them about pronouns and models introducing himself to new people by saying, *"Hello, I'm Lonnie, my pronouns are he/him."* The kids have had a babysitter whose pronouns are she or goddess and Lonnie has a coworker whose pronouns are they/them. Lonnie practices using these pronouns with the kids when the babysitter and coworker aren't around so they can use them correctly when they are together. Lonnie models using a gender-neutral pronoun when referencing a stranger who hasn't shared their pronouns and helps them think of more inclusive language to use in general. When the kids mention moms and dads, Lonnie adds parents to the list and reminds them that families can be made of one or more caregivers who can be called all kinds of parent or caregiver names.

# Put It into Practice

Thinking about how to talk to children about gender identity can be overwhelming at first. You might feel like you have no idea where to start or that it's going to be awkward. This is some encouragement to trust your kids, trust yourself, and trust the process. Lonnie began by observing Justice and Marina. He normalized different gender identities, pronouns, and expressions with the use of books, modeling in his own conversations and questions, and examples of people in their social circle. Hopefully you'll find some of the suggestions in this section will help you be more prepared.

## *Do:*

- Know the difference between gender identity and gender expression. Be able to share a variety of gender identities with your child so they know that there are more than two options or ways to describe themself.

- Reinforce freedom of expression. Let your child know that they can express themself however they want and can have any interests they want regardless of their gender identity.

- Contemplate your own gender identity development process. What was it like? What could have been different?

- Understand how your cultural backgrounds view gender identity. Have knowledge on your own (and your child's if different) cultural backgrounds' historical views of gender identity. If you don't know and you're not able to easily find the information, who could you ask?

- Normalize the use of multiple gender identities in your daily language and life. What books do you get from the library or buy to keep at home? Instead of talking about men/women or boys/girls, how can you mention many gender identities, just as a matter of fact? Does your social circle need to expand so your children get to know people of various gender identities and expressions?

- Know that things we *don't* talk about affect kids as much as things we do. Openly talking with your kids can reduce the potential for shame and low self-worth if they happen to be gender expansive. Cisgender kids who grow up with open communication about gender identity can be more empathetic and speak up when gender-expansive kids are being mistreated.

- Validate that body parts aren't connected to gender. Let your children know that even if the doctor/midwife/you thought they were a certain gender at the time of their birth, you learned later that our body parts do not dictate our gender. Tell them they might discover they are a girl, a boy, nonbinary, genderfluid, or any other gender and that they can tell you if they feel differently from what they were assigned.

- Normalize using your pronouns. Get into the habit of introducing yourself to people with your pronouns, whether you think the person might be gender expansive or not. Practice with friends and ask them to remind you when they notice you not introducing yourself with your pronouns.

- Make friends with discomfort . . . or rather, with other people feeling discomfort. Not everybody has read books like this or has even heard that there are more than two genders or various pronouns. Others have heard it and

don't like it! When you use gender-inclusive language or introduce yourself with your pronouns, some people might feel a certain way about it. That's all right. It's about them and where they are in their own development journey, not about you, so let them sit in discomfort and you can keep it moving.

## *Don't:*

- Don't forget that cisgender (cis) boy or cis girl are also gender identities.

- Don't project the impression that something is "wrong" if a child is expressing themselves in gender-expansive ways.

- Don't forget to emphasize that femininity, gentleness, and softness are for everyone, not just "girls."

- Don't think that just one conversation about gender identity is enough to balance all the other messaging your child might be receiving from society about gender identities and gender roles. Make this a regular part of your own dialogue and thought process.

- Don't underestimate your child's ability to understand. Kids seem to grasp these concepts faster than adults a lot of the time.

- Don't fall into the trap of thinking that if you talk about gender identity it will "influence" your child to label themself as transgender if they're not.

# *Takeaways*

- You can do this! I have full faith in your ability even if you're a little nervous about getting started.

- You don't have to put a lot of pressure on the first time you bring this up. There'll be plenty of opportunities for more conversations since you're on the path to normalizing this in your daily life.

- Start noticing *all* the messages you get about gender identity around you. Some are subtle and others are blatant. Consider how you can talk about those with your children.

- Teaching young kids about gender identity creates a safer and more liberating environment for everybody.

- Have conversations with your friends, family, coworkers, and neighbors about gender identity. The more comfortable you get talking about it and the more often you discuss it, the more natural it will feel when you talk about it with your kids.

- Think about how you can create some emotional distance or protection for yourself if you get pushback or critique for talking with your children about this.

- Know that for us as a broader society, there's work to do to start making our world a safer place to grow up and live as a gender-expansive person. We all have our part to do and I believe that we can do it!

# 10

# Building a Safe and Affirming Home

Eight-year-old Nick and five-year-old Jasmyn are the children of Dan and Lance. Dan is genetically related to Nick and Jasmyn, and their other genetic donor is a close friend of Lance's named Nara (their surrogate). While Nara doesn't live in the home, she is involved in parenting Nick and Jasmyn and is a part of their lives through phone calls and visits. It's important to all three parents that they provide a safe and affirming home where the kids can be free to find out who they are, discover what they like and don't like, and learn how to be compassionate community members. They've had intentional talks among themselves, asked questions of parents and caregivers who seem to raise children in a way they admire, and they've done some reading to try to decide how they can go about doing this.

They knew that mutual respect was a big part of building a safe and affirming home. They also decided they wanted to give as many choices and options as possible and reserve what they restricted or said no to for safety concerns or dangerous situations. The adults also wanted to be upfront and honest with the children as much as possible, checking in with one another about how to find age-appropriate ways to share information while also knowing that adults might underestimate sometimes what children can comprehend.

Nara shared that the concept of bodily autonomy was important to her because it was preventative against child abuse, built confidence, and sent the message that children can know what is or isn't positive touch or interference with their bodies. For Nara this even extended to waiting to cut the children's hair until they communicated they wanted that. Dan and Lance agreed, and they noticed that in public strangers would almost always assume that long hair meant the child was female. Dan and Lance also observed how that assumption hurt children from cultures where all genders grow long hair, and limited the expression of cisgender and gender-expansive kids alike.

Dan's extended family comes over once a month for dinner and recently a few of them made jokes about trans people and used derogatory language about feminine men. None of the parents were okay with this, but they had to talk together about how they wanted to handle it. They knew it was important to address the negative comments in front of Nick and Jasmyn because they didn't want the kids to think it was okay to say those things or think their parents' silence equated to acceptance. Dan felt that, since they were his relatives, he should be the one to address it in the moment. Dan and Lance practiced ahead of the next family dinner what Dan would say. When it happened again, Dan first said in a firm tone, "I don't get what's funny about that." He went on to say that he didn't agree with the comments and that all genders and all gender expressions are good.

One day, Dan, Lance, Nick, and Jasmyn were watching TV together when a commercial came on depicting a masculine person dancing seductively and gracefully in a silk robe. The commercial was supposed to make the viewer laugh. Dan asked, "Why is that supposed to be funny?" which sparked a conversation about how boys, men, and people perceived to be male are discouraged from being graceful or liking things like silk and flowers. By modeling asking questions, Dan and Lance build a safe and affirming home.

Later, when Nick and Jasmyn were playing with kids in the neighborhood, Lance overheard the neighbor Jeremy say, "Nick, here, give the pink one to Jasmyn. Pink's not a boy color." Nick replied quickly: "Colors don't have a gender!" This was good feedback that the parents' efforts to make their home a space where their children can like what they like and be who they want, regardless of assigned sex or gender identity, were paying off.

## Put It into Practice

Try playing a game called "What gender nonsense did you come across today?"
Here are some example answers:

*At school they said "boys only" on the basketball court. That rule stinks!*

*When I called the allergist to make an appointment for you, the first question they asked was, "Boy or girl?" Why do they need to know that to schedule an appointment, huh?*

*Nobody mentioned nonbinary people in any of my activities.*

*Today my shirt was purple with flowers on it and somebody told me it was "girly."*

You can have fun with it, making drum roll and cymbal crash sounds after each example, or giving "points" for each example. You can laugh and then, if you want, launch a discussion about how to respond when people say or do these kinds of things, just like when Nick answered that colors don't have a gender in the earlier example.

This type of activity raises everyone's awareness of the constant messaging going on about gender identity and expression, reinforces that your family recognizes multiple genders and freedom of gender expression, and emphasizes that you will support your kids and their friends in their identities and expressions.

## *Takeaways*

- Family members can actively work to create a safe and affirming environment for children to thrive in.

- Fostering a home where curiosity and questions are welcome is one part of making an affirming home.

- Make sure your child has a sense of agency over their body and their self-expression.

- Show your child that you'll confront transphobic and homophobic comments, as well as more subtly biased actions or statements.

- Encourage your child to explore all types of interests, clothing choices, hairstyles, activities, etc. Observe any hesitation that arises in you related to a certain expression or interest and allow yourself to be free of that bias.

- Actively listen to your child. Make space to be open to whatever your child is communicating.

# 11

# Encouraging Your Child's Gender Expression

Six-year-old Jafar wraps a colorful scarf over his head and tells Noor, "I'm going to wear *hijab* when I get older!" Noor, who wears hijab, smiles and warmly says, "Okay, that sounds good." Noor will observe if this is something Jafar says again and knows that she can ask more questions later to learn what Jafar thinks and feels about gender identity and gender expression. For the moment, she simply enjoys seeing Jafar happy and having a good time and expresses support for Jafar's wishes.

Kathy provides childcare every day for her four-year-old grandson, Charlie. Kathy makes sure to have a wide variety of toys for Charlie to play with: dolls, animal figurines, blocks, a tea set, trucks, etc. Charlie's parent sends him to Kathy's house dressed in stereotypical "boy" clothes and usually only in blue, brown, and green colors. When Kathy takes Charlie shopping for a piece of clothing, she takes him down the "girl" and "boy" clothing aisles, making positive comments about different items in all sections and asking what Charlie likes and wants to try. When Charlie wanted a rainbow tutu once, she bought it and talked ahead of time with his parent about not making any negative comments about him wearing it. Kathy tells Charlie he looks "pretty" wearing the tutu. Kathy pays attention to her words and notices if she's leaning toward only calling him "handsome" or "buddy" and avoiding words like "pretty" or "sweetheart." She asks herself why that is and works to remind herself that these words are for anybody unless they explicitly say they don't want to be called a certain term.

Eight-year-old Anton is playing pretend and says to their Uncle Mendo, "I'm Ezilie Danto!" (Ezilie Danto is an *lwa*, or spirit, in Haitian vodou.) Mendo asks, "Why do you like to be Ezilie Danto?" Anton answers, "Because she's fierce and smart and takes care of children, too." Mendo says, "Yes, I see why you're Ezilie Danto!" Mendo remembers later to talk about how Anton is also fierce and smart and nurturing. He tells Anton that nonbinary people, girls, boys, and other genders can all have these traits and ways of expressing themselves. Mendo says, "I wonder what other ways you like to express yourself," as a way of inviting more conversation if Anton wants to share more.

Ten-year-old Lanette likes to wear basketball shorts, tank tops, baggy tees, and snapbacks. Lanette plays basketball and football at recess and video games after school with friends. Sometimes kids tease Lanette and ask, "Are you a boy or a girl?" or make hateful comments about Lanette's alleged genitals. Her mom, Debra, has been working with Lanette to come up with how she

wants to answer those kinds of questions or bullying behaviors. Debra is also working with the school staff on intervening more when those things happen. Recently they had a family funeral to attend and Lanette asked to wear a button-down shirt and tie. Her mom knew some relatives might not like that, but she wanted Lanette to feel good in the clothes and decided to handle any disapproving comments herself. She showed pride in Lanette and took a photo of her in the shirt and tie.

## Put It into Practice

You can be proactive in affirming all gender expressions and in creating a safe home environment for your child to be themself and to try out things that feel good. You can offer your kid all options, affirm their communication about how they want to express their gender, and help them learn how to handle other people's biases or limited perspectives on gender.

- Praise all children based on their unique traits, skills, and interests. For example, "*You were so kind today when you comforted your friend who fell*"; "*You're such a fast runner!*"; "*You make really funny jokes!*" Focus less on their appearance.

- Provide a dress-up/dramatic play box. Include a wide range of props, outfits, and accessories so your child has an opportunity to freely and comfortably play and express themself in ways that feel good to them. Thrift stores, yard sales, and hand-me-downs from friends are all great ways to fill a play box. Tap into your imagination! Play dress-up with your child and let yourself move out of your day-to-day comfort zone with it.

- Keep your assumptions in check. Watch out for any assumptions you form about what your child will or won't want to wear or do.

- Support your child's choices. Be supportive of how your child wants to wear their hair, dress, use a nickname or chosen name, and take on various roles.

- Notice implicit bias. It could come in the form of viewing a boy's aggressive behavior as "displaying leadership" or "taking charge" and the same behavior by a girl as "bossy" or "spoiled." Describe behaviors you see regardless of who is doing it. For example, if you witness a boy and a girl fighting over the same toy, you might say, "I see that you want to use this toy right now and that Jamie is using it. I wonder how the two of you might work together to come up with something that works for both of you. Maybe you can take turns?"

- Engage with your child to discuss bias. If your child, or another child, says something like, "Itai's wearing an apron and playing in the kitchen but that's for girls," ask questions. "Hmmm, have you heard someone say that aprons or kitchens are only for girls? What do you think about that? Have you seen any people who aren't girls cooking in the kitchen or wearing aprons?"

- Reinforce gender-neutral messaging. Reinforce the messages that clothes are clothes. Everybody gets to wear anything they like. All colors are for all people.

- Expose your child to a variety of gender expressions. Make sure your child is exposed to kids and adults with a variety of gender expressions. Be intentional about your own social circle, the media consumed, and books and activities that are available.

# *Takeaways*

- Create opportunities for your child to explore different ways of expressing their gender.

- Encourage thoughtfulness and reflection on gender-related comments or stereotypes.

- Notice any assumptions or stereotypes that might have crept their way into your language or ways of viewing your kid's behaviors. Think about how to shift those.

- Talk about gender expression and point out different ways of expressing gender in the world around you. If you don't see much variation in your own circles, it's time to mix it up and broaden your world!

# 12

## Following Your Child's Lead

Millo, age five, was assigned female at birth. Millo recently told the family, "I'm not a girl, I'm just me." Millo also said, "I want to cut my hair to look like Mr. Keyon's."

Recently, Millo was reprimanded at kindergarten. The teacher had addressed the class by saying, "Good morning, boys and girls," and Millo responded with, "We aren't all boys and girls." Millo's answer flustered the teacher and it was considered rude to interrupt and correct an adult, so the teacher sent a note home with Millo.

Millo's family came to therapy for support and help thinking through how to handle these situations. The family members were unsure what was going on with Millo related to gender, especially since Millo wasn't saying, "I'm a boy." They didn't want Millo to be perceived as rude to adults, but they also wanted Millo to be comfortable advocating for themself. Millo's grandfather said, "You need to decide whether you want to be seen as a boy or a girl because that's what the world understands. It's too confusing when you tell people you are neither one." Millo was hurt by this but did not want to be seen as correcting or arguing with an elder. One of Millo's titis was very nervous that the family was about to "have to start Millo on hormones and all that." In therapy, the family acknowledged discomfort and fears and talked about slowing down and really listening to Millo. They were given information about the age range hormones would be an option (not at age five) and pubertal suppression medications, so they were familiar with possible future options, but with the reminder that they were following Millo's lead. They talked about ways to ask follow-up questions to understand more about what Millo might be feeling or thinking in natural ways. They considered how to approach the topic without putting a lot of pressure on it. The family started to implement some of the things they had discussed.

Over the next few months, Millo continued to reinforce, "I'm not a girl, I'm just me," and started to avoid wearing the dresses in their closet, gravitating instead to overalls or pants with colorful tops. At one point, some family members bought some "boy clothes" for Millo. They seemed disappointed that Millo was not excited about the gifts. Their therapist reminded the family

about following Millo's lead and not assuming anyone knew where things were going with Millo's preferences. The family recognized that they might have assumed and shifted into simply complimenting Millo's choices and referring to Millo as "kid" or "my child."

One of the cousins gave Millo a haircut "like Mr. Keyon's" and everyone could see Millo's happiness. A few months later, a parent asked Millo, "Do you still want to be called Millo?" Millo said, "For now, until I think of a different name." At times, family members would say it was uncomfortable when strangers would gender Millo in different ways and that they didn't know what to do when people called Millo "boy" or "girl." Their therapist advised them on how to have that conversation with Millo, finding out how Millo felt in those moments and what might feel good for family members to say or do.

The family discussed with their therapist how gender identity and gender expression are different things, although sometimes they might overlap. They watched videos of different people with different genders and gender expressions and discussed them, recognizing all the possibilities that Millo has in terms of gender identity and expression. The family started to think about ways that Millo might be able to learn more about those possibilities, too, since that would help Millo's own process of understanding and communicating their gender identity at some point in time.

## Put It into Practice

It's challenging that many parents, relatives, and caregivers have been taught that children should not be leading the way on anything. We're trained to believe that adults will always know what is best for kids and that kids must be shown what to do and when to do it by their adults. The notion of following a child's lead can go completely against what we were taught it means to be a good caregiver, and doing it can have some of our relatives

shaking their heads at us. For example, Millo's family had taught Millo to respect and listen to elders but also wanted Millo to be able to advocate for themself. It was confusing for Millo to know how to respond to the teacher or their grandfather in a way that would be seen as acceptable within the family and cultural values. Millo's caregivers could have asked what Millo wanted to say when adults said hurtful things and helped Millo practice assertive and respectful responses.

You may be working on aligning your beliefs with the parenting practices described earlier in the book, with the goal of a deepening understanding of your child versus trying to convince them that your way is right, and listening past your own biases and assumptions. Following your child's lead also means matching their level of emotional urgency. If they seem distressed or struggling, that needs to be taken seriously and responded to quickly. If they seem to be feeling good and doing well, you can match that mood even if your child is gender expansive. Sometimes Millo's family members wanted to rush ahead of Millo in thinking about hormone therapy or clothing choices instead of slowing down to listen and observe. Sometimes this is about the anxieties the family members are experiencing rather than what's going on for their child. You can notice your own emotions in order to work with them so that you're able to separate what you're feeling from what your child is feeling.

You can trust your child's internal sense of self and intuition about who they are, while giving room for exploration, play, and trying out different terms, labels, or expressions. Following a child's lead means that sometimes we adjust course, sometimes we pivot, and sometimes we go with the flow. Your child may present and identify one way at a young age and then later identify or express themself in a very different way as a preteen or teen. It doesn't mean their identity isn't real, right? I know you already know that if you've made it to chapter 12!

Here are some tips to follow your child's lead with their gender and gender expression:

- Resist urges to direct toward or away from something: Notice if you feel yourself wanting to steer your child away from or toward any activity, style, mannerisms, etc., and be willing to honestly ask yourself where this urge is coming from. We've all absorbed social messaging about gender expression and identity and can commit to actively unlearning and releasing it.

- Practice humility when your child identifies a misstep or misunderstanding. Many times young people tell me that their parents or family members get defensive when told they've done something hurtful, even if unintentional. We can take a moment, take a breath, and practice humility if our child reminds us that we're not using the right name, pronouns, or words to refer to them.

- Accept that your child's understanding of themself will grow and change over time. This includes many aspects of them, including possibly gender expression and identity.

- Have regular casual check-ins. Ask questions, like Millo's parents asked: "*Do you still want to go by Millo?*"; "*When you heard me answer the stranger about whether you were a boy or girl, how did you feel about that answer? Is there something different you wish I'd said?*"; or, "*You know some people change their pronouns from week to week or at different times in their life. Last month you liked _____ pronouns. Does that still feel good?*" And then *listen* and keep it moving.

# *Takeaways*

- Observing with an open heart means we are not attached to the outcome. We just want to actively support our child with whatever is happening with them in any given moment in time.

- Being gender expansive or transgender isn't an emergency or a problem to be fixed. Like any aspect of a person, it's something to be celebrated and appreciated. If you aren't sure what your kid might be communicating with their words and actions, or don't know how to respond, seek out a professional who is experienced with working with gender-expansive children, or better yet, has lived experience and works with gender-expansive children, to be a support for you in your journey to follow your child's lead.

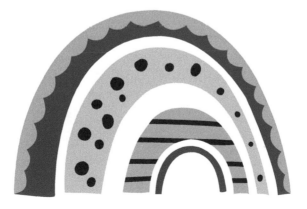

# 13

# Observing without Assuming

Mia is sitting on the ground watching two-year-old Mo play. Mo toddles over and spends a few minutes playing with a wooden hammer and tool chest. Mia narrates Mo's actions and says, "Look at you go, hammering those nails! You got one!" and, "It makes a loud sound when you hit with the hammer, huh?" Mia watches Mo move on to a toy piano and Mia comments, "Listen to those keys. You're playing the high notes and now the low notes." Next, Mo picks up a baby doll and starts to rock the doll and brush its hair. Mo kisses the doll. Mia observes, "You're taking care of that baby." Mia has heard adults, like her mother and a daycare teacher, make assumptions about Mo when Mo chooses a certain toy or activity. But Mia has made a choice to unlearn assumptions about gender based on gender stereotypes and binary views.

Nate is outside playing with three-year-old Niama. They're playing pretend and Niama wants to be Black Panther. They run and jump around the playground. Next Niama decides to be Spider-Man. They climb and run around the playground. They laugh and squeal. Nate doesn't make any assumptions about why Niama wants to be Black Panther and Spider-Man. He just lets the moment be fun and free.

Paul is playing pretend "house" with five-year-old Preston. Preston puts on an apron and says, "I'm the mom and you're the kid. I'm going to make you some lunch and then I'm going to put on some makeup." Paul jumps into his role and starts pretending to be a young kid. He doesn't draw any conclusions from Preston pretending to be a mom.

Isabella notices that some days, four-year-old Ignacio chooses to wear clothes like green sweaters with brown pants or black athletic track pants, and other days he wears purple sparkly shirts with pink leggings and a matching headband. Isabella chooses not to assume meaning in Ignacio's choices and just praises Ignacio for getting dressed and compliments each outfit. Isabella is committed to creating an environment where all gender identities and expressions are embraced and conversations about each person's own gender journey are normalized.

## Put It into Practice

You've heard that saying—that to assume makes an *ass* out of *you* and *me*? As adults, we make assumptions to manage information, navigate situations, or predict and control outcomes. We all do it, whether we realize it or not. And many of us really don't like when somebody else makes an assumption about us, do we? I know I don't!

When we assume, we so often get things wrong or we miss seeing the whole picture. All kids, whether cisgender, gender-expansive, or transgender, can benefit when the adults around

them are able to simply observe without making assumptions about their gender. It doesn't mean an adult would never ask questions about patterns or try to understand more, but rather that parents and caregivers are careful not to assume or tell themselves a story about something without open and clear communication. A lot of times, our assumptions come from messages about gender we've internalized or from our own personal experiences. When we let go of assumptions, we can truly get to know our children for who they are.

It's easy to assume, but assumptions are roadblocks to getting to know your kids and building a trusting relationship. When you notice that you're drawing conclusions, challenge yourself to practice grounding and coming back to the present. Check in with your child and actively listen without judgment. Commit to releasing expectations and seeking understanding. Kids and youth of any age can express their gender identity in different ways. This may or may not mean they are gender expansive, trans, nonbinary, etc. Observing without assumption keeps us open to all possibilities.

Below is a step-by-step guide to observing without assuming:

1. Notice when you have an assumption.

2. Identify the exact thought you're having. Examples:

    *There's something wrong because my kid likes unicorns and fairies.*

    *It's weird that she's pretending to shave her face.*

    *Is my kid gay because he plays with dolls?*

    *My child must be transgender because she wants to use a nickname that sounds like a boy name.*

3. Identify the emotion caused by the assumption (worry, fear, confusion, disgust).

4. Reexamine your thoughts and identify only the facts you've observed; remove any opinion or assumption you're adding to the observation.

> Examples: *My child sometimes likes to play pretend games about fairies and unicorns.*
>
> *My child just pretended to shave her face.*
>
> *My child likes to play with dolls.*
>
> *My child wants to go by a new nickname.*

5. Remind yourself that anything beyond the facts is a "story" your mind is inventing without evidence provided by your child communicating something to you. Ask yourself if there's any learning you need to do to better understand what you're observing.

6. Ask yourself, "How do I want to respond to this moment? What does my most confident, generous self want to do?"

## *Takeaways*

- Observe without judgment, opinion, or assumption.

- Believe that whatever your child's gender, however they express themself, and whatever they like is glorious and wonderful.

- Stay in the present to accept who your child is today.

- Empower your child to be their full, true self.

- Radiate confidence in your child's unique brilliance.

- Validate your child's identity and expression.

- Ease up. Release expectations and assumptions.

# 14

# Asking the Right Questions

On certain days, five-year-old Cassius would say to his family, "You can call me Cassie today." On other days Cassius would say, "It's alright to call me Cassius today." Cassius's mother and grandmother, whom he lived with most of the time, observed this, as well as Cassius's father and father's boyfriend. They weren't quite sure, but on the days of going by Cassie, the mannerisms, expressions, and even tone of voice sounded more feminine, and on the Cassius days the body movements and clothing choices seemed more masculine.

The family all talked together and were on the same page about not making assumptions and being supportive. They also wanted to open the door to conversation in case Cassius wanted to talk about inner feelings or what was going on in terms of gender identity and expression. The family realized that, although they had all tried to create a safe home environment, there might have been some things they missed in teaching Cassius/Cassie from the beginning about gender identities and expressions. They decided they needed to ask clear questions and give clear information in order to support their growing child in the best way possible. They wanted to really understand whether their kid was playing, trying things out to learn what felt good, or communicating gender fluidity or another gender identity so that their family could be actively affirming.

## Put It into Practice

Children can understand at very young ages that it's not body parts that make someone "boy," "girl," "nonbinary," "gender fluid," etc., but rather how they feel on the inside, in their heart and mind. You can talk to your kids from birth about how there are lots of ways to be a girl, lots of ways to be a boy, and lots of ways to be other genders. Kids can also be taught very early that we can't know somebody's gender identity from looking at them, reminding them that people of all genders can look all kinds of ways. It benefits all children, whether cisgender, gender expansive, or trans, to learn these things. It can lead to the creation of more harmonious and respectful friendships and communities.

You can teach your child from a young age to ask what pronouns people use, and model introducing yourself to people with your own pronouns. You can ask your child each day or week what pronouns they want to go by. This models that pronouns can change and shows that you'll respect and honor your child's decision.

Here are some questions to ask your child as a regular check-in:

- What pronouns do you want me to use for you? At home or with everybody?

- What name do you want to be called? At home or in certain places/with certain people?

- What do you want me to call you to other people—child? Son? Daughter? Something else?

- What kinds of clothes do you like? What colors or patterns?

- What do you like to do for fun? What games do you like to play?

- What kinds of toys or supplies do you like to have?

If your kid has shared with you that their gender is different from what they were assigned at birth, you can thank them for sharing that with you, tell them you're proud of them, and then you can ask these questions:

- Where do you see yourself on the gender spectrum?

- What words have you heard for gender identities, and do you have a sense of what feels right for you?

- Is there anything you want to change right now in how you express yourself? How can I support you in those changes?

- How long have you felt this way? How were you able to tell me now?

- Is there anything else you want me to know or learn about your experiences?

- How can I make things easier for you?

Here are some things NOT to say:

*This is hard for me. I'm going to have to grieve the loss of my little girl/son/etc.*

Your child may have worried about sharing this information with you because they don't want to be a source of pain. Instead of voicing your emotions to your child, you can process them with a trans-affirming therapist or friend. It's a chance to ask yourself if you're really grieving the expectations and social norms that come along with assigned genders. It's a chance to adjust and accept knowing your child more fully.

*Well, I support you, but I don't want you to tell Granddaddy. He just wouldn't understand and his health's not good.*

You might have an urge to say this to protect your kid from any hurtful words of other relatives, but the message received can be that your kid's identity is too much, something to be embarrassed about, or something that will cause harm to someone. Instead, you can reassure your child that you'll talk to relatives about it and address any hurtful comments that might happen on your own as their advocate.

*You can wear whatever you want at home, but when we go out in public you need to dress like _____.*

While it's true that safety risks can vary from family to family and location to location—you may have to consider and weigh those risks—you don't want to give your child the message that the way they want to express themselves is wrong, bad, weird, or something to hide.

*Are you sure this is how you feel? I know you have a friend at school who's transitioning and I want to make sure this is really you and not you over-identifying with your friend.*

Take the time to educate yourself and learn about gender expansiveness in children and young people. You are on that path and reading this book is an important step toward that education. The exploration of gender identity and expression can be difficult, and that process is different from when kids and teens experiment with different hobbies/interests/music/clothing styles. When mainstream society isn't reflecting the many gender identities that exist and in many cases still rejects the fact that there are more than two, once a child or teen reaches a point where they're introduced to people of other genders and is able to independently learn about the existence of those, it may make it easier for them to identify the ways they've been feeling inside. This can coincide with meeting classmates or teachers who have other gender identities, knowing a friend who has come into understanding of not being cisgender, or reading stories online of real people with various gender identities. It can be a process. For example, I've used several different terms to describe my identity over the years based on what I knew about myself at the time or felt accurate in certain ways. That doesn't mean that any of the previous terms were necessarily invalid or wrong for me, just that I continued to grow in understanding of myself and what resonates with me.

*You're too young to be talking about this stuff. Wait until you're older.*

Don't fall into the trap of underestimating what children understand and sometimes even comprehend better than adults do. So much of the time, kids are doubted by adults or not taken seriously because we think we know them better than they know themselves. Let's trust our children's ability to understand who they are and remind ourselves of our parenting values—that we celebrate who our child says they are today, that we stay curious about who our child will become, and that we let go of assumptions so we can decrease any subconscious limitations we might place on them.

# *Takeaways*

- Ask questions with the goal of deepening your understanding.

- Come into the conversation with curiosity.

- Commit to parenting from a place of love, releasing fear as often as you can.

- Process your own emotions alone and with other adults.

- Let your questions have a positive tone.

- When your child gives you answers about what kinds of things would make life easier for them related to their gender identity or expression, do your best to do those things. If you don't know how, ask someone who might.

- Remember, you've got this! And your kid's got this!

# 15

# Preparing for Puberty

S imon is eight years old and his parent, Alix, gave him two books about puberty: *Sex Is a Funny Word* and *Puberty Is Gross but Also Really Awesome*. Alix chose those books because they're inclusive of a range of gender identities and bodies and Alix knew that in Simon's school health class, information on puberty wasn't going to be shared in a comprehensive, inclusive way.

They set up a time to talk together about the books while Simon ate his favorite snacks. Simon was assigned male at birth, but in their discussion of the books, he let Alix know that he was worried that some of the pubertal changes he might go through like growing facial hair and having a lower voice weren't going to feel good to him. Alix asked open-ended questions with curiosity and really listened to Simon's responses. Based on what Simon shared, Alix decided that they should make a consultation appointment with a pediatric endocrinologist to ask questions about puberty blockers and whether this might be a medication that would benefit Simon. The medication would give Simon more time to learn about what he was feeling in terms of gender identity.

Given some of Simon's comments, Alix really wanted to have this consultation before puberty started to spare Simon any distress or turmoil that might happen if these pubertal changes did not align with Simon's gender. Alix was glad to have given Simon the books and made the time to have a talk about them in a relaxed way. Alix noticed some of their own anxiety creeping in and decided to call a friend to process that away from Simon.

## Put It into Practice

Do you remember the class you took in school, or maybe the talk you had with a parent, about puberty? I do, and let me tell you that neither was detailed or inclusive enough to be useful to me in my life at the time. Did you have a gym teacher showing outdated videos about menstruation and erections? A nurse putting condoms on bananas? A parent quietly sliding a book about pubic hair and armpit sweat under your door and never mentioning it again?

I know from talking to lots of young folks that those classes and talks aren't going too much better today. These conversations might be uncomfortable or awkward, or we just might

not really be sure how to go about them, but it's important that we ensure our kids have access to comprehensive and inclusive sexual health information. This is another important time to review the fact that body parts are not gendered, to use inclusive language in talking about body parts, to share exactly what can be expected with different pubertal changes, and to openly listen to how your kid feels about the possible changes. It's another good time to reiterate the concept of consent and bodily autonomy.

Consider how to talk about bodies in ways that don't center on cisgender identity or erase intersex people. I've had lots of parents of young trans youth ask me to talk with their kids about sex because "I don't know how trans people have sex so I don't know what to say." As a parent or guardian, you can learn that information yourself and share it with your child. *Trans Bodies, Trans Selves* might be a good resource for you in learning how to be inclusive in your conversations about these topics. Talking to your kid about puberty isn't a one-and-done conversation. There'll be lots of moments you can ask more questions, listen, and offer information and yourself as a supportive resource.

You'll also have lots of opportunities to engage with your child about media that they consume or are exposed to and what you both think about the references or reactions to puberty that come up. Be real and authentic in those moments! Let your child know that you're not afraid to broach those topics.

**NOTE:** *Not all trans, nonbinary, and agender kids and teens have dysphoria about their bodies. Dysphoria may happen more because of being misgendered out in public or over the phone, for example.*

*Dysphoria is different from a cisgender youth feeling self-conscious about the pubertal changes happening to their body. A parent once said to me, "Well, I felt weird when I started wearing a bra, too. I didn't like that boys at school could see the straps. Everybody feels uncomfortable about puberty."*

*The difference is that the self-consciousness or feeling weird or awkward wasn't about being a girl or being viewed as female because of starting to wear a bra.*

**Pubertal Suppression (Puberty Blockers):** Blockers can come in the form of leuprorelin (injectable, either monthly or every three months) or a histrelin acetate implant (slow release over one year). They can be prescribed by a pediatric endocrinologist, primary care pediatrician, family doctor, or nurse practitioner trained in their use. When the medicines are stopped, puberty (or gender-affirming hormone therapy) resumes, so this is not an irreversible treatment. If puberty has started before beginning blockers, breast reduction or testicular reduction will occur. Phallic growth will stop. Frequency of erections will decrease. Pubic hair, body hair, facial hair, and acne will not go away. The time that a child might start blockers can vary depending on the situation. If your child has been expressing or showing signs of gender expansiveness, you can talk to a prescriber about options and even seek out a therapist or support group as you work on being an even more affirming parent than you already are.

## *Takeaways*

- You can talk with your child about puberty long before it begins.

- Share accurate information with your child so they can make the best decisions for their body and spirit.

- Learn about the ways that gender dysphoria can present and understand the differences between gender dysphoria and general discomfort that cisgender youth might have during puberty.

- You can get support for yourself and your kid as they're approaching puberty, including trans-knowledgeable medical providers.

- Remember that if your child expresses gender dysphoria, they don't have to experience pubertal changes that might not be right for them. There are medications that can put a pause on puberty.

- Coming up on puberty is another time to call in your village. Who do you know that could also talk with your kid and is trusted by them? What stories or books do you want to use to round out your talks with your child? Who do you know who can be a good resource for you as you help your kid approach puberty?

# 16

# Preparing for Social Transition

F ive-year-old Rocky was assigned male at birth and has been identifying as "not a girl or a boy" since age three. Rocky now wants to be called Remy, use they/them pronouns, and wear clothes that are stereotypically masculine and feminine without people calling them a girl or boy. Remy wants to use the single stall, all-gender restroom, as well as the "girls" bathroom at school. Remy's family is supportive, but their parents aren't sure how to help Remy socially transition.

Remy's family hears of another family in town whose child also uses they/them pronouns. They talk with the family about their questions and that family's story and experience. After this conversation they felt less anxious and more prepared. They also decided to see a trans therapist who works with young children to make sure they have plenty of support throughout the process.

# Put It into Practice

Remember that transition is unique to each person. There's no formula or format to follow, but there is overarching guidance on how to support your child. Social transition is a highly individualized process in terms of what steps are taken and when but can involve changing name, pronouns, and/or outward gender expression. It can take some adjustment as people around the young person may be using different names or pronouns for them based on whether they've been told about the transition or if they're a stranger gendering the youth based on assumptions. It can be challenging to hold the emotions around these mixed experiences, to manage nervousness about how different people will react to the transition, while also feeling a sense of "rightness," relief, or joy when somebody uses a new name or pronouns correctly. Some young people start to feel more comfortable in general in life and sometimes that they have more capacity to engage fully with the world as they transition.

- We honor the principle of following the child's lead and listening to what's communicated. This means trying to avoid making assumptions while actively asking questions and seeking to understand the responses. It means going at your child's pace rather than trying to speed something up or slow something down.

- Social transition is not irreversible or unchangeable. It's okay if your child changes their mind about their name or pronouns. This does not invalidate their identity or cause them harm. You can *state this clearly* to your child, normalizing that they may feel differently or speak differently about their gender at various points in life and it's okay.

- A kid's gender identity propels the social transition, not the other way around (Yong, 2019). A desire to use different pronouns or names indicates a strong association with another gender.

- Talk about how body parts do not determine gender identity. Make sure your child has examples of lots of combinations of body parts and genders. They can work together on how to respond to comments or questions about body parts from child peers or adults. The family can continue to assess whether puberty blockers might be needed and consult with a medical provider for information and guidance as well. Parents can also discuss whether changing the gender marker on birth certificates, passports, etc., is a helpful step.

Some people don't consider children who identify as nonbinary, agender, "not boy or girl but something else," or other nonbinary genders as wanting or needing to socially transition. I presented Remy's story as an example because I think it's important to understand that they *are* communicating a gender identity, and some things socially will need to shift for that child to feel affirmed, just as trans children with binary gender identities need some social changes.

Remy had expressed identifying as "not a girl or a boy," using they/them pronouns, using their new name, and restroom choice as being important. Together with Remy, the parents took a series of steps to provide Remy with support for social transition. Let's review how Remy's family approached it:

- The family identified the most supportive people in their social circle. At first, Remy was just using their new name and pronouns at home but would now expand the circle. They decided how to bring up the topic and talked with Remy about how they might answer questions about these changes.

- They looked through Remy's clothes with them and made a list of pieces of clothing or accessories that could expand the options they have for gender expression and a plan for getting some of those.

- After learning about their rights, the family met with school administrators to inform them of the transition and discuss a plan for letting all relevant teachers know. They talked about how Remy's new name would be noted in school records and rolls so that even substitute teachers would not call out the old name.

- The family was able to ask questions about how teachers would handle misgendering and respond to any student questions about Remy's restroom use. They discussed privacy and honoring Remy's decision-making about how to respond, too.

- The family asked how Remy's teacher would avoid using phrases like, "Okay, boys and girls," or dividing kids into activities by "boys" and "girls," and they donated a couple of children's books on gender identity to the classroom. They provided a recommendation for a consultant to the school if the school could benefit from ongoing guidance and support with the transition.

- The family talked about what they would say about the changes to people who were in more outer rings of their social circle, like neighbors or coworkers.

Parents often ask me about online posts they've come across about "de-transitioners" (a person who no longer identifies as trans or feels they are now a gender different from the one they previously identified as) or "desistance." I let them know that those comments are based on very few, scientifically flawed studies. For example, they conflated gender expression with gender identity and made assumptions about participants who dropped out of the study. Also, most previous research studies are flawed in that they start from a worldview of binary gender identity—male and female—as well as binary thought: One is either this or that, always and forever. As Diane Ehrensaft says, "Why are we asking a child to conform to something that is not them because society hasn't done its learning yet? It's time to teach society."

Studies show that less than one percent of people who report "transitioning" report "detransitioning," but there are those rare individuals. It doesn't have to involve a sense of regret. And for those people who do report regret, it often has to do with unsatisfactory surgical results or surgical complications, rather than regret about aligning with their gender identity. Sadly, a reality is that some feel they have to detransition due to transphobia leading to loss of housing, employment, family rejection, etc. The media has sensationalized some of these complex stories, and anti-trans groups have completely exaggerated the occurrence of this phenomenon, using it to try to deter family members and communities from supporting trans individuals.

Working with a trans-identified therapist who has experience working with children can offer families insight informed by lived experience, as well as potentially relieving a family's fears, since a lot of people may not know an "out" trans adult or have worked with a trans professional before. Trans therapists are also usually well connected to local and national community resources and may have had personal experience with various settings and providers that inform their referrals. There are definitely cisgender therapists who are trans affirming and knowledgeable to assist

young kids and their families. Think of the powerfully positive message you are sending a child who might be questioning their gender identity or exploring gender expression if you choose a trans adult to work with.

Research shows that embracing and affirming your child's gender identity and assisting with social transition decreases depression and anxiety compared to children whose families don't provide unconditional love and acceptance nor allow social transition (Olson et al., 2016). Social transition can make a child more comfortable with making friends and participating in family outings and activities, and more able to focus while learning.

Parents and caregivers can help children come up with ways they want to respond to questions or comments. For example, if another classmate says, "*Last year you were a boy,*" a response might be, "*No I wasn't, some people just thought I was*" or "*My name is _____ and I go by _____.*" Some youth might feel comfortable responding, "*I'm trans.*" Responses can be in line with that child's personality and natural way of speaking, and it can help build their confidence to practice. Another example could be helping your child decide how they want to answer if somebody says, "*I love your name! How did your parents pick that?*" (if your child chose their name). You can reassure your child that they get to decide what they disclose to strangers or acquaintances and give the tip that they can evade a question they don't want to answer directly or lie about by responding in a roundabout way: "*Thank you! My name was inspired by/means/ sounds good with . . .*"

Sometimes problems might escalate into bullying. You should let your child know that bullying can come from peers but also adults. Encourage your child to assess their safety in situations and what they might need to be safe, including asking for help from nearby adults or bystanders. You can practice with them how to communicate confidence, strength, and groundedness while removing themself from an escalating situation. If you or your child are concerned about possible physical bullying or

attacks, you might think about enrolling them in self-defense class, martial arts, or what might be available even online, to feel that they have more physical defense strategies if needed. Sit down with your kid and help them look up local and online support groups and networks so that they can get support from other gender-expansive and trans youth, and make sure they have the number to an appropriate crisis line. Gender Spectrum is one place to start for national online support groups, and the Trevor Project has a chat crisis line, as well as a phone line. Trans Lifeline is a trans-led and trans-staffed crisis line. If your child is experiencing bullying, a non-affirming school environment, or just doesn't know many other gender-expansive young people, you might want to seek out a summer camp for trans kids and youth so they can have a positive experience with peers and adults.

## *Takeaways*

- Recognize that social transition may help children feel their gender identity is accepted, interact more confidently with peers, feel more securely a part of their social groupings, and experience less anxiety when facing new situations and new people.

- Keep the benefits in mind when you're dealing with hard moments in the process.

- Intentionally communicate acceptance and offer reassurance to your kid.

- Parents and caregivers might be surprised by the range of emotions they feel during a social transition with their child. Find others who have gone through similar experiences to help decrease any sense of isolation and offer encouragement. Sometimes professional support can give the same benefits.

- Notice any nonverbal messages you may be sending without realizing it. Did you decorate your assigned-female child's bed with pink and purple while your assigned-male child's bed was green and blue? Are there choices you made that might have communicated limitations on who your child could be? If so, talk with your child about this and what you've learned since making those decisions.

- Model confidence for your kid in how you state their identity or pronouns and answer questions from others.

- Ground yourself in love. Let love guide instead of fear as much as possible.

- Remind yourself that affirming your child in who they are is not wrong!

- Let yourself feel good in the knowledge that you're actively showing unconditional love to your child.

# PART IV

# Frequently Asked Questions, Answered

I want to take an opportunity to answer some frequently asked questions about gender identity, gender expression, raising gender-expansive children or trans teens, and more. These are things that come up when I'm in trainings with people, working with family members of therapy clients, or just talking to other parents in conversation. This is not an exhaustive list of questions, but hopefully you'll find something here that you've been wondering about.

# Question #1

*This is all kind of new to me and something I've never thought much about before, but I am really trying to now. I want my kids to be free to be themselves. I'm sure I need to change some things, but I'm not sure where to start. What advice do you have for parents and caregivers who are trying to get away from gender stereotypes and gendered language?*

Thanks for being ready to shift your language and thoughts about gender! We all have things to unlearn, and this means we all have things to practice.

The first step is to recognize how often you're using gendered terms or thinking in stereotypical ways. Ask your kids or your friends to "buzz" you every time they hear a gendered word, phrase, or stereotype. This can be a lighthearted way to practice and can raise your awareness about how you use language. Next, think about more inclusive ways to say certain things (such as talking about "parents and caregivers" versus just "moms and dads"). Practice this and teach these ways of saying things to your kids, too. When you notice somebody around you gendering someone they don't know, you can tell them, "Say 'that person.' We don't know their gender by looking at them." This is a reminder to you and others that gender identity can be different from gender expression, and that gender identity is not dependent on appearance.

Notice when the children in your life are discouraged from doing certain things because of their assigned gender, and challenge those beliefs so that your kids know you support them in doing what feels good and right to them. Read and watch or listen to things by people of a variety of genders, who use a range of pronouns and honorifics. This can help you absorb more of this vocabulary.

**Take Action:** Take one news article, social media post, or section of a book and notice any gendered language. Practice rewriting those lines using gender-inclusive terms.

Enlist the help of a friend, family member, coworker, or neighbor and set a timer for 15 minutes. Have a conversation and ask them to listen for any time gendered words are used. Discuss how those things could be said differently.

Start a "gender stereotype" jar. Every time you or anybody in the family observes (or has directed at them) gender stereotypes in society, put some change in the jar. When the jar is full, you get to donate the money. Your child can help decide where to donate, such as finding a program for houseless trans youth, a program that provides education on gender identity and expression to schools or faith groups, or one that donates binders, packers, and other gender-affirming items to kids and youth who need them.

## Question #2

*I want to teach my kids how to be nonjudgmental and inclusive. But sometimes they say things that I know would be hurtful to someone or that sound offensive. I know part of it is their age and developmental stage, but I still want to work on this with them. How can I do more to raise open-minded kids?*

When our kids say something that sounds judgmental, is within a binary framework, or is outright hurtful, we can ask questions that might prompt them to think about things from a different perspective. We can watch our own language and the ways that we talk about others so that we're modeling inclusive, open, and respectful ways of thinking of others. We can make it clear when they've said something hurtful that it's not okay and explain why it's hurtful or offensive. Celebrating diverse identities, maintaining a diverse social

network and community, and speaking positively about other people are ways to model nonjudgment and inclusivity to our kids. We can play an "empathy game" with them where we act out different scenarios and ask them to model empathy and how they would respond in a situation. This provides safe practice space and chances for feedback in a way that your child might think is more fun than just a conversation.

**Take Action:** Take turns playing the "empathy game" with your child. Act out a scenario and ask them to show empathy, and then switch places.

Assess your own social circle. If it's not representative of different identities and expressions, think about how you can build real relationships with a more diverse group of people. Does your community have groups for trans, nonbinary, Two Spirit, and gender-expansive people? Could you volunteer your time to support their work and invest in that group of people? Attend their public events and donate to their work? If not, maybe there's a general Pride center or group. Otherwise, how could you expand your networks in general? Think about activities or community spaces that draw a diverse group of people and how you might get involved.

Model speaking about other people in respectful ways. Let your child "buzz" you, do a hand signal, or somehow communicate when they hear you say something judgmental about another person.

## Question #3

*My child is five years old and has been raised with knowledge of multiple genders, taught to ask people for their pronouns, and has been around people of various gender identities. When she was three years old she said that she is a girl. Over the past year or two she's become very rigid and*

*kind of judgy about gender. She imposes stereotypes ("boys can't wear lipstick"), genders people she doesn't know even though she was taught not to do that, and lately has even been saying she only wants to play with girls and women. I'm at a loss because we tried hard to avoid this kind of thinking and am not sure where it's coming from or how to handle it.*

First off, thank you for the work you did to teach your child about multiple genders and about asking for pronouns versus assuming. I mentioned earlier in the book that despite our best efforts at home, our kids are going to be around other people and other ways of thinking, sometimes spending many more hours a day with limited views of gender. Along with that, young children are trying to make sense of the world in their own way, and sometimes it might feel easier or comforting to them to have rigid "rules" or categories. As parents and caregivers, we can continue to reinforce the values and knowledge that we have as well as to ask questions to prompt thought (for example, *"How do you know that person's pronouns? Did they tell you?"* or, *"Why do you think that person is a girl? Is there any other gender they might be? Have they told you their gender?"*). Continuing to foster relationships with people of various gender identities and expressions can be a balance to any more binary or limited environment your child is in.

**Take Action:** Ask thought-provoking questions. Mix up the media, making sure your child is exposed regularly to representations of a range of folks. Foster relationships with a diverse community. Teach and model empathy and kindness.

*I've told my kids they can play with whatever they want and do whatever activities they like, but they still seem to gravitate toward stereotypical things based on their assigned gender. Is that because it's just what they naturally like or some other reason? What else can I do?*

It's hard to answer this without knowing you and your family, but I usually ask about gender stereotypes in the home among the adults. What's modeled or demonstrated at home? How are household chores divided? What types of jobs do people have and what roles do people take on in the family? How do the adults express their gender? Most of us aren't raising children in a bubble, so they're absorbing social messages, observing what behaviors and expressions are validated and which are punished or discouraged. Familial influence isn't the only factor, and in many cases, home is the place children are spending the least amount of their time. It may be the case that your kids truly do like the things they're gravitating toward, or you may learn later they didn't but felt pressure to conform. Doing the strategies and recommendations in this book can help you create an affirming home environment that can feel supportive if your kids want to identify in a new way or express their gender in a different way.

**Take Action:** Check in with yourself about any other gender stereotypes that might be unintentionally happening at home beyond toys or kids' activity choices. Be thoughtful about what types of activities you plan and offer as options for the family and your kids. Make sure they know there is a range of opportunity and that you'll support any interest they might have, even if it's something they don't witness a lot of other people doing or that seems to be centered on gender binaries. Communicate out

loud about gender stereotypes and give examples. Help your kids think about why those stereotypes exist and how they can reject them if they want to. Know that your child's interest might fluctuate through time.

## Question #5

*If I'm cisgender and heterosexual, what are some ways I can make sure my kids have exposure to multiple gender identities and expressions besides trying to expand my social network?*

One thing you can do is to seek out cartoons, music, YouTube and TikTok personalities and shows, books, and other media that includes characters with multiple gender identities and expressions. Preview them first and then talk about them with your kids. Most of the media your kids are exposed to centers on cisgender and heterosexual people. There are gender-expansive people who are animators, writers, musicians, and more. Make sure your kids have the opportunity to experience gender-diverse content so they are growing up with exposure to all the possibilities open to them.

**Take Action:** Set up a preview party night with your friend or partner and watch cartoons, YouTube videos, TikTok videos, movies, or music videos featuring gender-expansive characters and people. Discuss them and select a few to schedule a watch party with your kids. Make it fun! To make sure that this content is being woven into and normalized with your child's media consumption, be intentional about scheduling times (you don't have to call it anything, it can just be a typical movie night) to watch the content you've curated. You can also ask your kids if they've seen or heard of any gender-expansive characters or shows you don't know about.

*My four-year-old child has been telling me that she's a boy. I've been noticing her smile drop when I say, "Hey girl," "Girl, please!" and other similar things to her. She asked me the other day if she would grow a penis when she grows up. She hasn't been wanting to go to preschool and I've started feeling bad when I drop her off because she's so upset. This seems like some things I've heard about gender dysphoria. I'm starting to wonder if I should be saying "he and him" for my child. I feel scared about where this might be heading but I don't want my child to be depressed or in pain. What should I do?*

Thank for you noticing and taking seriously the things your child might be trying to communicate to you. If you haven't yet, you may want to start by letting your child know what you're observing and hearing from them, asking them to tell you more and help you understand. You can ask your child, *"If there was a magic wand that could change anything, what would you want to be different?"* Let your child know that you'll be on their (or his, her, or other pronoun) team and help find whatever resources might help.

When you know more about your child's wants and needs, it might be clear to you that a social transition would really decrease gender dysphoria. If you're feeling lost and like you really need support to know what's best or what's going on, I would encourage you to find a support group online or in person for parents of gender-expansive children, as well as a trans-affirming and knowledgeable clinic or child therapist for your family. Those can help you and your child figure out the best process for social transition and give you support along the journey.

**Take Action:** Ask your child questions about things you think you're observing, and offer ideas or scenarios up to make sure they know about possible options for themself. Seek out your own support along the way.

## Question #7

*My seven-year-old, Jayce, was assigned male at birth and likes to wear skirts, tutus, and nail polish sometimes. Our family supports this and have said that "any clothes are for any body." But I get nervous when Jayce plays outside in those things and goes places in public. There've been a couple neighbors who've made comments like, "Jayce, are you wearing a costume today?" or, "Is that your sister's skirt?" I'm waiting for the day they say something worse or somebody asks a question when we're out in the community and Jayce is wearing a tutu and nail polish. I don't really know how to respond to those comments.*

It can be hard to know how to respond to certain questions or comments about your kid's gender expression, especially if you know some people don't have much knowledge of, or exposure to, gender expansiveness.

It can help to determine ahead of time which relationships might call for more dialogue or explanation from you. You might decide there are certain folks you want to talk to about the fact that Jayce likes wearing skirts and nail polish, explaining that you support it and hope Jayce's community will support it, too.

Then there may be strangers or casual acquaintances you bump into now and then. You might decide to have some planned responses up your sleeve for comments and questions. For example, a question such as, *"So, is your kid a boy or*

*a girl?"* could be answered with, *"Jayce is a boy." "Is that a boy in a dress?"* can be met with, *"Yes, dresses are for anybody who wants to wear them,"* or, *"I support my child's self-expression. We support people of all genders and expressions in our family. Isn't it sweet/dope/awesome/beautiful/[your* word of choice] *when kids can be themselves? I hope we all get to do that."* Conversations with kids asking questions may be different than with adults. It might be a chance for a short educational moment with another child on the playground.

Get support for yourself and ask other parents and caregivers about their favorite ways to talk to other people about their child. If you don't know anybody local, you can find groups online who share these kinds of experiences and ideas with each other.

**Take Action:** Ask your kid how they might want you to respond to these kinds of questions or comments. Practice your own responses so that when the time comes, you'll feel confident that you have an idea of what to say.

## Question #8

*I think that kids at school are bullying my child. They've come home crying a few times and have told me that several kids have been saying hurtful things and laughing at them. One kid is getting other kids to laugh and say the hateful things, too. I'm so angry and so sad for my kid. They were excited to be able to be themself fully at school and now they just seem withdrawn. I don't want to make things worse for them. What should I do?*

First, talk with your child. Let them know you care, are listening openly, and want to hear about their experience. Next, speak with the school and ask about their policies for addressing bullying. Advocate for concrete actions and open

communication with you about the steps they take. You can work with your child to develop self-esteem and confidence. You can suggest that it takes strength and confidence to move away and not engage with bullies. Sometimes it might also be more effective for your child to respond to a bully calmly, quietly, and confidently before moving away. You might help them think of what they would want to say. For example, *"Say what you want, but I know who I am. It doesn't matter what you think; I like myself. My gender is something you just don't understand, but that's not my problem."*

You can also help your kid expand their friendship base and support system. Encourage your child in making friendships at their school, at other community spaces with other kids, and with trusted adult mentors, too. If there are chances for them to talk with other kids with shared gender identities or experiences of being bullied, that's good, too. A therapist or parent group might be able to help with those connections. Check in with your child. Show nurturing, compassion, and genuine admiration to your kid.

**Take Action:** Bullying can have serious and long-lasting effects, so it's important that parents and caregivers take action rather than ignoring or waiting. You might feel like raging, but be careful your actions don't escalate the situation or increase the bullying toward your child. Allow any processes the necessary time to be tried. You might need to increase your advocacy for your kid if the school isn't addressing it or if the processes aren't effective. It may help to talk to several of your friends who would give you objective advice on how to handle things, or even your own therapist. Think about the skills and traits that you can help your child develop to build confidence around bullies, as well as to build resilience. Foster healthy friendships with other kids around the same age as your child, as well as adult mentors who'll affirm your kid. Having adult mentors who share your child's gender identity can benefit them, too.

*I want to find a therapist to help my family as we start to think about my child's social transition. What should I be looking for and what questions can I ask a potential therapist to know if they might be a good fit for us?*

Many therapists advertise as LGBTQ+ friendly but it's important to ask specifically about the "T" and their experience with trans and gender-expansive care. In this case you can look for a therapist who has both lived experience and experience with gender-expansive kids and youth. When you call or email, you can ask potential therapists if they have lived experience and how many gender-expansive children they have worked with. If you can't find somebody in your area who fits both categories, you may have to prioritize one.

You should ask whether the therapist has knowledge of local resources and would be able to assist you in knowing your rights in school, providing referrals for physicians who prescribe puberty blockers and gender-affirming hormone therapy, offering information on support groups, etc. If the therapist works within a larger agency or clinic, ask what type of interactions you could expect from support staff and whether all staff are trained in being affirming of multiple genders. You can ask about whether the therapist provides something called superbills for you to submit to insurance for reimbursement, or whether they are in-network with your plan, and how both of these scenarios work. Know that if either you or your child aren't comfortable with the therapist when you meet, or you find that they're not able to help you in the ways you need, you can ask for a referral or just let them know you'll be looking for another provider. Of course, you can also seek out therapists who share racial or ethnic identity with you or your child, and if you speak with a

trans-affirming clinician who doesn't share your race, you can ask them for trusted referrals who do.

**Take Action:** You can make a list of questions to ask potential therapists. You may want to rate your priorities to consider in your decision. Word of mouth can be a good way to find out about therapist options, and there may be online lists of therapists vetted by trans people in your region.

## Question #10

*I'm supportive of my kiddo and feel like we've created an affirming home environment. But I've noticed that out in public, sometimes I have emotions I'm not proud of because I don't like drawing attention to us. The other day my six-year-old announced to the playground, "I'm nonbinary!" and when I saw some of the other parents there look at me, I felt dread, worry, and embarrassment. I'm ashamed to admit that and kind of surprised that I'm having these reactions in those kinds of moments, but I am. What can I do about these feelings?*

Thank you for being honest about your emotions and wanting to know what to do about them. It may be that a shift in how you think about these moments would lead to different feelings. You could try thinking of this in the way you'd think about your kid exploring any aspect of themselves or proudly expressing other parts of themselves. Remind yourself that it's a positive thing for your child to be able to tell other people who they are. When other people don't understand or don't like it, it might feel awkward for a minute, but what's the feeling you want your child to take away in that moment? That their parent was embarrassed, or that their parent was proud and celebratory? Thinking of things in the long term and big picture can sometimes help us let go of some of the other emotions.

You can also get support for yourself. Meeting other families in similar situations can really normalize your experiences and boost your confidence and courage. Sometimes parenting can bring out our own insecurities that haven't been resolved. It may take addressing those with our own healers, therapists, or spiritual leaders to be able to parent from our best place in those moments.

**Take Action:** Write out what your "big picture" goal is for your parenting and your child's experience of life. Write out specifics on how you can do your best to make the big picture happen. Practice self-compassion. Parents are people with all kinds of feelings. It's what we do with the feelings that matters. Find your own support, identify and address insecurity or fears, and surround yourself with people who can boost your self-esteem and courage in parenting.

## Question #11

*My three-year-old grandson likes to have his nails painted. I'm supportive of gay people and trans people, but I think he's too young to know about that stuff, so I don't think we should let him have painted nails. I promise I'm not homophobic and if he decides when he's a teenager or adult to do it, then I'll fully support him. Do you agree that we're on the right track with not letting him paint his nails again?*

With situations like this I encourage family members to first pause and reflect before deciding or reacting. Some questions to ask yourself: Does my grandchild like painted nails because they're colorful? Because adults my grandchild loves have painted nails? Why am I associating nail polish with sexual orientation or gender identity? Am I thinking about those things because of something else my grandchild has expressed, said, or done? Why do I want to shield a young

child from knowing about various gender expressions or identities (or sexual orientations, though those are different from gender expressions)? Usually being willing to honestly consider these types of questions will lead you to the answer.

**Take Action:** First pause and take a breath. Then reflect. Identify the thoughts and anxieties that are present for you. Be honest with yourself and ask questions. Commit to erring on the side of affirmation over fear.

## Question #12

*My 10-year-old niece is living with us after being removed from her parents' care. We realized she's been taking my son's boxer briefs and wearing those instead of her own underwear. Does this mean she's transgender? What should we do? We don't want to be shaming but we should probably do something.*

Thank you for wanting to support this young person and avoid shaming. You can talk about this at a time that seems relaxed and comfortable, if possible. You could say something like, *"There's no judgment here. I've noticed that you've been wearing Sean's underwear and I'm wondering if you'd like for me to pick up the same kind for you to have as your own. I know we're still getting to know each other. You can safely share anything about yourself here, whether it's anything to do with how you feel on the inside, how you like to dress, how you like other people to see or relate to you, or who you're attracted to."* Open the door for the conversation, practice your active listening skills, and see where that takes you. Remember that we want to avoid assumptions, while emphasizing that it's valid to be whoever you are and express yourself however you want. We also want to make space for the fact that sometimes people are figuring it out and we need to let them have their process.

**Take Action:** Avoid assumptions and open up conversation at a time when everybody is most likely to be calm and relaxed. Make sure the person you're caring for knows that you believe in all genders and gender expressions and will support them in being themself. You might be the first person to say this to them! Remove as many barriers as you can to your child being able to express themself fully.

## Question #13

*As an adult I can understand that there are more than two genders, but won't that idea just confuse my child? I think they're too young to introduce this. A neighbor's child seems confused because I hear them call their teddy bear three or four different pronouns.*

Young kids can understand that there are multiple genders when it's presented in a matter-of-fact way that's in line with their developmental stage. Sometimes they understand it better than some adults do! Young children may even be talking about where they are on the gender spectrum or try to communicate this in various ways. Sometimes how they're describing their gender to you may not fit with what you were expecting, but letting them know you realize there are many genders can help them feel supported. Very young kids are learning how to use pronouns even when they're only exposed to two, so it can take some time before they understand what pronouns are and how they're used. Introducing more pronouns doesn't cause ongoing difficulty with this.

**Take Action:** Start explaining to your child at a young age that there are more than two genders, even if not everyone around them knows this. You can match your language to their age and development, but simply let them know the facts. This helps your child understand their own gender identity, as well as being empathetic to people of all genders.

*My child is already at risk of mistreatment for other reasons. If I encourage them in being transgender, they are going to be set up for even more risk and mistreatment. What should I do?*

This is really real. And the problem is not that your child wants to be themselves, but that there are those out there who are transphobic and anti-trans. When faced with this reality, we can place the emphasis on addressing transphobia and anti-trans bias around us, in our family, our neighborhood, our faith community, our school system, etc. We can call on allies to do that work, too, to create a safer world for our child. We have to understand that not allowing our child to be themself also poses a serious risk to their health and well-being. We can work with our children on how to navigate risks of bullying or violence, while understanding that the problem is not in who they are.

**Take Action:** Ask your school, faith group, family, friends, and trusted advisors what practices, teachings, and policies are in place to ensure everyone is learning about multiple genders and gender expressions to make a safer environment for all. Recommend trainers and resources. Call on allies to further the work. Consider what might help your child have increased safety in different settings.

## Question #15

*I know a family in my area who hasn't assigned a gender to their infant and uses "they" pronouns for the child until the child can tell the parents what their gender identity is. How is this different from how I'm raising my kids, which is*

*that they can play with or wear whatever they want regard-less of whether they are a girl or boy? Aren't both examples of "gender-neutral parenting"? If I've already assigned a gender to my child from birth, is it too late?*

Raising kids with the label of the sex or gender they are assigned at (or before) birth and encouraging them to explore interests and express themselves however they want, even outside of gender stereotypes, is creating an affirming home for gender expression and interests. However, this is different from not assigning a gender to your child from birth and waiting until the child lets you know who they are. Families who take this approach (which can also be cultural practice for some people) are introducing from birth that gender is not assumed based on genital configuration, but that they will honor the felt gender identity of the child. Families using this approach intend that their infant and young child won't have to experience some of the subconscious stereotyping and ways of relating that occur when people know a child as "girl" or "boy," leading to more freedom to determine for themself how they feel on the inside and what they like and don't like. If you've already assigned a gender to your child and they're conscious of what they're called, you can tell them, *"We thought you were a _____ at birth, but there's a chance we aren't right about that. There are a lot of different genders. If you think you're not a ____, you can always tell us."*

**Take Action:** You can decide not to assign a gender at birth to your child, even if you have older children to whom you did assign a gender. If you already assigned a gender at birth, you can have a real, honest talk with your kid about assumptions made and open things up for the possibility that you assigned the wrong gender. This talk can be revisited from time to time as a reminder. Whatever your child's gender identity or expression, you can create an affirming and freeing home environment.

*My 11-year-old has been going by the same name for the past couple of years and we're ready to do a legal name change so he can start middle school with only the chosen name in the records. What's the process for this? Are children allowed to legally change their first name? Will we need a lawyer and a court hearing?*

Legal name change laws and required procedures vary from state to state. You should be able to look up the process for your state and county. Usually, you'll need to file in the county your child lives in. If you need help or direction on how to find the information, you might reach out to your state's trans rights group (if there is one) or contact Transgender Law Center or National Center for Transgender Equality. See the Resources section on page 135 for more information. You may also be able to get a packet from the county clerk of court.

In general, one parent or guardian can file an application (or petition) to the court for the name change, but if your child has more than one legal guardian, all of them might need to be in agreement unless there are some stipulations met. You may want to provide documentation and evidence that the name change is "in the best interest" of your child. The documentation could be letters of support from a physician, a therapist, etc. Some states may require "affidavits of character," parental consent forms, and copies of the birth certificate and any previous name changes. Some states require publication of the petition for name change in a local newspaper or posting within the courthouse. In those states, sometimes you can request a waiver to the publication requirement. A hearing may be scheduled if all legal parties have not signed consent or if the judge has questions. You're required to pay for any filing and publication fees, as well as copies of

a signed court order for name change. You can usually do the filing process yourself, although some families hire an attorney to do the whole process for them.

**Take Action:** Contact your local or state trans rights organization for information; if one doesn't exist, reach out to a national organization like the Transgender Law Center or National Center for Transgender Equality if you're not sure where to start. They can advise on "reasons for name change" that have been accepted in your region, but you might also consider "this is the name that is preferred" or "this is the name the child goes by," especially if publication is required. Contact your child's county of residence clerk of court to ask for a minor legal name change packet. Gather all the required documents, identify fee amounts, and seek consent from legal guardians, as well as any affidavits or letters required.

## Question #17

*My child's been on puberty blockers for a couple of years now. He wants to start gender-affirming hormone therapy soon, but I thought you had to be 16 or older to do that. He's 13 now. I'm nervous about this. What about his fertility and what if he wants to have biological kids someday?*

You're right that 16 and older used to be the required age to start gender-affirming hormone therapy. However, many prescribers are prescribing to younger adolescents who have been on blockers. This is to help young people be on pace with peers experiencing puberty, as well as to allow for more results with hormone therapy. It's true that it can be hard at age 13 to know if you'll want biological children when you're older. At the same time, not all people do want to become parents in that way—or parents at all—and ultimately, in

valuing bodily autonomy, we support young people in the decisions about their body, right? And as parents we can be there to support them in the future if they have any unfulfilled desires, no matter what they are.

**Take Action:** Schedule a consultation with your child's prescriber to ask questions and open communication about hormone therapy. Practice active listening with your child. Ask yourself what you might need to let go of in your own expectations or dreams. Give yourself space to process those emotions away from your child.

## Question #18

*My 13-year-old transmasculine child is socially transitioning. Aside from using a new name and pronouns, what else does this entail? What other things should I be thinking about? They already presented the way they wanted in terms of hairstyle and clothes before.*

Well, the first thing I'd do is talk with your child about what else they might envision for their transition. Without knowing them, it's hard for me to answer this, but some transmasculine people find chest binders or packers to be helpful. If your child wants to bind, it's important to know how to do it safely and to get the right size. A binder company like gc2b or the New York Toy Collective can help with this, as well as some trans-affirming physicians. There are also packers (prosthetic penises) that can be worn and made in youth sizes found at places like New York Toy Collective. Your child may want to do a legal name change or shift certain roles they have in various activities if there are things they're involved in culturally or spiritually that were assigned by binary gender.

**Take Action:** Ask your child about their vision or dream and offer some possibilities to find out if they are aware of those options or interested in them or not. Some of these are things like packers, stand-to-pee devices, chest binders or double layered sports bras, breast forms, gaffes or tucking underwear, etc. You could share ideas about ways to honor and celebrate a name change or shift in cultural practices if those are relevant.

## Question #19

*My 17-year-old college freshman who is trans wants to do a summer study abroad program in a country that is not known to be an affirming place and maybe not safe to be out. He hasn't changed his legal name yet and the program coordinator said that he should "present" in alignment with his legal name while there. I don't know if this is the right thing. I'm worried about the dysphoria this could cause to someone who's been living as their true self for a while now and has to be "in disguise" or "in the closet," so to speak. My kid really wants to go, but maybe this isn't the right place to visit, or maybe we need a different program? Should I advocate more with the coordinator?*

What does your kid say? What do they want? What do they fear? You can have this conversation first. You can get more information from the coordinator by asking questions like: Who in the program or the other country would be accessing your child's identification documents and comparing them to presentation (how realistic or widespread is any risk or threat)? What are the documented statistics on treatment of known transgender citizens of the country, as well as visitors? Are there any legal ramifications there for being trans? What would the living situation be? Would there be privacy in terms of restrooms/changing areas?

When you have all the needed information, you and your child can decide what the risk really is and whether the risk level is one that is tolerable or not. Then you can approach the coordinator with a plan and request, or you can research other programs or other locations and advocate for a safer placement if needed. You may need to provide information and education to the coordinator, too, if the plan is to move ahead with your child presenting consistently with their gender identity versus stereotypes based on identification documents.

**Take Action:** When concerned about your child's safety, talk with them to learn what they feel are the risks and what information they might still need to gather. Ask questions of those "in charge" and advocate for your child when needed and when appropriate.

## Question #20

*Why does it seem like so many transgender and nonbinary people have so many problems? Is their gender identity due to childhood trauma? They really don't seem happy to me so I'm not excited about the thought of my child possibly identifying as trans or nonbinary or being gender expansive in some way.*

Gender identity is not due to any external experiences, but instead based on the internal sense of self. Gender-expansive or transgender children and youth can experience trauma in the form of family rejection, peer rejection, social discrimination, abuses, and more. The response to these experiences can be feelings of sadness, isolation, hurt, shame, fear, depression, and anxiety, especially if the young person is in an unsupportive setting. Trans, nonbinary, and gender-expansive

kids and teens do best in affirming environments. Affirming homes and other settings can provide a balance to other painful experiences.

**Take Action:** Remember that you can take actions to create more affirming spaces for young gender-expansive, trans, and nonbinary people. This increases the ability of all youth to experience joy and confidence. You can be a supportive person who celebrates all genders and gender expressions and models that for those around you. You can challenge anti-trans discrimination and exclusion in your own personal sphere and in the region where you live.

## Question #21

*Some of our extended family have been asking personal questions like "So what surgeries are you gonna get?" I don't want my child to feel that just because an auntie or grandparent asks, they have to share information they don't want to. At the same time, my 10-year-old has been asking at what age they would be eligible for gender-affirming surgeries and I don't know the answer.*

Your child (or you, if the question is directed to you) can answer invasive questions about their body and medical interventions with responses like *"That's not a question that's appropriate to ask people," "I'm not comfortable talking about that," "I don't talk about my genitals to people,"* or *"Are you asking about my private parts?"* These are just a few ideas, but the basic message is that your child does not have to give information to anybody that they are not comfortable giving. In terms of surgery ages, that will depend on a particular surgeon's age requirements. Some surgeons will provide surgeries for under age 18 and others do not. The WPATH

Standards of Care state that the decision on what age to perform gender-affirming surgery is individualized to that particular youth and their care team. So, the broad answer is that it depends on your child, their journey and desires, and collaboration with any providers who are working with your family.

**Take Action:** Teach your child that they have autonomy over what information about their bodies they want others to know and give them concrete examples of how they can respond to questions from others, especially other adults. If your child is curious about surgery for themself, you can research surgeon policies in your region and connect with local family support groups where people often share word-of-mouth information and referrals.

## Question #22

*My child is experiencing online harassment from anti-trans and transphobic people on various social media platforms. Are there any steps we can take? How do I help them cope with this?*

You can screenshot and save the messages and report them to the platforms. You can block the senders and adjust privacy settings to the most restrictive or even de-activate accounts for a period of time until the harassment has stopped. If the actions qualify as a hate crime, you may want to report and seek help from legal representation, cyber investigators, or other authorities. Harassment and bullying, especially in a public forum, can have serious negative impacts on the target. Seek professional support and social support for your child if they've experienced this.

**Take Action:** Do your best to make your child's social media and Internet use as secure and safe as possible. Learn about all the different current popular apps and sites your child might participate in and their privacy and location settings. You can create guidelines for safe use for your child. Take quick action if your kid is being harassed or bullied or even just being exposed to hateful rhetoric about their identity so they don't have to try to deal with it alone.

# RESOURCES

## *Online Resources*

Abrams, M., and G. Kassel. "LGBTQIA+ Safer Sex Guide." Heathline. August 31, 2020. Healthline.com/health/lgbtqia-safe-sex-guide #condoms-and-barriers

The Gender Book (ebook, hardback, and resources): TheGenderBook.com

Gender Spectrum: GenderSpectrum.org/resources

National Center for Transgender Equality: TransEquality.org

Radical Copyeditor: RadicalCopyeditor.com/2017/08/31 /transgender-style-guide

Teen Health Source: TeenHealthSource.com/topics/sex

Trainings, consultation, speaking engagements, and therapy services: HawnTherapyAndConsulting.com

Transgender Law Center: TransgenderLawCenter.org

Trans Youth Equality Foundation: TransYouthEquality.org /for-parents

TransYouth Family Allies: IMATYFA.org/parents.html

## Books

*Beyond Magenta: Transgender Teens Speak Out* by Susan Kuklin

*The Every Body Book: The LGBTQ+ Inclusive Guide for Kids about Sex, Gender, Bodies, and Families* by Rachel Simon, illustrated by Noah Grigni

*The Gender Creative Child: Pathways for Nurturing and Supporting Children Who Live Outside Gender Boxes* by Diane Ehrensaft, PhD

*Gender Identity Workbook for Teens* by Andrew Maxwell Triska LCSW

*It Feels Good to Be Yourself: A Book about Gender Identity* by Theresa Thorn

*Sex Is a Funny Word* by Cory Silverberg

*They, She, He Easy as ABC* by Maya Christina Gonzalez and Matthew SG

*Trans Bodies, Trans Selves: A Resource for the Transgender Community* edited by Laura Erickson-Schroth

*The Transgender Child: A Handbook for Families and Professionals* by Stephanie A. Brill

*Transgender Teen: A Handbook for Parents and Professionals Supporting Transgender and Non-Binary Teens* by Stephanie A. Brill and Lisa Kenney

*Who Are You?: The Kid's Guide to Gender Identity* by Brook Pessin-Whedbee

# REFERENCES

Bilal, Khadija. "Here's Why It All Changed: Pink Used to Be a Boy's Color & Blue for Girls." May 1, 2019. *The Vintage News.* TheVintageNews.com/2019/05/01/pink-blue.

Brooks, John. "The Controversial Research on 'Desistance' in Transgender Youth." May 23, 2018. KQED. KQED.org/futureof you/441784/the-controversial-research-on-desistance-in -transgender-youth.

Butler, Octavia. *Parable of the Sower.* New York: Four Walls Eight Windows, 1993.

———. *Parable of the Talents.* New York: Seven Stories Press, 1998.

Cook, Rachel E., Matthew G. Nielson, Carol Lynn Martin, and Dawn DeLay. "Early Adolescent Gender Development: The Differential Effects of Felt Pressure from Parents, Peers, and the Self." *Journal of Youth and Adolescence* 48, no. 10 (October 2019): 1912–1923. doi.org/10.1007/s10964-019 -01122-y.

Gender Identity Development Service. "Social Transition for Younger Children." GIDS.NHS.uk/parents/advice/social -transition-younger-children.

Eagly, A. H., Nater, C., Miller, D. I., Kaufmann, M., and Sczesny, S. "Gender Stereotypes Have Changed: A Cross-Temporal Meta-Analysis of U.S. Public Opinion Polls from 1946 to 2018." *American Psychologist* 75, no. 3 (2020): 301–315. doi.org /10.1037/amp0000494.

Ferguson, Sian. "What Does It Mean to Be Agender?" January 20, 2021. Heathline. Healthline.com/health/agender.

Halim, May Ling, and Diane Ruble. "Gender Identity and Stereo- typing in Early and Middle Childhood." In *Handbook of Gender Research in Psychology,* edited by J. C. Chrisler and D. R. McCreary, 495–525. New York: Springer, 2010. doi.org/10.1007/978-1-4419-1465-1_24.

James, S. E., J. L. Herman, S. Rankin, M. Keisling, L. Mottet, and M. Anafi. *The Report of the 2015 U.S. Transgender Survey.* Washington, DC: National Center for Transgender Equality, 2016.

Jones, Jeffrey M. "LGBT Identification Rises to 5.6% in Latest U.S. Estimate." *Gallup News.* February 24, 2021. news.Gallup.com /poll/329708/lgbt-identification-rises-latest-estimate.aspx.

Keo-Meier, Colt, and Diane Ehrensaft, eds. *The Gender Affirma- tive Model: An Interdisciplinary Approach to Supporting Transgender and Gender Expansive Children.* American Psychological Association, 2018.

Kuper, L. E., L. Wright, and B. Mustanski. "Gender Identity Devel- opment among Transgender and Gender Nonconforming Emerging Adults: An Intersectional Approach." *International Journal of Transgenderism* 19, no. 4 (April 25, 2018): 436–455. doi.org/10.1080/15532739.2018.1443869.

Levin, Sam. "'It Helps Me Be Myself': Trans Kids on the Healthcare Republicans Want to Deny Them." *The Guardian.* March 24, 2021. TheGuardian.com/us-news/2021/mar/24/trans-children -healthcare-ban-gender-affirming.

Littman, Lisa. "Parent Reports of Adolescents and Young Adults Perceived to Show Signs of a Rapid Onset of Gender Dysphoria." *PLOS ONE* 13, no. 8 (August 16, 2018). doi.org /10.1371/journal.pone.0202330.

Maas, Megan. "How Toys Became Gendered." December 9, 2019. *The Conversation.* MSUToday.MSU.edu/news/2019/how-toys -became-gendered.

Nanda, Serena. *Gender Diversity: Crosscultural Variations.* Long Grove, IL: Waveland Press, 1999.

Olson, Kristina R., Lily Durwood, Madeleine DeMeules, and Katie A. McLaughlin. "Mental Health of Transgender Children Who Are Supported in Their Identities." *Pediatrics* 137, no. 3 (March 2016). doi.org/10.1542/peds.2015-3223.

Olson-Kennedy, Aydin. "Parenting a Transgender Teenager in a Cisgender World," Annual Gender Infinity Conference, 2017, Houston, TX.

Rafferty, Jason. "Ensuring Comprehensive Care and Support for Transgender and Gender-Diverse Children and Adolescents." *Pediatrics* 142, no. 4 (October 2018). doi.org/10.1542/peds. 2018-2162.

Richards, Alikah S. *Raising Free People: Unschooling as Libera-tion and Healing Work.* San Francisco: PM Press, 2020.

Solomon, Jamie. "Gender Identity and Expression in the Early Childhood Classroom: Influences on Development Within Sociocultural Contexts (Voices)." July 2016. *Young Children.* NAEYC.org/resources/pubs/yc/jul2016/gender-identity.

Steensma, Thomas D., Roeline Biemond, Fijgje de Boer, and Peggy T. Cohen-Kettenis. "Desisting and Persisting Gender Dysphoria after Childhood: A Qualitative Follow-Up Study." *Clinical Child Psychology and Psychiatry* 16, no. 4 (October 2011): 499–516. doi.org/10.1177/1359104510378303.

"Supporting Gender-Expansive Children Creates Safe Spaces for All." Virtual Lab School. Accessed May 31, 2021. VirtualLabSchool.org/focused-topics/gender-safe/lesson-3.

Turban, Jack L., Dana King, Jeremi M. Carswell, and Alex S. Keuroghlian. "Pubertal Suppression for Transgender Youth and Risk of Suicidal Ideation." *Pediatrics* 145, no. 2 (February 2020). doi.org/10.1542/peds.2019-1725.

United States House of Representatives, History, Art, & Archives. "Postwar Gender Roles and Women in American Politics." Accessed May 31, 2021. history.House.gov/Exhibitions-and -Publications/WIC/Historical-Essays/Changing-Guard /Identity/.

Yong, Ed. "Young Trans Children Know Who They Are." January 15, 2019. *The Atlantic*. TheAtlantic.com/science/archive/2019/01 /young-trans-children-know-who-they-are/580366.

# INDEX

# Acknowledgments

I'd like to offer gratitude to all those who came before me who had the practice or tradition of not assigning a gender to their infant and waiting to learn who their child was. I'd like to thank the other writers and scholars who have shared their knowledge on this topic.

# About the Author

 **Tavi Hawn, LCSW,** is a licensed clinical social worker who has worked with gender-expansive children and transgender kids, teens, and adults for more than 12 years. Hawn is a multiracial Indigenous person who is also Two Spirit and nonbinary transgender. Hawn is parent to an incredible small human and is humbly learning all the new lessons parenting brings.

CPSIA information can be obtained
at www.ICGtesting.com
Printed in the USA
BVHW010158110723
667040BV00003B/29

# Contents

Afterword

*Speaking to the Heart and Equipping for the Journey*

Appendix 1

*Being a Sensory Smart Parent or Teacher*

Appendix 2

*Sensory Smart Classrooms on a Budget*

# Introduction

*Helping Children and Teens with a Traumatic Past*

Anya throws the crayons across the room and runs out the door. This isn't the first time she's done this; her teachers lost count long ago. Anya is an eight-year-old little girl who was born in Eastern Europe and spent the first three years of her life in an orphanage. The relative who dropped her off in the middle of the night gave no information about Anya's history, but to this day her precious little body speaks volumes about the abuse and neglect she experienced—as does her behavior. Eventually adopted by an American family, Anya is now part of a local after-school tutoring program—one where every week her teachers struggle with her frequent outbursts.

Luke's sad face and unkempt appearance tell his story, as does his out-of-control conduct. The six-year-old has been attending a children's church ministry for about a year. Every Sunday a family stops by his house to pick Luke up for church. The family members know only the basics about Luke's background, but they are aware that his home life is difficult. His father is an abusive alcoholic, while his mother works multiple jobs and is rarely around. Those who work with Luke every week know almost nothing about him. They also have little idea how to help him.

Johnny allows no one to get close, although many have tried. He entered the foster care system at age four and was adopted at six. Now fourteen, Johnny struggles with self-esteem and feelings of rejection. His adoptive parents, reluctant to share his history of severe neglect, have revealed little to his teachers. Although Johnny's teachers don't know his background, his disobedience and angry attitude point to a troubled past.

Where do we find children and teens like these—ones who've experienced serious trauma and other adverse childhood experiences? The simple answer is *everywhere*. Kids from difficult home situations are in our classrooms, on our sports teams, part of our after-school programs, in our churches, and at our summer camps. Yet how many of us who are involved with these kids from hard places feel equipped to face the challenges? How many of us know enough to be the safe adults these kids need in order to heal?

Perhaps that is why you picked up this book.

## A Decisive Link

I (Jayne) taught school for ten years before entering social work. I struggled, like so many teachers, with misbehavior among my students and how to correct it. I wish I would have known then what we are about to share with you now.

**It is often not what's *wrong* with children that leads to misbehavior but what *happened* to them.**

And it's not just children like Anya, Luke, and Johnny. Take twelve-year-old Susie, for example, who endured the chaotic divorce of her parents. Or Casey, just six, who lives with emotionally abusive parents yet tells no one. Or David and Ron, fourteen and sixteen, who've grown up with a depressed mother and an absent father.

What do all these kids have in common? Each of them has

experienced *complex developmental trauma*. Each one was set on a trajectory that often leads to a host of serious issues—developmental, social, emotional, and relational—which, without intervention, will likely show up in both childhood and adulthood in the form of high-risk behaviors, disease and disability, and sometimes even early death.[1]

## Recognizing the Need

When we began our ministry more than four decades ago, we didn't understand the powerful impact of childhood trauma. We were foster parents, adoptive parents, a pastor (David), and an educator and child welfare professional (Jayne), yet a familiar phrase described our experiences with troubled kids: We didn't know what we didn't know. Once introduced to the vast world of hurt and trauma, we decided to approach our work as lifelong learners. And we still learn new things every day—not only the *why* behind the behavior of kids from hard places, but the *how*, in terms of ways to help them heal.

As we continued to dig deeper, we recognized just how many people could benefit from the things we've learned. Everyone who touches the life of a vulnerable child—whether it be in church, at school, on the ball field, or at home—should learn what it means to look at life through the eyes of a wounded child. Behind the smiling and laughing faces, perhaps in more lives than we realize, are a host of hidden wounds: emotional pain, profound rejection, and psychological and physical abuse of all kinds.

We need to understand that spiritual and emotional care are inseparable. Adults who learn to see through a trauma-informed lens will be better equipped to create an environment where children from difficult backgrounds can grow and thrive. Our churches, schools, teams, and even homes can become places where healing happens.

In 2014, we were approached by Back2Back Ministries, an international orphan-care organization. They asked us to join them for one purpose—to help train their worldwide staff in what we now call *trauma-competent caregiving*. We developed a nine-module training curriculum based on the essential skills of trauma-informed care.[2] We had no idea at the time that the need for this material would increase exponentially.

In the years since the curriculum launched, we and the Back2Back training staff have shared our expertise with individuals from nearly seventy countries, and our material has been translated into nine languages and counting. The demand for training is ongoing because adults working or volunteering in local churches, schools, children's homes, and the foster care system are hungry for knowledge and practical tools. They want to be safe, nurturing adults in the lives of the children they encounter.

We've had the privilege of meeting thousands of dedicated caregivers, from orphanage workers to foster and adoptive parents—all of whom deal with children from backgrounds of abuse, neglect, and other trauma. We've had countless conversations with parents, teachers, and ministry workers. We've sat across the table from social workers and mental-health professionals as they've shared stories of overwhelming heartbreak and their desperate desire to help these precious children. This book was born in response to those who want a resource full of real-world examples and practical tips to guide them in this vital work.

## What's Ahead

Our journey into the world of trauma-informed care has been life-changing for us, and we hope it is for you as well. We now view children much differently than we did in the past, recognizing that there is always meaning behind their behavior. Compassion continually reminds us that what we see in these children is about what *happened* to them. Our journey of discovery has also impacted many of the adults we've encountered along the way.

Our goal for this book is to help you approach and implement trauma-informed care in a variety of settings. Joining us on this journey will

- lead you to a deeper understanding of how early-childhood trauma impacts the lives of teens and younger children;
- guide you in understanding the developmental issues of the children you encounter;
- help you understand how, if left unresolved, early-childhood adversity can have a lifelong impact into adulthood;
- show you how a child's traumatic history impacts the lives of those who teach and care for them, whether in orphanages, foster homes, adoptive homes, school, or churches;
- instruct you in how to bring healing and hope to children (and adults) from wounded places;
- guide you in learning and applying principles of the often-neglected practice of self-care; and
- equip you to create a trauma-informed environment wherever you work with children.

## Does It Make a Difference?

Does growing a team of trauma-informed leaders make a difference in the lives of children, teens, and families? The answer is a resounding *yes*! Kim Botto, director of kids' clubs and student ministries at a large, multicampus church, says, "Being trauma informed has changed the DNA of our kids' and student ministry. We all are growing in empathy towards these young people and are more willing to try new strategies."

She continues: "Foster, adoptive, and kinship families who felt isolated and rejected by their church because of the overwhelming needs of their children are finding community and support. We are gaining the skills that enable hurting kids and teens to connect in safe, welcoming, and fun environments where they can experience God and grow in their faith."[3]

As you walk with us through this book, it is our goal that you, too, will learn how to welcome kids from hard places with open arms and grow in your understanding of the children and teens you serve . . . and of yourself.

# 1

# "WHAT HAPPENED TO YOU?"

*Understanding the Lifelong Impact of Early-Childhood Trauma*

We see a child's behavior and ask,
"What's wrong with you?"
A better question would be
"What happened to you? Tell me your story."

Every Tuesday afternoon, seven-year-old Carli comes to Fire-Up, an after-school program at a church in her neighborhood. Occasionally, Katie, the program tutor, feels prepared for Carli. Most times she does not. Carli's behavior is erratic, and Katie never knows what to expect. In seconds, Carli can go from calm and quiet to out of control. Often, all it takes is a change of routine or hearing a simple "No, you may not play with those toys right now."

Katie knows a little about Carli's painful past. Carli, who looks more like a five-year-old than a seven-year-old, has experienced more neglect and abuse and witnessed more violence than most adults.

For the first three years of her life, Carli and her brother were shuffled around to various relatives, eventually landing back home in their mother's distracted care. Efforts to help the family failed, and Carli ended up in foster care. She lives with a family who attends the church where Carli participates in the Fire-Up program. The adults in Carli's life have been conditioned to focus on her disruptive behavior, but Carli didn't set out to create problems in the classroom; she was set up for it by her early life experiences.

Fifteen-year-old Kevin attends his church's youth group most Sundays. While present in body, he mentally distances himself from the group, avoiding conversations whenever possible. Jason, the youth pastor, is concerned about Kevin. If Jason can get him to interact at all, the conversation is usually focused on Kevin's chronic stomach problems and what a stupid, worthless kid he believes he is.

Jason knows that Kevin has lived with his grandparents since he was four—a result of his parents' traumatic divorce. Kevin's mother was unable to provide for him in a safe, nurturing way, and his father is totally absent from his life. Jason desperately wants to reach Kevin but has no clue how to do so. It's important for Jason to understand that Kevin didn't intend to be at such a hard place in his life; he was set up for it by his early life experiences.

The encouraging news is that Katie and Jason can play a helpful role in the lives of these two children, as well as in the lives of the many others who walk this broken road. Yet for adults like Katie and Jason to be effective in this mission, they must understand the impact of early-childhood trauma. Moreover, they need tools and strategies to help them interact with and guide the young people they love and serve.

## The Church's Role in Caring for Kids from Hard Places

"I never knew there was a world out there like this!" exclaimed Juan, a pastor attending our trauma training in preparation for becoming a foster parent. In that three-hour session, Juan learned about the impact of early-childhood trauma and the potential life-long effects if those traumatic events are left unprocessed. As he left the training, Juan stopped by to talk with the presenter.

"This day changes everything in ministry for me," he said. "This wasn't just for me to learn about becoming a foster parent— I want our church to be one that understands the impact of trauma and learns what to do to help our children and teens while there's still time to make a difference. I am taking this message back to my congregation."

Who better to lead children and teens on a healing journey than well-informed, well-trained adults who regularly encounter traumatized children as teachers, coaches, ministry leaders, and parents? This first chapter will examine what trauma is and its impact on a developing child. Subsequent chapters will help those uniquely positioned to implement healing interventions in a child's life.

Children are most often wounded as a result of broken interpersonal relationships, and they will heal only via healthy, nurturing relationships. There are three key tasks that, when learned and implemented, can empower caring adults to facilitate healing in the wounded children they encounter.[1]

**Understand the impact of trauma.** The first task is to recognize how children's earliest experiences can negatively impact them in nearly every aspect of their lives: brain, body, biology, belief system, and behavior. Carli and Kevin are both examples of that. To understand this is to comprehend the *why* behind the strategies we'll look at in the pages ahead. These strategies are evidence based, which means that research over time has confirmed their effectiveness. These strategies also have their roots in Scripture. Indeed, we are just now learning what God has known all along.

**Recognize trauma-based behavior.** The second task for individuals caring for kids from hard places is to recognize behaviors that are rooted in fear, anxiety, grief, and loss—these are by-products of a traumatic childhood. Our thinking can transform as we learn to change the question from *Why are they behaving so badly?* to *What happened in the past that caused them to respond in this way?* When we begin to understand the meaning behind a child's behavior, even when we don't know the whole story, we can respond with wisdom and compassion.

> When we begin to understand the meaning behind a child's behavior, we can respond with wisdom and compassion.

**Respond by building relational connections.** The third task is perhaps the greatest challenge: learning how to respond in a way that enables a wounded child to connect with a safe, nurturing adult. Once that connection is made, a child's or teen's heart can soften over time, and he or she will be more open to receive help and guidance.

## Understanding the Impact of Early Trauma

Trauma is an emotional response to a distressing event—or ongoing series of events—such that one's personal safety, or even one's life, feels threatened. The traumatic event(s) can cause the person to feel intense fear or a sense of helplessness.[2] But what might that look like in a child's day-to-day life?

Twelve-year-old Kathy and her two younger sisters have been attending church for three years. Their mother drops them off every Sunday and is often very late picking them up after the morning services. Kathy and her sisters have witnessed years of domestic violence at home. The siblings can never predict the environment they will walk into each day after school. Will it be peaceful? Will anybody be there? Will Dad come home in an angry mood? Will Mom leave in tears again, staying away for hours? Will Kathy have to find something for her younger sisters to eat?

The three girls' behavior during the children's-ministry time is unpredictable at best. Some mornings, they are cooperative and join right in. Other mornings, the slightest correction can prompt a meltdown similar to a preschooler's behavior. Although some of the adults at church know a bit about the girls' home life, they have little understanding (through no fault of their own) of the significant impact that stressful childhood experiences can have on every area of children's young lives.

Many who work with hurting children have yet to learn the true meaning behind much of their behavior. In other words, the adults who encounter them haven't learned how to view these children through a *trauma-informed lens*.[3] Why is this so important? Because so many children and teens come from traumatic backgrounds—what are known as *adverse childhood experiences* (ACEs). This term was coined in 1985 by Dr. Vincent Felitti, a physician and chief of Kaiser Permanente's revolutionary Department of Preventive Medicine in San Diego, California. ACEs were identified in the CDC-Kaiser Adverse Childhood Experiences Study, a groundbreaking public-health study that discovered that childhood trauma leads to the adult onset of chronic diseases; depression and other mental illness; violence and being a victim of violence; as well as financial and social problems.[4]

ACEs are commonly described as frightening, ongoing, unpredictable life stressors that children experience without an adult fulfilling a supportive role.[5] Whenever an adult who should be on duty is absent or negligent, a child can experience trauma. Researchers who study the consequences of early-childhood harm in relation to ACEs have identified several life events that can have a negative impact on a child:

- a parent or guardian divorcing or separating from the family
- a parent or guardian dying
- a parent or guardian serving time in jail or prison
- living with someone who is mentally ill, suicidal, or severely depressed for more than a couple of weeks
- living with anyone who has a problem with alcohol or drugs
- witnessing a parent, guardian, or other adult in the household behaving violently toward another (e.g., slapping, hitting, kicking, punching, or beating)
- suffering from or witnessing violent acts in his or her neighborhood
- experiencing economic hardship "somewhat often" or "very often" (e.g., the family finding it hard to cover costs of food and housing)[6]

Other types of trauma, particularly those not addressed in the initial ACE research, include bullying and environmental disasters. These experiences can harm children's developing brains and change how they respond to stress. Simply put, children like Carli, Kevin, and Kathy and her siblings live with chronic stressful situations.

Indeed, there is another term for what thousands of children live with. Science journalist Donna Jackson Nakazawa refers to it as *chronic unpredictable toxic stress*, or *CUTS*.[7] These stresses come from the relational and environmental events identified by the ACE research. I (Jayne) like to describe the impact of CUTS like this:

Imagine I am standing in front of you in a classroom, and on my desk is a vase filled with water. I pour some red food coloring into the vase, and of course the water turns red. I then take a regular household sponge and drop it into the water. By the end of our class time, the sponge will have turned red because it has absorbed the colored water.

This is what life is like for children who live in a consistently stress-filled environment. These kids are like sponges, absorbing the toxic events and emotions all around them. Stress-initiated chemicals continually flood their bodies, negatively affecting almost every part of them.

"Toxic stresses don't toughen up a child," Nakazawa writes. "They break down a child's or adolescent's brain so that the child is less able, throughout life, to handle the next thing, and the next."[8]

## Understanding Adverse Childhood Experiences (ACEs)

Before we go any further in our discussion of the ACE research, let's take a look at the questions that explore the life experiences of childhood.

The first five questions apply to what has happened early in a child's life, such as instances of abuse or neglect:

- Did a parent or other adult in the household **often** . . .
  - swear at you, insult you, put you down, or humiliate you **or**
  - act in a way that made you afraid that you might be physically hurt?

- Did a parent or other adult in the household **often** . . .
  - push, grab, slap, or throw something at you **or**
  - **ever** hit you so hard that you had marks or were injured?
- Did an adult or person at least five years older than you **ever** . . .
  - touch or fondle you or have you touch their body in a sexual way **or**
  - try to actually have oral, anal, or vaginal sex with you?
- Did you **often** feel that . . .
  - no one in your family loved you or thought you were important or special **or**
  - your family didn't look out for each other, feel close to each other, or support each other?
- Did you **often** feel that . . .
  - you didn't have enough to eat, had to wear dirty clothes, and had no one to protect you **or**
  - your parents were too drunk or high to take care of you or take you to the doctor if you needed it?

The second five questions deal with what has happened in the home, such as substance abuse or divorce:

- Were your parents **ever** separated or divorced?
- Was your mother or stepmother . . .
  - **often** pushed, grabbed, or slapped, or did she ever have things thrown at her **or**
  - **sometimes or often** kicked, bitten, hit with a fist, or hit with something hard **or**
  - **ever** repeatedly hit over the span of a few minutes or threatened with a gun or knife?

- Did you live with anyone who was a problem drinker or alcoholic or who used street drugs?
- Was a household member depressed or mentally ill or did a household member attempt suicide?
- Did a household member go to prison?[9]

The more times an individual answers yes, the higher their ACE score.

Carli, Kevin, and Kathy's ACE scores, for example, would most likely be very high, and we would see evidence of this in their physical health, behavior, and overall ability to function in challenging situations.

ACEs can also damage a child's immune system so profoundly that the effects are still evident decades later. People with high ACE scores often experience chronic disease, mental illness, cognitive impairment, relationship failures, high-risk behaviors, disabilities, and even premature death.

**Long-Term Impact of Trauma (ACEs)[10]**

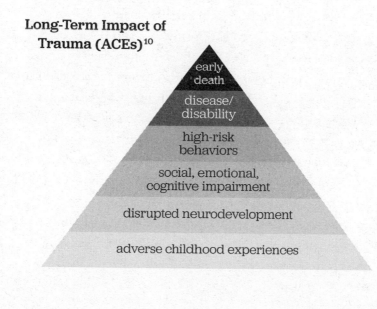

early death

disease/ disability

high-risk behaviors

social, emotional, cognitive impairment

disrupted neurodevelopment

adverse childhood experiences

*Toxic Stress Impacts the Brain*

Remember the sponge illustration? Children who live in a toxic environment have marinated in stress hormones for weeks, months, or even years. They are not the same children they would have been had there been a safe adult on duty, buffering those harmful experiences and helping those children cope and recover.

Healthy brain development requires that a child experience stress events that are both *positive* and *tolerable*. A closer look at three teens helps us understand the different levels of stress:

- Micah, our college-age grandson, is a very skilled pole-vaulter. I can't imagine launching my body to the heights that he does. As Micah prepares for each vault, the adrenaline in his body ramps up. These are *positive* stressful events that he has learned to manage in his pursuit of improved performance.
- Bobby is a thirteen-year-old boy in our community who lived with his parents in a nearby apartment. Their apartment complex caught fire one day, and Bobby, his parents, and his beloved dog all (barely) escaped. This type of stress is called *tolerable* because Bobby had healthy adults in his life to help him process the event.[11] One of Bobby's teachers at school knew that he needed to talk about it—a lot. Over time Bobby felt more calm and regulated about this traumatic event.
- Both of Susan's parents were alcoholics. At only seven, she regularly witnessed the physical abuse of her mother and older brothers. Her father also visited her at night in her bedroom, but this ongoing sexual abuse was a well-kept secret because her father demanded her silence. Susan's stress was neither positive nor tolerable and would thus

fall under the harmful category of chronic unpredictable toxic stress (CUTS).

Of the three, Susan is obviously at the greatest risk of long-term effects from chronic stress. The toxic hormones coursing through her system make it more likely that her brain development is impaired, resulting in cognitive, self-regulatory, and behavioral delays and challenges. Due to brain developmental delays, some children who live or formerly lived in a CUTS environment are assessed with emotional and psychological maturity barely half of what it should be at their ages.

### Toxic Stress Impacts the Body

Jonathan is twelve years old, but due to being raised in a severe toxic environment, his physical stature is more like that of an eight-year-old. He suffers from ongoing digestive issues and misses a lot of school and other activities due to illness.

> Children living in a CUTS environment can have half the emotional and psychological maturity they should at their age.

Children from chronic stressful environments often experience multiple physical problems, such as recurrent headaches or stomachaches that appear to have no obvious cause. They may experience autoimmune disorders, respiratory or digestive system dysfunction, or problems with coordination, balance, or body tone. High levels of the stress hormone cortisol can also impede normal growth.

### Toxic Stress Impacts Biology

Carrie experienced a level of childhood abuse that defies comprehension. She often spent weekends with her grandfather, who repeatedly sexually abused her. Her single mom knew nothing about it because Carrie's grandfather would tell her, "This is our little secret." In her late forties, Carrie contracted breast cancer. Before beginning treatment, her oncologist did some blood work and posed a question Carrie was not expecting.

"Did you experience abuse or other trauma as a child?" he asked.

"Yes," she replied. "Why are you asking me that?"

"I see it in your blood work."

The doctor explained that when a child experiences traumatic events, his or her body enters "fight or flight" mode as a means of self-protection. If neither of those natural responses is possible, if the child cannot run or fight, she freezes—essentially disassociating from what is happening. By disassociating, the adrenaline that would be expelled through flight or fight is trapped in the body, turning into toxins that can show up at a cellular level even years later.

Research shows that when a child grows up in a chronically stressful environment, natural biological functions are altered, and those biological alterations can be carried into adulthood. These alterations might include hormonal dysfunction, immune system dysfunction, or altered genetic expression. In other words, one's organs, tissues, and even cells can pay the price.[12]

### Toxic Stress Impacts Behavior

How we view a child's behavior is critical to how effective we are as adults who want to help. When we see aggressive behavior or a child who seems out of control, will we immediately define that behavior as "bad," or will we first examine the meaning behind the behavior?

Children who grew up in a chronically unpredictable, toxic, or abusive environment often view their circumstances through the lens of self-preservation. They have developed unconscious survival strategies that are automatically triggered by real or perceived threats. For example, one of Carli's involuntary survival strategies is to respond with anger and meltdowns when adults attempt to correct her behavior. Kevin's survival strategy involves isolating himself in a protective emotional shell, allowing almost no one in. Kathy copes with her environment by engaging in toddler-like tantrums and defiance. (We will discuss various ways to manage and respond to these behaviors in a later chapter.)

### Toxic Stress Impacts a Child's Belief System

Kevin is an example of a young man whose belief system defines almost everything about him. In response to his belief that he is stupid, unlovable, and worthless, Kevin has walled himself off from the world around him. Why would he believe anything positive or good about himself? The adults in his life have failed him. They weren't there to meet his physical, emotional, or relational needs.

Belief systems are an incredibly powerful part of who we are and, as children, who we eventually *become*. Belief systems are formed by the words we hear and the experiences we have, and they often establish a trajectory for the rest of our lives.

Some researchers suggest that our belief systems begin to form in the womb.[13] Prior to birth, they say, we hear our mother's voice and experience—at least to a degree—our mother's world. For many fetuses, that world is safe and peaceful. For others, stressful chemicals flood their developing brains as a result of domestic violence or chronic depression or anxiety in their mother's life. Some newborns have already experienced starvation due to malnutrition in the womb.

Children who grow up experiencing physical abuse face a host of conflicted beliefs. *If I was loved, my parents wouldn't hurt me.*

Children who experience neglect might doubt their worth. *If my parents valued me, they would meet my needs.* These children and teens, many of whom attend our churches, schools, camps, and other ministry settings, have harmful belief systems formed by the words they've heard (verbal and/or emotional abuse) and experiences they've endured (physical abuse and/or neglect). Emotional and psychological abuse comprise a consistent pattern of derogative words and bullying that result in damage to a person's self-esteem and mental health.[14] Research indicates that the deep emotional damage done by verbal abuse can be just as severe as that resulting from physical abuse.[15]

What are some of the hurtful words that many children hear?

- "You're stupid."
- "You're ugly."
- "God doesn't love you."
- "We never wanted you."
- "We don't love you."
- Sometimes there are no words at all, which is another kind of abuse. Complete disconnection and lack of interaction equals emotional neglect.

Less extreme statements can also impact a child's belief system:

- "Why can't you be more like your brother/sister?"
- "You never make the right choice."
- "You look fat in that outfit."

It's been said that what one believes fuels the emotions and sets a trajectory for behavior: "For as he thinks in his heart, so is he" (Proverbs 23:7, NKJV). The apostle Paul knew the power of the mind when he encouraged his fellow believers to "be transformed by the renewal of your mind" (Romans 12:2).

So if children have formed negative belief systems about themselves due to traumatic words and experiences, then how do we help them renew their minds and form new beliefs? By giving them new words and new experiences. We will discuss this at length in a later chapter.

## The Good News

We know this information is a lot to take in, but there is hope! Why do we say that? Because Scripture tells us that we are "fearfully and wonderfully made" (Psalm 139:14). God created us in such a way that, over time, our brains and bodies can heal, and this includes our behavior and our belief systems. Scientists refer to the brain's ability to adapt and change throughout one's lifetime as *neuroplasticity*. This means, among other things, that new words, new experiences, and new relationships with people and with God can open doorways to healing, despite the effects of early-childhood trauma.

In the next chapter, we will discuss how the powerful presence of safe adults can profoundly promote healing for children and teens from hard places.

## Key Takeaways

1. Children and teens who have endured adverse childhood experiences are all around us—in our churches, in our schools, on our teams, even in our homes. Understanding the impact of trauma, recognizing its effects, and responding with caring connection will help any adult better care for wounded and vulnerable children.

2. Chronic, toxic, traumatic stress can impact a child's entire being, including the brain, body, biology, behavior, and belief system.

3. There is hope! Our brains grow and change over a lifetime. New, positive experiences and safe relationships with caring adults can help repair a child's brain and open the door to healing from past trauma.

## Discussion Questions

1. The first paragraph of this chapter briefly mentions Katie, an after-school tutor, who "occasionally . . . feels prepared for Carli. Most times she does not." Does this remind you of some of the kids you interact with? How did reading this chapter change the way you think about those kids and their behavior?

2. Do you agree or disagree: "Who better to lead children and teens on a healing journey than well-informed, well-trained adults who regularly encounter traumatized children as teachers, coaches, ministry leaders, and parents?" Have you seen examples of this being done well? What do you see as the biggest obstacle(s)?

3. The word *trauma* is used a lot these days, with varying degrees of understanding. What is one thing you learned about trauma from this chapter?

4. Earlier in the chapter, we wrote: "How we view a child's behavior is critical to how effective we are as adults who want to help." What do you think the children described in this chapter would want others to know about them or their stories? What would help us view their behavior differently?

5. You probably felt a range of emotions as you read this chapter. What emotion did you feel most strongly? Why do you think that is?

## Application Strategies

1. Chapter 1 encourages us to start viewing children's behavior through a different lens. This week, allow yourself to consider what might have happened in the life of a child you interact with. *(We see a child's behavior and ask, "What's wrong with you?" A better question would be "What happened to you? Tell me your story.")*

2. Consider how the words and experiences you share with children are impacting their belief systems. Are you reinforcing a child's sense of being unlovable, or are you giving them words and experiences that speak to their value?

3. Ask God to show you children who need your presence as a safe adult. Pray that God will enable you to learn to mend the broken road in the lives of hurting children.

# 2

# THE POWER AND NECESSITY OF THE MIDDLE CIRCLE

*Creating a Bridge to the Resources They Need*

Every child who winds up doing well has had
at least one stable and committed relationship
with a supportive adult.

CENTER ON THE DEVELOPING CHILD, HARVARD UNIVERSITY

The visitor raised his hand first, then stood up. "I have something significant to share about the very thing you are teaching," he said. "May I?"

"Of course," I (David) replied. I had just finished a portion of trauma training based on the principle that healthy relationships are foundational for healing. I invited the gentleman to share.

It turned out that the man was a minister named Raphael, and he shared an incredible story. Pastor Raphael serves people in Armenia, a country devastated by an earthquake and decades of harsh Soviet-era domination. Armenians are survivors, traumatized by circumstances beyond their control and with very little outside aid or resources to help them cope.

The story I heard that day was one I will never forget, so I asked him to write it down. Here is Pastor Raphael's story in his own words:[1]

I was in my office when the police chief of the department of the teenagers [the juvenile officer] came in with his assistant. They wanted to talk to me.

"What's the problem?" I asked.

The police chief said, "We have a fourteen-year-old boy from an impoverished part of the city, and he is out of control. He doesn't have a father. His mother lives in one of the containers [literally a train-car container] in the part of the city where there are many of them. This boy does terrible things there, stealing and doing whatever he wants. We don't know what to do. He beats people, and he grabs people—he takes stones and hits people's heads.

"We've taken him to the police headquarters; we've even beat him, but he is also beating us. We beat him until he becomes unconscious. We've tried every method. We beat him, and we talked to him. Nothing helped. We cannot kill him; we cannot change him. The city is afraid of him. And now we came here. Can you help us?"

"Where is he now?" I asked.

"He's here in the next room."

I asked them to leave quietly. I went out from my office to visit the young man. I walked over to him, and he stood up. I looked him in the eye, smiled at him, nodded, and hugged him. And I said, "I am so happy you are here. I want you to be here for some time so that I can help you. Please, stay here and spend some time with me, as my friend."

This young man was very cold in the beginning. I showed him hospitality, and I figured that he was hungry.

We gave him something to eat, and that simple gesture was the start of a lifelong relationship. Sometimes he stayed at the church overnight, and sometimes he went back to his mother's train container.

Once he took some money. I hugged him, kissed his head, and I said, "Don't steal from me. If you need some money, just tell me." He was surprised. Nobody had ever showed him love like that. The church people began to love him too.

Little by little, the young man saw that when he did the wrong thing like stealing from someone in the church, the people still loved him and treated him well. He asked, "Why you do this for me?" So I told him about God and what a relationship with Jesus Christ could mean in his life.

Broken, the boy began to cry. I told him, "You don't have a father, but God is your Father."

He started to change. He began to do good for others. He began participating in church services, and he started to pray with his friends. God changed him. He became a new creation.

When nothing else worked for this young man, Pastor Raphael's simple gestures changed the trajectory of this boy's life. What did Pastor Raphael communicate with those gestures?

- Walking into the room where the boy sat, he communicated: *I want to be in your presence.*
- Looking the boy in the eye, he communicated: *I see you.*
- Smiling at the boy, he communicated: *I approve of you.*
- Nodding and hugging, he communicated: *You are welcome in my world.*
- And so on.

## Being the Middle Circle

Pastor Raphael filled what I call a "middle-circle" role in this boy's life. A middle circle is a person who serves as a facilitator in someone's life—creating a bridge or connection between that person and the resources they need to thrive.

Over time, Pastor Raphael helped the troubled young man by serving as the stable adult that virtually every child desires. Almost anyone can serve as a middle-circle person in the life of a child, teen, or even another adult; someone who connects with them through meaningful relationships. Scientific studies in the neurological, biological, and behavioral disciplines have concluded that life cannot be fully successful apart from connection with others. We are made for relationships.

## What Does the Middle Circle Look Like?[2]

Throughout my ministry, I have used a simple diagram to illustrate the principles of the middle circle:

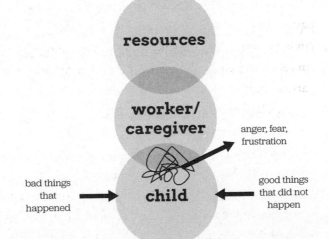

- The **bottom circle** represents a child from a hard place—or, more broadly, the countless children, teens, and even adults who come from difficult backgrounds. The trauma from the past has such a person's brain and nervous system in a tangle. Not only did bad things happen to them (abuse), but good things also did *not* happen. (This is what we call *neglect*, which is sometimes even more damaging than abuse to a developing child.[3]) These negative life circumstances create an environment of anger, fear, and frustration.
- The **top circle** represents the necessary resources a child needs to grow and develop in a healthy way. These resources include things that meet the child's physical, emotional, social, spiritual, and educational needs.
- The **middle circle** represents an individual who helps connect the hurting child with these necessary resources. A middle-circle person is a safe, nurturing adult—often a parent, caregiver, counselor, coach, pastor, or social worker. An effective middle-circle person is intentionally present, safe, and consistently helps meet the child's deeper needs, particularly
  - attachment with a safe adult and
  - orientation regarding values, goals, and future plans.

At some time in our lives, we all need a middle-circle person to connect with us, guide us, and offer us support. In human history, there is one perfect example of a middle-circle person:

## Jesus as Our Middle Circle

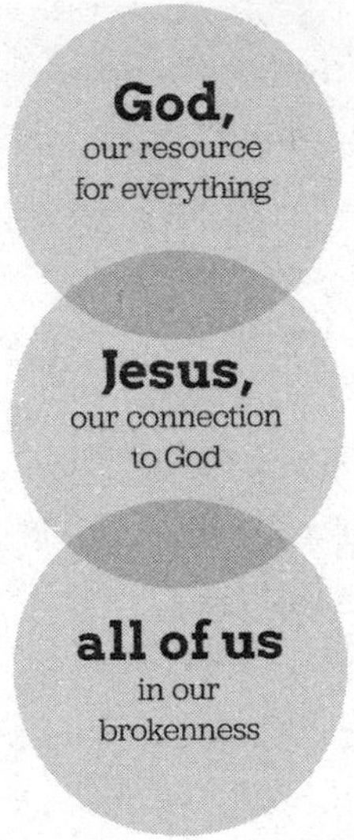

**God,**
our resource
for everything

**Jesus,**
our connection
to God

**all of us**
in our
brokenness

From a biblical perspective, the **bottom circle** represents every person who has ever lived. The Bible describes us as *lost, confused, separated, dead*. Our condition is bleak, and we are unable to save ourselves.

The **top circle** represents God the Father, who has infinite resources to meet every need we have. The problem is that our sin has separated us from God and His resources.

The **middle circle** represents Jesus Christ, the One who serves as the connection—the bridge—between us and God. Jesus came to offer us access to God and the *abundant* life He offers (John 10:10). Jesus becomes our middle circle when we come into a relationship with Him. That's when we experience what Peter refers to:

May grace and peace be multiplied to you in the
knowledge of God and of Jesus our Lord.

His divine power has granted to us all things that
pertain to life and godliness, through the knowledge
of him who called us to his own glory and excellence,
by which he has granted to us his precious and very
great promises, so that through them you may become
partakers of the divine nature, having escaped from
the corruption that is in the world because of sinful
desire.

2 PETER 1:2-4

The middle-circle concept is a way to illustrate how the
Kingdom of God works as described by Paul: "In Christ God
was reconciling the world to himself" (2 Corinthians 5:19).
Simply put, God the Father sent Jesus the Son to invite us into
a relationship with Him; and in that relationship, God provides
all the resources necessary for us to be redeemed and healed. In
other words, God is the source of all things needed, and Jesus
is the middle circle (or delivery system) who connects us to the
Father.

We all are called to be middle circles in one way or another.
Of course, most parents and grandparents already fulfill that role
to some degree, but there are
surely others outside our homes
who need someone to serve as
*their* middle circle. It might be
a child, teen, or even adult in
your church—someone who is
isolated or alone. It might be a
youngster across the street or a teen on your sports team. If you
are open to filling that role, you need to know four essential
characteristics of an effective middle-circle person.

> "The LORD is my shepherd;
> I shall not want."
>
> PSALM 23:1

### A Middle-Circle Person Understands the Universal Need for Attachment and Orientation

We have spent countless hours in orphanages in eastern and central Asia. One scenario in particular played out in virtually every country we visited. When we'd first arrive, orphaned children would routinely stream out the front doors and into our arms. In the beginning, we thought this was a happy occurrence. I (Jayne) loved to hug on them, but then it dawned on me: *These children don't even know us, yet they cling to us like long-lost family members.* A young boy named Victor, who was six at the time, was—like most of the children—starved for attention and attachment. I will never forget the sadness on his precious face. Victor desperately wanted to look into the eyes of a safe adult, someone who would be there for him. Yet he had no one.

Regardless of our age or station in life, all people need *attachment* and *orientation*.

Think of a young child in foster care, moving from one home to another. The youngster is losing any attachment to the adults he knew in his prior home and is now entering a new home with no one to guide him—no one to help him find his way. He doesn't know the environment, the rules, or what is expected. He feels alone and detached.

Think of a young college student, heading off for his first year away from home. He knows no one else at this school. He doesn't know the campus or where anything is located. He probably doesn't even know his roommate. He feels alone and detached.

Think of an elderly person moving into a nursing home, losing all that she has known all her life. She knows no one; she has no idea how to navigate even to the dining room. She feels alone and detached.

Attachment and orientation are the foundations for healing.

We all need someone with whom we can attach—someone who can guide us where we need to go.

Dr. Gordon Neufeld, a prominent author and developmental psychologist, defines *attachment* and *orientation* like this:

- *Attachment* results from healthy emotional and psychological intimacy. Attachment is that deep soul connection to another person, like a newborn to his mother. To experience attachment is to have a place of safety and security.[4]
- *Orientation* is the drive to get one's bearings and become acquainted with one's surroundings.[5] Orientation is basically teaching someone the way to go and what to do when you get there.

Dr. Daniel Siegel and Dr. Tina Bryson put it this way: "Children who form strong bonds—secure attachments—with their parents at a very young age lead much happier and more fulfilling lives."[6]

Tragically, this bonding doesn't happen in many families, but any safe adult can help meet this need. They only need to understand that attachment is the connection and orientation is the guiding force, creating a way to impart positive values, beliefs, and other resources necessary for healthy development.

Siegel and Bryson say parents and caregivers should ask this question: "What is the single most important thing I can do for my kids to help them succeed and feel at home in this world?" Their answer is simple yet profound: "Show up."[7]

Yet many children today do not have a healthy adult relationship nor the life-enriching benefits it brings. This is where the middle-circle person comes in. You might be thinking that—at least in your church—everyone is just fine. But if you overheard a conversation among the teens in your church's youth group, you'd probably learn that many of them are not "just fine." They don't have safe, connected adults in their lives. They don't have adults to guide and support them, or even simply to speak words of encouragement.

A middle-circle person understands that fostering a sense of attachment, connection, and orientation is merely the first step.

### A Middle-Circle Person Understands That Heavy Lifting and Loving Are Required

> When [Jesus] returned to Capernaum after some days, it was reported that he was at home. And many were gathered together, so that there was no more room, not even at the door. And he was preaching the word to them. And they came, bringing to him a paralytic carried by four men. And when they could not get near him because of the crowd, they removed the roof above him, and when they had made an opening, they let down the bed on which the paralytic lay. And when Jesus saw their faith, he said to the paralytic, "Son, your sins are forgiven."
>
> MARK 2:1-5

Four men, acting as middle circles, carried their friend to the source of spiritual and physical healing. But it wasn't easy. Can you envision getting a paralyzed man up onto a roof using a stretcher, digging a hole in that roof, and then working with your friends to lower the full-grown man down to Jesus without letting him fall? This man's life might never have changed had someone not picked him up and carried him to the source of healing. These men did some heavy lifting—and loving.

A middle-circle person knows that it won't always be easy. Unrealistic and unmet expectations in every area of life can lead to disappointment and discouragement. Middle-circle service often requires sacrifice and even suffering.

In Galatians 6:2, Paul instructs his audience: "Bear one another's burdens, and so fulfill the law of Christ." Yet if entering a burden-bearing relationship with another fulfills "the law of Christ," then what is this law? I describe it as VRS, or *voluntary redemptive suffering* for the sake of another.

Voluntary redemptive suffering is what Jesus, our middle circle, did for us. He suffered on our behalf, for our redemption. Christ also served as a model for us to follow. Jesus is certainly a tough act to follow, since emulating Him requires heavy lifting and loving.

Our friends Shirley Garrett and Sean Barret have firsthand experience with heavy lifting and loving. Every Wednesday night, a blue van pulls out of the church parking lot in Dayton, Ohio. The youth ministry leaders and van drivers—Shirley and Sean, her son-in-law—have a single mission: pick up youth from the surrounding area for the church's evening activities.

Shirley and Sean have been doing this not for one year, not for five years, but for twelve years. Thanks to their efforts, more than sixty inner-city young people show up each Wednesday for activities, Bible study, and connection. Some teens have been coming for years. More than 90 percent of these young people come from single-parent homes. For Shirley, Sean, and the others who help each week, this sort of commitment requires heavy lifting and loving in spite of challenging circumstances.

One young man named Donte, whose family life was particularly chaotic, benefited greatly from the positive influence of Shirley and other church volunteers. "If you asked some youth workers about Donte," Shirley said, "the response would jar you:

'He's a bad kid. He will never amount to anything. I don't want him in my class. He is out of control.'

"Many saw him as a lost cause," Shirley explained. "But we didn't. We took every opportunity to speak into his life, literally for years. He had no adult doing that. He needed consistent guidance and consistent loving, even in the hardest of times."[8]

As part of their ministry work, Sean and his wife, Darlene, tutored students from underperforming schools. They made a concerted effort to connect with kids like Donte. "We did that for four or five years," Sean said, "and were able to invest in him and others on an academic basis."

Now that he has graduated from high school, Donte is now working a full-time job and supporting himself. What's more, Shirley says, "He still comes on Wednesday nights."

Donte represents hundreds of young people whose lives have been transformed thanks to a single church's teen ministry. Heavy lifting and loving aren't easy, but the hard work comes with some incredible rewards.

Recently, during a church service dedicated to honoring Shirley's lifelong commitment to youth ministry, more than one hundred teens and young adults shared their appreciation.[9] Shirley heard comments at that event that she will likely never forget. Here are just three:

"Miss Shirley, I don't know where I would have been without you helping me."
FROM A COLLEGE GRADUATE

"Thank you for making such an impression on my life, and thank you for your effort and your patience."
FROM A GRADUATING HIGH SCHOOL SENIOR

"Miss Shirley, you helped me stay on track by keeping in touch."
A YOUNG MAN WHOM SHIRLEY WOULD TEXT WHEN HE WAS IN COLLEGE TO MAKE SURE HE WAS UP IN TIME FOR CLASS

These are the rewards for heavy lifting.

### A Middle-Circle Person Understands the Need to Establish and Maintain Boundaries

I (David) was speaking several years ago at a large church in Ukraine. After I finished the message, I invited anyone who was interested to come forward for a blessing and prayer. I had no idea what would happen next. Hundreds came forward. The surge of the crowd was intimidating, and the crush pushed me back against the platform. Other pastors and leaders came forward to help pray for all the people.

I later wondered why so many came. The church's pastor said something I will never forget: "You in America have access to many resources to meet your needs. Here we have only God."

The point of this story? When someone assumes the middle-circle role, he or she might be overwhelmed by the number and complexity of the needs that emerge. Without establishing proper boundaries, middle-circle people will likely face burnout, exhaustion, or loss of family relationships, among other issues. Many middle circles have trouble saying no and feel guilty when they do. Yet refusing to say no is actually the surest way to experience not only burnout but also unhealthy relationships that ultimately hinder growth for both parties. (We'll discuss this in further detail in our chapter on soul care.)

Connections Homes, a Georgia-based ministry that connects young adults with families, began as founder Pam Parish's own family story:

We have eight daughters—six of them came from trauma—and I began to look around at the statistics of eighteen-year-olds who exited foster care or ended up homeless without safe and stable families. I wanted to know why these eighteen-year-olds ended up at our doorstep. If four of them could find their way to our home, then there's got to be a lot more out there.

I began a search for an answer to the question *How many more youth were out there?* It was heartbreaking to learn that about seven hundred kids age out [of foster care] every year in Georgia. Even more tragic, across our country nearly twenty-one thousand youth age out of state foster care programs, often lacking skills and relationships that will aid them in becoming successful. We were at critical mass in our own home, but I had the idea that there must be other people out there who could step up and connect with these teens.

Connections Homes opened in 2014. Its purpose is to recruit, train, and equip families to mentor teens who need a stable, safe relationship to guide them through young adulthood. Since then, we've connected almost 180 kids with mentoring families. We also continue to train and equip our mentoring families.[10]

Parish learned that serving as the middle-circle person for scores of teens required her to learn the vital skill of establishing boundaries. She developed some principles that she, her husband, and her ministry partners practice in order to avoid burnout and protect their existing relationships.

"For me, learning to maintain boundaries also came with learning some self-care," Parish says. "I think a lot of foster and adoptive parents that you meet are type A personalities. It is that strong personality that believes you can conquer anything. One of the downsides of a type A personality is that they don't rest. And self-care is not easy for them."[11]

Parish says that maintaining boundaries means setting aside time for herself and time with her husband. "I have learned not to be afraid to say no to my kids when what they want interferes with my established boundary. People in ministry need to learn to do the same thing, but another principle is key to that."

She goes on: "Saying no when you have to for your own well-being is important, but even before that, you need to clearly communicate what those boundaries are."

If texting you after 11:30 at night is off limits except in cases of a literal emergency, then you need to say that. And you need to say it clearly. Popular author and researcher Brené Brown says that "clear is kind,"[12] and I use that phrase all the time because clarity *is* kindness when it comes to relationships.

"I try to practice those words with our girls," Parish says, "but it's often hard to do—especially when you're also trying to empathize with their stories and not be too hard on them. Reframing *clarity* as compassion for yourself and for your children can help you distinguish between the *I'm being selfish* mindset and an *I'm caring for us by caring for me* mindset. Because if I don't care for *me*, then *we* are not good. Boundary setting is a vital task for a middle-circle person."[13]

### A Middle-Circle Person Understands the Need to Keep Showing Up

I (David) was a pastor for many years, and one Sunday morning I decided to reveal my secret for success in ministry . . .

I keep showing up.

Showing up in any context is essential, especially in parenting and ministry. Consistency in showing up is critical for a middle-circle person who wants to foster attachment, connection, and orientation in children and youth. Conversely, inconsistent involvement will not meet these basic needs.

It bears repeating: "Children who form strong bonds—secure attachments—with their parents [caregiver, pastor, coach, etc.] at a very young age lead much happier and more fulfilling lives," write Siegel and Bryson.[14]

"When children experience this type of reliable behavior and connection, they are freed to learn and develop without having to use attention or energy to survive," says psychiatrist and professor Bruce Perry.[15]

Bishop Aaron Blake and his wife, Mary, understand the power of consistently showing up. As parents to six grown children and foster/adoptive parents to six teenage boys, they kept showing up in difficult circumstances.[16] Middle-circle people intervened in Aaron's life when he was a child, so he later turned around and did the same for others, as he describes in the following story:

> I was a vocational pastor and a social worker/counselor/
> whatever when I first met Melvin, who was sixteen at the
> time. He came into my office at the high school where I
> worked and uttered four words: "Can you help me?" At
> the time, Melvin was in the foster care system, and he
> was distraught. I remembered myself as sixteen-year-old
> Aaron Blake, who did not have a father in the home.
> My mother also struggled—she was a day worker who
> cleaned houses for a living.
>
> I called my wife, Mary, and told her about Melvin.
> She agreed it would be fine for him to move in with us.
> Our six biological children were all now adults and living

on their own, so we had plenty of room. We didn't have any idea what would be coming next.

After Melvin, five more teenage boys—all on the football team with Melvin—walked into my office, one or two at a time, with the same plea: "Can you help me?" They all were in foster care with the same common theme in their lives: early-childhood trauma.

Eventually they all moved in. The day those boys walked in our door, I told them they were not going to be moved; they were not going to be bounced to another home; they would forever be in our home. I call all of them my "grafted sons." Those boys were grafted into our family tree and our hearts, and they are still connected with us now.

Living with six boys who have a history of trauma might be the hardest thing you could imagine. Aaron Blake understood that. But he had no idea that his commitment would be tested by fire. Literally.

In the midst of living and loving these boys through many challenging issues, there came a moment when I thought, *It's over. I can't do it anymore.* That's when our house caught on fire. It started with one of the boys playing with fire in his bedroom. When it happened— and I recall this as if it was yesterday—there was a moment when I thought one of my boys was still in the house. I went to the back and my eyebrows were singed and my hair was singed. I thought the fire department could get the fire out and save the house, but it burned to the ground.

It was the dead of winter. It was cold that night, and Mary and I were standing on the sidewalk across the street from our house. We had sent the boys to the church to wait. When I saw that the house was not going to be saved, the grief was overwhelming. That house was where my six biological kids had grown up, and all our pictures, all our memories, everything was gone. We had no place to go.

I looked over at Mary with tears in my eyes.

"I'm sorry," I said. "I can't do this anymore."

Mary looked back at me and said, "Let's go to Walmart."

*Go to Walmart?* I thought that was odd.

"We need to get clothes," she said. "The boys have to go to school tomorrow, and you have to go to work. Come on, this is what families do."

The next day I went to get the boys after school, but I couldn't find them. I eventually found them in the gym. The coach told me that they'd been there all day.

I went up to the boys and asked, "What's going on?"

"Come on, Pop," they said. "Tell us if we're leaving. Tell us, please. We don't want to be embarrassed when someone comes to pick us up."

I'd said it before, and I said it one more time. "I want to remind you guys that you are grafted into our family; you are connected. Nothing has changed. You will always be family."

Aaron and Mary Blake, their six biological children, and their six "grafted sons" continue to enjoy the lifelong relationship called *family*. The Blakes now enjoy a household full of grandchildren. Because the Blakes continued to *show up*, even in the hardest of times, their six grafted sons—all now adults—have someone to call Mom and Pop, and those sons' children have someone to call Grandma and Grandpa.

∞

It's nearly impossible to overstate the importance of middle-circle people who consistently show up. Children from difficult backgrounds have typically experienced neither predictability nor consistency, and promises to them were rarely kept. Middle-circle people provide attachment and orientation; they know that heavy lifting is required; they understand the importance of healthy boundaries; and they keep showing up.

This is the role—and the blessing—of the middle circle.

## Key Takeaways

1. A healthy life requires human connection. The hurting kids you work with need to know that a safe adult sees them, wants to be in their presence, approves of them, and welcomes them.

2. A middle-circle person is a safe adult who helps connect those in need to resources that will help them. There are four characteristics of a middle-circle person:

   • They understand the need for attachment and orientation.
   • They know that heavy lifting and loving are required.
   • They establish and maintain boundaries.
   • They keep showing up.

3. Jesus is our middle circle. He connects fallen, sinful people to the Father, who offers abundant life. And He modeled VRS (voluntary redemptive suffering) for us.

## Discussion Questions

1. What were your thoughts as you read the story of Pastor Raphael at the beginning of the chapter? Did the child in the story remind you of anyone in your own life?

2. None of us has everything we need on our own to be successful. We *all* need Jesus to bridge the gap between us and our Father, and we also need other people. God designed us to need others. Share a story from your own life of someone who was the middle circle for you.

3. On page 37, we read, "When someone assumes the middle-circle role, he or she might be overwhelmed by the number and complexity of the needs that emerge." Do you have experience with this issue or fears about it? Discuss what healthy boundaries might look like in your church, school, home, and so on.

4. As you consider becoming a middle-circle person (or if you already are one), which of the four essential characteristics comes most easily? Which is the most difficult for you?

5. How do you see the gospel in the story of Aaron and Mary Blake? Does knowing their story change your perspective about the potential cost of being the middle circle in the life of a hurting child, teen, or adult?

## Application Strategies

1. God asks many of us to practice living out VRS. What is one action step you can take this week to respond to such a calling?

2. Once you've identified which characteristic of a middle-circle person is most challenging for you, try working on that characteristic at least one time this week. Ask God to help you grow in that area.

3. The story of the Blakes shows us forgiveness in action. If you felt let down by someone you were trying to help, what could you do to foster forgiveness?

# 3

# BOUNDLESS HOPE

*Transforming Hearts and Minds of Those Who Serve*

No child is too far gone that we can't have
boundless hope for who he can become.
Didn't Jesus think that way?

KIM BOTTO

Alex, screaming at the top of his lungs, had a meltdown at second base when he was called out. He picked up the base and threw it into the outfield. The practice stopped until he calmed down and returned to the dugout.

Afterward, the coaches got together. This had become a common occurrence since the twelve-year-old had joined the team. Alex's behavior was challenging, to say the least; if he didn't get his way—or worse, if he was called out—the result was usually a major explosion.

"I don't see how we can keep this kid on our team," one of the coaches remarked. "He is a bad kid and so disruptive. I have no idea why he acts like this and no idea what to do." What those coaches didn't know was that due to a history of early-childhood trauma, Alex had a very short fuse when it came to disappointments, especially his own. He had learned early on in his birth family that failures or mistakes were costly and usually resulted in harsh physical consequences.

How do we view challenging children and teens in our programs or classrooms? Do we label them as "bad" kids? Do we respond with frustration and disconnection? Are we actually glad when they don't show up, or are we grateful for the opportunity to make a difference in their lives?

In her book *The Deepest Well*, Dr. Nadine Burke, former surgeon general of California, states an incredible truth: "Trauma isn't a zip code."[1]

We often associate children and trauma with poverty and other socioeconomic issues. Until a gym teacher discovered Alex's physical abuse, no one would have guessed that the boy endured severe abuse, especially considering the nice, middle-class neighborhood where his parents lived. Alex is safe now, living in a new town with his grandparents—but that means he's also far from friends and familiarity.

Kids from all socioeconomic levels, even from families who appear healthy and stable on the outside, can and will experience trauma. The global community recently came through a coronavirus pandemic that caused significant trauma for millions. But even before the pandemic, the mental and emotional health of our children and families was already cause for alarm. Here is what we know:

- Nearly 40 percent of American kids have been direct victims of two or more violent acts, and one in ten have been victims of violence five or more times.[2]

- More than three million American kids are victims of bullying each year.[3]
- It's estimated that 94 percent of kids have viewed pornography by age fourteen.[4]
- Almost 10 percent of children have witnessed one family member assault another family member, and more than 25 percent have been exposed to family violence during their lives.[5]
- Most adult drug addicts began using before the age of eighteen.[6]
- Suicide is the second leading cause of death for people ages 15 to 24.[7]

Whether we are teachers, coaches, ministry workers, or parents, we will likely encounter children and teens who've experienced some degree of trauma. Some live in dysfunctional home environments, and others are witnessing painful divorces. Some of those children and teens have experienced domestic abuse—either physical violence or emotional abuse or both. Some try to downplay the pain of bullying, yet it comes out in their behavior. Others live in foster or adoptive homes where they have encountered heart-wrenching abuse and neglect. The list is endless.

So how do we *react* to out-of-control behavior? Are we like Alex's coaches, who wondered, *What is wrong with him?* There is a better *response*, however—one that requires careful consideration: *What happened to him?*[8] Acknowledging the difference between the reaction and the response can lead to a paradigm shift in our relationships.

The immediate *reaction* (*What's wrong with him?*) leads us toward negativity and judgmental attitudes. It's quick, it's often unthinking, and it looks at nothing beyond the immediate behavior. This misunderstanding happens in our schools and churches, and it happens to teens who find themselves in juvenile court. Ongoing misunderstandings of trauma-related behavior have had a profound effect on our educational, mental-health, and juvenile-justice systems.[9]

The thoughtful *response* (*What happened to him?*), however, asks God to help transform our minds and fill our hearts with newfound compassion for wounded ones whose behavior is their vocabulary. A carefully considered response completely changes our perspective as we work with every troubled youngster, teen, or adult we encounter.

> There is a better response—one that requires careful consideration: *What happened to him?*

What adjustments should we make in how to help these wounded kids? Once we understand that the same concepts for working with people from adverse experiences apply to virtually everyone, there are three key principles that form the foundation for a trauma-informed program. These principles have grown out of twenty years of work with children and teens who came to us from very hard places.[10]

## Three Foundational Principles for Creating a Trauma-Informed Environment

### First Principle: Examining the Mindsets Where It All Begins

"What are some of the beliefs we have about the difficult kids in our ministry?" This is the first question Kim Botto, former Kids' Club director for Crossroads Church in Cincinnati, Ohio, asks as she begins training program volunteers about childhood trauma.

"I ask them to be real and write down things that come to

mind," Botto says. "We have to start here because what we believe will impact everything we do." It can be a tricky question, she admits, but she says that it's vital for adults to consider their beliefs about working with troubled kids.

These are additional questions Botto asks:

- Do you ever think a child is a waste of time and energy?
- Do you ever think a teen has gone too far and any effort expended on that kid is wasted?
- Do you ever think, *This is just a bad kid*?
- Do you ever say to yourself, *This kid is going to be just like her parents*?
- Do you ever say to yourself, *This kid is unreachable*?[11]

It's critical to consider how our belief systems influence how we interact with children exhibiting behavioral problems. What we believe about them impacts our emotions (what we feel) and directs our behavior (what we do).

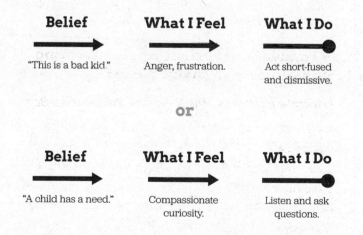

| Belief | What I Feel | What I Do |
|---|---|---|
| "This is a bad kid." | Anger, frustration. | Act short-fused and dismissive. |

or

| Belief | What I Feel | What I Do |
|---|---|---|
| "A child has a need." | Compassionate curiosity. | Listen and ask questions. |

*Second Principle: Embracing Boundless Hope*

Another of our essential transformational principles is that we believe in something called *boundless hope*.

"People with boundless hope are interested in a child and his story," says Botto. "They imagine what he could become in the future and commit to a relationship of walking alongside." This means that "any kids' ministry, or anywhere a child or teen is, is a place where we invite every kid regardless of their unique needs, background, or energy level. We want people who have a growth mindset to believe that no child, teen, or even adult is too far gone and that we have boundless hope for every child."[12]

> "People with boundless hope are interested in a child and his story. They imagine what he could become in the future."
>
> KIM BOTTO

What does a "growth mindset" look like for adults who work with children and teens? To explore this question, let's first compare two different mindsets: growth and fixed.[13]

- A **growth** mindset says, *I am willing to learn what a child needs.*
- A **fixed** mindset says, *We have always done it this way.*

- A **growth** mindset says, *I have never served in that type of ministry, but I am open to new ways of interacting with wounded children.*
- A **fixed** mindset says, *I would never work with those types of children.*

- A **growth** mindset sees potential in every child and says, *I will love that child the way Jesus does—in a way that is compassionate and connecting.*
- A **fixed** mindset never allows one's heart to be open.

We can think of few things more exciting than learning how to reach the hearts and minds of hurting kids, using methods found in both science and Scripture. We have learned that having a growth mindset is indeed a scriptural principle. "An intelligent heart acquires knowledge, and the ear of the wise seeks knowledge" (Proverbs 18:15).

### Third Principle: Seeing the World through the Lens of a Wounded Child

Our final essential principle involves building empathy.

Willy is a fifteen-year-old boy from a broken home, and he looks mad whenever he attends teen ministry meetings at church. Willy lives with his grandparents, who, if asked, would say they don't want Willy to live with them. But they had no choice—it was their house or foster care.

Every Sunday morning, Willy's grandparents insist that he join them at church. Willy slouches in the back seat on the drive there, grumbles when they arrive, and shuffles inside with his eyes glued to his phone. Willy invariably sits in the back of the room, slumps in his chair, and scowls.

One's first reaction to a teen like Willy might be to simply ignore him and hope he keeps his attitude to himself. Yet a trauma-informed response, one of *curious compassion* based on empathy, would seek to know his story.

Why empathy? According to Jason Weber, national director of the Foster Care Initiative for the Christian Alliance for Orphans, *empathy* is the starting place for seeing the world through the eyes of a wounded child:

> We cannot even address the issue until we feel, to some level, what kids have experienced. When we know more about the why and the cause of the things that hurt them, it goes a long way in helping us feel with them and understand them. It is like the idea of God with us as Immanuel, and we carry that into empathic relationships with our kids.[14]

Let's make it clear that there is a difference between empathy and sympathy. Michael Miller of Six Seconds—an organization dedicated to promoting the skills associated with emotional intelligence—writes, "Empathy means *experiencing* someone else's feelings. . . . It requires an emotional component of really feeling what the other person is feeling. Sympathy, on the other hand, means *understanding* someone else's suffering. It's more cognitive in nature and keeps a certain distance."[15]

Viewing life through the lens of a wounded child requires empathy and can help us better understand the child's behavior. It means we know at a much deeper level that abused and emotionally neglected kids do not see through a clear lens, untarnished by life. Instead, they see through a broken lens, distorted by the abuse and neglect that has stolen their innocence. On this journey toward understanding a wounded child's needs, we've learned some life-changing lessons from studying under Dr. Karyn Purvis.[16] Two of Dr. Purvis's statements transformed our belief system, our emotional reaction, and our behavioral response to children and adults:

- Behavior is the language of children who have lost their voice.
- There is always meaning behind the behavior.[17]

Many children learn early on to adjust their behaviors to mask their feelings—mostly fear. They learn to adapt, to survive, through responses like fight, flight, or freeze. "Many children who manifest acting-out behaviors have inner needs they are unable to vocalize," writes Donna Jackson Nakazawa, "and therefore the needs continue to go unmet, and the negative behavior continues."[18]

Neither Alex nor Willy viewed adults as safe people. And why would we expect otherwise? They've had no safe adults around to demonstrate the empathy and compassion they need in order to heal. The people they've interacted with (and that might include those of us who work with vulnerable children) likely have little understanding of the impact of trauma.

So how do we intentionally overcome these attitudes and instead create an environment of empathy?

Says Botto: "We build empathy through science and stories."[19]

## An Important Note about Science

Science has a lot to say to those of us who are not personally connected to the tragedies of life that these kids have experienced. According to Jason Weber,

> Children and teens with a history of adverse childhood experiences have noticeable brain differences. Their brains are physically different from children who have grown up in a loving and nurturing environment, and they often have significant cognitive, emotional, or social delays.
>
> We are used to responding to the brain differences with children who have obvious disabilities, but kids with a traumatic past don't necessarily display any external cues. Instead, we see those brain differences most often in their behaviors. When we approach our work with

hurting children from a posture of empathy, we won't see them or treat them as "bad" kids. Dr. Karyn Purvis rarely left a speaking engagement without saying, "I have never met a wounded child who cannot receive some level of healing."[20]

Although brain science is not everyone's favorite subject, we need to appreciate just how important it is to our understanding of wounded kids. A child like Alex, for example, is probably much younger—at least emotionally and socially—than other children his age. So is Willy. I (Jayne) wish I would have known this when we were foster parents, adoptive parents, a schoolteacher, a friend to hurting adoptive families—and the list goes on. It would have transformed my thinking. Understanding and compassion would have hopefully kicked in as a default response to a child's behavior.

We discussed in chapter 1 how CUTS (chronic unpredictable toxic stress) impacts the body, brain, biology, belief system, and behavior.[21] Almost every day, we encounter children and adults who've spent most or much of their lives in a CUTS environment. The value of their experiences outside that environment—whether in a classroom, after-school program, church, sport, or other setting—depends on how the people managing those programs view them and seek to understand their circumstances.

"It is simply amazing to see the blinders come off people [who are] working with children," Weber says. "They acknowledge that they didn't know all of this. They now understand with a new level of empathy that they cannot expect the same things from kids that have experienced trauma. So we can learn to minister differently to their hearts and minds."[22]

Recognizing the science behind these differences helps us have realistic expectations and celebrate every success—big or small.

## Gathering Stories

Stories can be invaluable in understanding kids from hard places.

"When we learn the science, we can then connect the science of trauma with the compelling stories of the children, teens, and adults we serve," Botto says. "Every child has a story. We use a little bit of science—the facts of how trauma affects the brain and behavior—and then we share stories of children who are in our ministry. We protect the child's story by keeping it anonymous, but it's often shocking when volunteers learn of the trauma, neglect, or abuse some of our kids (and adults) have experienced. So we tell our team that every kid has a story, and this story impacts their behavior."[23]

Here's an example of one such story, related by Kim Botto:

Although Louie was only four at the time, the children's ministry workers knew he would be a challenge the moment he was dropped off in his church classroom.

As program director, I got a call that morning about a kid who was being combative and had been removed to the hall because he was perceived to be a possible danger to the other kids. When I arrived, I sat down with him and started to talk—not scolding him; just trying to get to know him. He immediately became angry and told me to shut up, adding in some expletives. I didn't know this child's story, but I knew he had one.

"It seems like you're angry," I said calmly. "We don't talk to each other that way. Could you ask me more kindly?" He was expecting me to yell at him. Instead, he turned and said, "Stop talking please."

I happily complied. After a few minutes, he started talking again, sharing some of his favorite toys and a bit about his family. I would have lost the opportunity to connect with him if I had immediately jumped to punishment because of his R-rated language.

When it was time for the church service to be over, I saw his mother walk around the corner. She saw us in the hallway and her head dropped. At that moment I knew she had been in this hard place before—perhaps many times.

As she approached us, I introduced myself and told her how much fun I had getting to know Louie. Her startled look told me she had never heard that before. I asked her to take a walk with me. Louie was calm enough to remain in the classroom.

As we walked down the hall, I learned that this was their first Sunday at our church. She started crying.

"Every place I go," she said, "Louie does something to ruin the day. I cannot manage his behavior. I can hardly take him anywhere."

She told me a lot in a few moments about the early life of this child. There had been significant domestic violence. He had experienced unspeakable loss in his short life, and just making ends meet proved a daily challenge for their family.

I wanted to connect with this mom. I asked her a simple question: "What does Louie need from us for him to feel safe in our Kids' Club? And what do you need?" Those two questions changed everything for this mother and child.

Three years later, Louie and his mother are active members of our church ministry. By partnering with parents, regardless of their child's behavior, and doing it in a kind, gentle way, we get all sorts of stories from the parents that help us help them.

Staff and volunteers from other churches often ask me, "When should I start training to be trauma informed, because we don't have any kids with any trauma." I say to them, "Actually, yes, you do. Every kid has a story with challenges that have impacted their life. Based on the statistics, you *do* have kids who've experienced trauma, and these strategies work for every child and teen."[24]

## Learn the Tools to Respond to Children Differently

Tools for responding to children in our programs are changing. Not long ago, the focus was on managing behavior instead of looking at the possible meaning behind the behavior. Teachers followed a simple formula:

- First, give the child a warning.
- Second, put the child in time out, away from the other children.
- Third, contact the parent.

Both parent and child suffer the consequences of those disconnecting actions: isolation, guilt, blame, and shame, without ever getting to the source of the problem. Now, however, we are learning a better way.

According to Botto, going straight to discipline without connection is counterproductive and ineffective in changing behavior. For many kids already in survival mode, discipline increases their fear, and fear increases challenging behaviors. "There is great value in focusing on building a connection that creates a safe place for kids. Once kids feel safe, their behavior improves."[25]

Later on we will share practical tools and the experiences of others; we will follow the science and, most importantly, the Word of God to provide strategies for creating a trauma-informed ministry.

For now, as we conclude this chapter, we want to share comments from others who have worked with children and teens with a trauma history. They have found transformation, not only in their ministry outcomes but within themselves:

When kids are acting out, I used to think that they only wanted attention. I think the truth is, yes, one way to say it is that children want attention. But I now know when a child is also saying, "I'm seeking connection, I just don't know how to ask for it." Learning this and applying this has been huge for me, not only in ministry but as a father of three children.
KIRK MARSHALL, STUDENT MINISTRY CREATIVE DIRECTOR

I teach junior high and high school Bible classes and mentor several teenage girls one-on-one. Learning about trauma-informed care has impacted the way I teach and interact with students for the better. I now look at behaviors and ask what's happening inside that student rather than focusing on the behavior. My goal is to encourage students to make a lifelong commitment to dealing with the issues and needs beneath their behaviors from the viewpoint of the Bible.
ROBIN WIENTGE, CHRISTIAN SCHOOL BIBLE TEACHER AND COMMUNITY IMPACT TRAUMA TRAINER

Becoming a trauma-informed organization has been transformational for Back2Back. We have gained knowledge that has led us to change or create new programs, review our policies, and speak with a new vocabulary. Additionally, Back2Back now has a separate organization called Trauma Free World, dedicated to providing trauma training. Above all, it has created new opportunities for hope and healing for the vulnerable children and families we serve.

TODD GUCKENBERGER, EXECUTIVE DIRECTOR OF BACK2BACK MINISTRIES

## Key Takeaways

1. We start by examining our mindsets toward the children we serve. We need to honestly evaluate whether we approach difficult kids with boundless hope or as a waste of our time and energy. What we believe will influence our emotions and our actions.

2. Building empathy requires that we recognize the emotions connected to kids' stories. This requires that we spend time with them, listening to them and working to understand.

3. By developing the tools to engage with children differently, we can more easily get to the source of their issues and better engage with their hearts.

## Discussion Questions

1. This chapter opened with a quote about boundless hope that asked, "Didn't Jesus think that way?" What would Christ-centered hope look like when working with hurting children?

2. If we want our work with kids to be trauma informed, it helps when we all approach the task together. Why do you think this is so important?

3. Wounded children often see adults as unsafe people because adults' lack of understanding can result in judgmental attitudes toward those who have survived trauma. How does knowing this affect your heart toward the kids you work with?

4. Knowing the difficult life circumstances of the kids in our programs can help us view them with greater empathy and compassion. If you have experience getting to know the story of a child you've worked with, discuss how it changed your relationship with that child.

5. In this chapter we read about how Louie and his mother experienced acceptance and compassionate curiosity from Kim Botto. What was the key to Louie opening up? What was the key to his mother opening up? What do you think kept them coming back to church?

## Application Strategies

1. It can sometimes feel like it's easier *not* to know the hard things that kids face. But if we don't know, it's harder to help them. Our first application strategy is to name those hard things. Consider the kids you work with: How many have experienced bullying? How many have been victims of violence? How many have been exposed to violence within their own families?

2. Think of the kids in your program whom you find particularly challenging. Review the questions listed under the first principle for creating a trauma-informed environment to help reassess your mindset about these children.

3. Knowing the story of a child you interact with can dramatically shift your relationship with that child. Commit to fostering that relationship and being compassionately curious. Begin with just one or two children—write down their names and begin talking with them and praying for them.

# 4

# "AM I SAFE HERE?"

*Creating an Environment of Felt Safety*

Felt safety is not found in a place. Felt safety is
first and foremost found in the context of a warm,
nurturing, protective relationship.

BARBARA SORRELS, *REACHING AND TEACHING CHILDREN
EXPOSED TO TRAUMA*

The Sunday-morning notification is every parent's dread. Whether
it's a text message on your phone or your child's number appearing
on a screen, every parent who's ever dropped off a child in the church
nursery or a Sunday school classroom knows about the dreaded notification. It means simply one thing: *Come and fix your child.*

Sharen Ford, director of Focus on the Family's foster care and
adoption efforts, shares the following story:

> I can still see Alicia's face. She was a foster mom with
> some challenging children. She attended a pretty large
> church and wanted her church leaders to get on board

with creating a ministry for families who were doing kinship care, foster care, or who had adopted kids from the child-welfare system.

The pastor didn't acknowledge the need for such a program.

"That's just children's church," he told her. "Just bring the kids, and you will know where they are. They can be in children's church while the families are in either weekday Bible study or when they're in the services on Sunday or Saturday evening."

But that didn't work for Alicia. She looked forward to sitting in a service and having a break from serving in children's ministry, yet she would no sooner get settled in her row when the number for one of her children would start flashing.

*Come and get him—fix him—so we are not interrupted.*

"I got tired of being that family member who got called out to go deal with my kid," Alicia told me. "No sooner had I come back and gotten settled in my seat, you know, trying to catch up with the service, when my number started flashing again. And it usually wasn't for the same child. It was for a different one."[1]

Whether it's a flashing light, a text to your phone, or a tap on the shoulder, it's still embarrassing, says Erin Arant, a licensed occupational therapist and mother of three—two by adoption who have traumatic histories.

"It feels like a subconscious judgment of your parenting," Arant says. "When the light flashes, someone stands up. And when they do, the whole congregation looks. You might call me a frequent flyer."[2]

Parents of kids with trauma-related behaviors or special needs are particularly tired. They need time to experience worship and ministry as much as anyone—if not more.

Alicia turned her frustrations into action by paying attention to whose numbers were flashing. She discovered that most of them were parents who were fostering, had adopted children, or were grandparents caring for their grandchildren.

"We needed to be able to share in the worship service without interruption. Our children need a safe place where the staff understands them."

The church eventually responded by helping educate families and, in particular, ministry staff on the needs of troubled children—especially those with a history of trauma.

For more churches to catch this vision, something needs to happen first: Our churches need a mindset that welcomes complex, challenging, and complicated family situations.

## Welcoming the Messy

About twenty kids piled off the bus parked in the church parking lot. It was the beginning of a new ministry—reaching out to children in a nearby inner-city neighborhood. The idea was a good one—bring the kids to church and provide a meal for them—but it wasn't working. The new children's behavior was very disruptive.

Most of the children came from a CUTS (chronic unpredictable toxic stress) environment.[3] As a result, they found it challenging to adapt to the orderly, peaceful situation that the church workers were familiar with. The kids were simply recreating the chaotic environment they were used to. It was essentially their "working model."[4] The church staff and congregation, however, didn't understand this.

Many of the existing church families started keeping their children in the services because of the "negative" influence in the kids' classrooms. It wasn't long before the bus ministry stopped. It wasn't any single person's fault—*no one* was prepared to welcome the kids in the way they needed. The church workers *didn't know what they didn't know.* In short, they were not trauma informed.

"Part of the reason churches struggle with dealing with youngsters from difficult places," says Dr. Ford, "is a fear of the unknown.

> Many church families are foster or adoptive parents, and their kids are often viewed as *'bad kids.'* Think back to the vast number of children who experience chronic traumatic events—even among those who are living with their biological families. As Dr. Karyn Purvis says, 'Their behavior is their voice.'[5] Many people think, *It's the kids' problem, these bad kids; that's why they act like that* or *That's why they are in foster care.*[6]

Says Dr. Kayla Pray, a Christian clinical counselor, "When I hear the idea of *messy* about difficult children or teens, I think of them as *unrefined.* They need time, nurture, and structure to grow into the person God created them to be.

"So what we consider an outburst of anger—or what we sometimes call controlling, demanding, or attention seeking—is a passion that God is going to refine. We need to learn how to welcome in those diamonds in the rough.

"We want to acknowledge that it's easy to feel overwhelmed by the task, but these kids are *always* worth the effort."[7]

If you're not sure where to begin, Dr. Ford says she always encourages people to start with prayer: "*Okay, God, what is my piece?* If my part is just to continue to pray, that's fine. But if God is stirring you into action, what's that actionable piece that He wants you to do? Are you willing to have courageous conversations with others so they can come alongside you? God may be calling you to become that essential person in a child's life."[8]

Our churches and programs should be places where kids feel safe, and they should also be safe places for families. We want our churches and programs to be places of healing and strength, where families don't feel isolated, alone, or—even worse—shamed. But what does felt safety look like?

## What Is Felt Safety?

A child's sense of safety is the bedrock of everything that is to follow. When I (Jayne) think about the concept of *felt safety*, I see it as the core of everything else. Think about when, as a child, you walked into a new school for the first time. Try to recall your thoughts and emotions. Remember how your body physically responded to the new experience. If you were like many of your peers, you didn't feel safe. It was unfamiliar, unknown, perhaps even intimidating. Yet over a relatively short period, you were able to adjust to the new environment because you had the skills to do so.

> A child's sense of safety is the bedrock of everything that is to follow.

That's not the case for children with a history of trauma.

"Children from hard places come into the new place. They are wired for survival mode, meaning that they have experienced trauma," says Cindy Lee, LCSW, cofounder of the Halo Project.[9]

"They gear their behaviors around making sure that they can survive," Lee says. "And so, when they come into a new, safe environment, they don't automatically feel safe.

"New people plus an unpredictable climate equals fear—the very opposite of safety. Fear activates a child's internal alarm system, and the brain is stuck there. Easy adjustment does not happen quickly—or at all."[10]

Even though Siegel and Bryson primarily address parents and caregivers in *The Power of Showing Up*, their research-based findings also apply to those in education and ministry. For example, they write that "safety is the opposite of threat. It is the first step toward building a strong attachment. A caregiver helps the child *be* safe and therefore *feel* safe."[11]

Our ministry and educational environments can likewise be those safe places.

## What Felt Safety Looks Like

Creating a place of *felt safety* requires that the adults in charge arrange the environment and adjust their behavioral responses so that the children in that environment can feel profoundly safe.[12] They have two primary jobs when it comes to keeping their kids safe and making them feel safe. The first is to protect them from any harm. The second is to avoid becoming the source of fear and threat.[13] The atmosphere is an essential component in that process, and we will address that later in the chapter. But for now we will look at the most critical aspect of *feeling* safe, and that begins with fostering a healthy relationship with an adult. The following graphic depicts what can happen when a child feels safe in the presence of a trusted adult and within a secure environment.

Our brains are designed to do many things, but two things stand out here. First, the brain's job is to guard and protect us.

Second, the brain helps us learn and develop. Yet the brain can't prioritize both tasks at the same time. For example, if a child is overwhelmed by fear, there will be little to no learning because his brain is in protective mode.

When behavior becomes an issue, we need to first consider the child's history. We shouldn't be thinking, *How can I change this behavior?* We don't know what happened to him before he came into our program. Our attempts to modify behavior can do more harm and reinforce the child's belief that he isn't safe. The question we should ask ourselves is *How can I strengthen my relationship with this child so he feels safe?*

One young woman learned this lesson well:

Emily, a youth pastor at an average-sized church, was stumped. One of her students, Katie, had just turned fifteen when she and her family started attending the church. Katie came into their teen program each week with an attitude that screamed, *Don't get near me!* She wouldn't let anyone get close, emotionally or physically. Each Wednesday Katie walked to the back of the room, sat down, and essentially endured the hour-long program. She often kept her hoodie over her head.

Finally, some of the adults in the youth program suggested in a team meeting that they ask Katie why she even comes. "At least we could ask her to straighten up and come closer to the front," said one frustrated volunteer.

Emily disagreed. "What have we learned?" she asked. "There is always, always meaning behind the behavior. I am going to ask her mother's permission, and when Katie comes next week, I am going to slip her a note and ask to take her out to lunch."

Emily did just that. She handed Katie the note. At the end of that night's program, Katie just walked out without acknowledging the note. The following two Wednesdays, Emily gave Katie two more encouraging notes and reminded her of the lunch invitation. Finally, on the fourth Wednesday, Katie handed Emily a note that read, *I guess I will go if you want me to. I can go on Friday.*

The lunch was awkward. Katie barely talked, but Emily was determined to break through the shell surrounding this troubled teen. They set a date for another lunch, and then another. During the third lunch date, Katie asked Emily why she was doing this. "I care about you and want to help you," Emily replied.

Tears rolled down Katie's face. "No one has ever said that to me."

As the tears came, so did the conversation. "You see my parents on Sunday, and they look like the perfect couple. But the truth is that they are getting a divorce. They are hiding it all right now. I hear them arguing over who has to take me. My family doesn't want me; why would anybody else?"

That conversation opened the door for Katie to have a safe, caring adult in her life. Over the next few weeks, Emily and her team made an intentional effort to connect with Katie in meaningful ways. Katie slowly got involved with the youth group and made significant progress in relating to her peers. And Emily learned how felt safety involves a trusted adult creating emotional space for kids from hard places.

I (David) counsel a lot of hurting teens. When working with these very wounded young people, I want to create emotional space for these teens so they know that I want to *hear them*. I might ask, "Is there anything you've faced that you do not like and cannot change?" This is a powerful question, and in my experience, it opens them up to more conversation. (We will look more closely at the power of this particular question in chapter seven.)

"Creating space starts with remembering that emotions are synonymous with children," says Dr. Pray. "You think of tantrums in the toddler stages, and how behavioral problems emerge in the elementary years. Then the rebellious teenage streak going into the teen years. It's all about emotions. They're angry. They're sad. They're grumpy. They're difficult. They're irrational. Therefore, we want to create space for emotions . . . and not be disciplining for emotions."[14]

Sadly, emotions are not welcome in many homes, and the kids there have learned that it isn't safe or worth the time to try and share what is going on inside.

If young people know that emotions are welcomed by a safe adult and that they will not be reprimanded or condemned for sharing those feelings, Pray says, then most of them will be open to talking about their behavior once those emotions are out in the open.

"It is important to note that some feelings are so raw and personal, you will need to allow for time and private space with the child or teen."[15]

According to Josh Shipp, a youth expert and motivational speaker who also spent time in the foster care system, "What kids don't talk out, they act out."[16]

At the church Pray attends, one way they are creating room for emotions is through story time.

"The kids come in, and the teacher opens with story time," Pray says. "Then the teacher asks, 'What are some fantastic things that happened this week? What are some sad things that happened this week?' Getting the kids to talk about what's going on in their lives lets them know it is safe to feel and talk. She then gives the kids lots of time for prayer requests."[17]

## Principles for Creating an Environment of Felt Safety

Erin Arant, whose story was mentioned at the start of the chapter, is an adoptive mom and an occupational therapist whose work focuses on children and teens with a history of trauma. Arant suggests that the principles of felt safety should be practiced with every child.

"Although my expertise is with children with special needs, if we respond to those kids differently than anyone else, they will pick it up and feel isolated," Arant says. "They feel different, and that sets them apart. It's not fun to be different."[18]

"We need to set up our children's program so it is inclusive to all children, regardless of any special needs," says Cindy Lee from the Halo Project. "And I mean *all* kids. And when they first walk through that door, they have to see right away that it's different. Then you know what will happen? You'll get good behavior. They're thinking, *What is this place?* If the whole environment is different than anything they've ever experienced, they will come back."[19]

If program leaders and volunteers apply the following principles across the board, and if they respond to each child in a consistent manner, the result is typically a newfound passion among the staff—and a new vision that helps change lives.

### *Principle One: Feed Them Healthy Snacks*

One thing Carlos's parents count on when they go to church each week is that their son will no longer come out of his classroom with a sugar high. Eight-year-old Carlos used to love the donuts in class, but he loved them way too much! Before his Sunday school teachers could get to him, he was usually on his third donut. That's all different now.

The first principle in fostering felt safety isn't actually psychological or spiritual but rather physical: Providing healthy snacks should be a priority. An occasional donut isn't the end of the world, but high-sugar snacks can spike glucose levels and lead to challenging behavior. In Carlos's case, his parents had to deal with his hyperactive behavior—behavior that threatened the peacefulness of their after-church meal.

The classroom teachers didn't make the switch immediately, but they eventually made an announcement that the Sunday snacks were going to change. They introduced samples of the new snacks, spent a couple of weeks weaning the children off donuts, then made the switch complete. If we want kids to pay attention and build self-control, we also need to empower their bodies to function well.

The effectiveness of this principle is apparent at the Back2Back Ministries location in Cancun, Mexico. According to Erick Mowery, director of child and family development for Back2Back, "Our community center is right in the middle of an impoverished rural area. They work with over thirty-four families, both dads and moms, parenting scores of youngsters. Three days a week after school, nearly seventy young people come to the center to get help with homework, take classes, do a Bible study, play games, and receive counseling. However, before any of that begins, they walk into the kitchen to pick up healthy, nutritious snacks."

Research shows that hydration and nutrition are essential for learning and self-regulation because dehydration can cause irritability and aggressive behavior.[20] The following is a list of healthy snacks:

- water (instead of soda or high-sugar juices)
- granola bars
- fruit
- cheese sticks
- meat rollups
- peanut butter
- crackers
- nuts (as with other snacks, pay special attention to potential allergies)

By offering healthier food options, the Cancun staff met other needs that build trust—consistency and predictability. Kids from a CUTS environment desperately need both. Research shows that predictability and consistency—along with managed transitions (see more on this below)—are essential to promote feelings of safety and reduce feelings of fear.[21]

If you know that some children in your program come from a background of neglect, you might notice their food-related behaviors in the classroom. According to author and educator Barbara Sorrels, "the primary goal of dealing with food issues with maltreated children is to take away the fear regarding availability. Let them self-select snacks throughout the class period. This strategy eliminates the need for another transition to a group activity, keeps sugar levels stable, and helps children learn to read their internal cues that indicate hunger."[22]

For many children who hoard food, their behavior stems from a fear that there won't be enough. Don't be surprised if a child with such a history visits the snack table often in his first few times in class.

### Principle Two: Manage Transitions Well

Some children show up to our programs bounding with enthusiasm. Others, especially those who are new or have separation fears, might cling to a parent or caregiver. Managing the transition to and from the classroom is vital. What does that look like for the adults in charge?

"I love to stand outside and watch the little ones come in," says Cindy Lee. "We have an opening and closing ritual for each age group. The teacher or therapist gets down on the child's level and directs three questions to the parent/caregiver:

- 'Can I be their boss while they're here?'
- 'If they ask for a hug, can they have a hug?'
- 'If they would like a snack, is it okay if I give them a snack?'"[23]

The three statements above—addressed to the parents but intended for the children to hear—send messages that are important for children:

- *Your voice matters.*
- *Your opinion matters.*
- *I will listen to you.*

"With our middle schoolers," Lee says, "they have a special handshake that's like a family handshake. In the context of [middle-school] ministry, kids often arrive at the room without parents. When they come in, teachers greet the children with the handshake of their choice. Some teachers may think that doing

77

all of this takes away from teaching time. However, it is essential to remember that when children feel safe, the amount of teaching will be far more effective."[24]

### Principle Three: Celebrate with Character Praise

Jamie no longer dreads picking her eight-year-old son up after children's ministry each Sunday. It used to be that every Sunday she would get a list of all his behavioral challenges. But things have changed. Now when Connor walks out of the classroom, his teacher comes out with him and shares a short list of what we call *character praise*.

"It doesn't take much to become intentional about looking for the good in our youngsters," Lee says. "I encourage staff and volunteers to handle the classroom behaviors [themselves] and, instead of sharing behaviors (parents likely already know about the behaviors), offer positive character praise to the parents. Find three things you can share with the parents when they arrive to pick them up. *They are so kind; they are so generous; they are so creative in their artwork.* It's almost better if it's not behavior-related, but parents will take anything positive they hear. They aren't used to getting that.

"Adopting this routine also creates an environment where children feel safe. It's an environment where adults manage behavior, and praise is a high priority. What would that look like coming from the adults? *Good job putting your shoes away.* And you can then add character praise: *You are so respectful. You are so thoughtful and kind.*

"The way to change behavior is to change a child's damaged belief system by offering new experiences and new words. Unfortunately, these words of praise may be the only time many children hear them. Scripture tells us how powerful words are: 'Death and life are in the power of the tongue'" (Proverbs 18:21).[25]

Over time, a child's behavior will likely improve. But until it does, this third principle also creates felt safety.

### Principle Four: Remain Calm in the Moment

Staying calm in the moment is usually easier said than done. When a child's behavior escalates to a meltdown (we typically think of this as a tantrum, but there is a difference),[26] it immediately takes us out of our comfort zone. Instead of responding to the child's needs, we react to their behavior.

If we could encourage readers of this book to do just one thing, it would be this: Children who are escalating need *us* to remain calm, to stay peaceful.

"If you can stay calm in whatever they're offering," Lee says, "you are automatically different; you are automatically somebody they can trust. So we tell our church volunteers and teachers—whatever you need to do to stay calm during this time, do it. That's what they need from you more than anything. It's a tall order, obviously, but it's not a tall order for a certain amount of time."

"I suggest that adults don't show emotion at that moment," Lee says. "Of course you'll want to debrief with someone later about your experience and how you felt, but in the moment, staying calm is going to be what anchors that child. The child is learning, *I can say and do whatever, and this human, this adult—this strong, loving adult in charge—is going to stay calm. And I know that I am safe.*"[27]

### Principle Five: Staff Your Children's Ministries with Consistent Personnel

In an ideal world, it would be great to have the same adults staffing our programs each week, but that is a challenge even in the best situation. There are several reasons why recruiting and retaining volunteers is a challenge:

- Many potential volunteers don't feel like an hour or two each week can really make a difference (even though it can!). Second Corinthians 6:2 refers to a "favorable time," what some translate as "an opportunity of favor and grace in time." This is the sort of moment that can make a difference in the life of a child. It might be the opportunity to speak a word of encouragement or word of love. It might be a tender touch on the shoulder or a smile that changes everything. So yes, one hour can make a difference!
- Many potential volunteers don't think they can manage difficult behaviors. Training staff from a trauma-informed perspective can change that. We created this book to be that needed resource.
- Many former volunteers have tired of the same old ways of doing things with little or no improvement. Thus they've lost their passion. Creating a new vision for the ministry as presented in this book can help energize them again.

Until leaders in search of volunteers pay attention to the reasons above, the challenge of attracting and retaining volunteers will likely remain.

Although children benefit from predictability in relationships, that is rarely available when volunteers rotate serving from week to week. With that in mind, Lee offers a way to help children with the consistency they crave.

"If teachers are rotating, then I would probably create a wall or bulletin board calendar," Lee suggests. "I would have all their pictures somewhere on the wall, on a visual calendar or something like that, so the kids could see which person is supposed to be next week. Then, when they walk into the room that next week, it's not a surprise. Predictability helps the brain to organize itself and be ready to learn.

"Another helpful idea is to post the current teacher's picture on the outside of the door, so as children walk up to the class, they connect with the teacher even before they enter the room.

> "Predictability helps the brain to organize itself and be ready to learn."
>
> CINDY LEE

Then, as teachers prepare to close the class, they could walk over to the visual calendar and say, 'Hey, guys, I am here today. I'll be back on this day. I can't wait to see your smiling faces again. It's going to be so great.'"[28]

### Principle Six: Have a Plan to Manage Sensory-Related Issues

Keith wasn't in his class very long each Sunday before he melted down crying on the floor. While the rest of the classroom was buzzing with music and children's voices, the teachers didn't know what to do with Keith. As usual, his parents were quickly alerted. They often ended up sitting with Keith in class.

Unbeknownst to Keith's teachers, his parents had left out a significant detail about their son. He had sensory issues related to hearing. Loud noises and loud classrooms easily overwhelmed him. Keith's parents hoped he could manage the one hour in class, but he couldn't. As a result, the staff lacked two things—knowledge of Keith's specific needs and a plan to address them.

"If a child with a cast on his arm walks into your children's ministry, you don't have to think hard about the fact that you might have to adjust what you're doing that day based upon the fact that this child has a cast. Maybe they won't be able to put the glue on 'just so' or write or color. You just see the cast and you adjust. And if you were in the presence of a child who was running a fever, and you took their temperature, you don't think about it, you just enact your plan—contact the parents. Or if a child comes to your house to visit and she is in a wheelchair, you're going to make adjustments to make sure that it's accessible."[29]

In each case, Lee says, there is a signal. In the first case, the cast is the signal. For the second situation, it's the child's temperature. And for the third scenario, the wheelchair is the signal that tells us we need to enact our plan.

"If I see any special behavior," she says, "that's the signal that tells me I need to enact a plan. Sensory issues are signals. Trauma-type behaviors, survival behaviors, are signals. So I would educate my people: If you see a signal, you need to enact a plan."[30]

Here are some examples of what such a plan might involve, though there will always be some trial and error:

- If it's a sensory signal, the child might need a quiet space designated for them. Parents could provide noise-canceling earphones, or the program might purchase some that children can use.
- If it's a trauma-related signal, the appropriate plan typically begins by making a connection with the child. Think about this scenario to connect with them on something else:

> If Timothy is banging on the wall, I would say, "Hey, Timothy," to get his attention. "You know what we have for snacks? Today we have granola bars. Do you like granola bars?"
>
> "No, I don't."
>
> "Well, guess what? We have other snacks. You want to go and look?"
>
> Then we're connected, right? So I keep going until we're connected. Once connected, I sit down with him and say, "I see that you were banging on the

wall. I'm wondering if something's bothering you. Or maybe you need something. Let's talk about it."

We deal with the behavior once he has calmed down and we are connected.[31]

*Principle Seven: Ask Yourself, "Did I Connect Today?"*

One of the most powerful principles of felt safety happens at the end of the day. Lee suggests that every staff member and volunteer do a self-connection check:

> When you lay your head on the pillow at night, before you go to sleep, I want you to ask yourself: *Did I connect with every one of the children in some capacity?* It doesn't have to be anything other than just a few solid seconds of eye contact, meeting a single need, or whatever. This is a great accountability question.
>
> If staff and volunteers do this self-check each week, what you should see is an increase in their desire to connect with children, an interest in developing more creative ways to do that, and genuine enjoyment in the time they spend with the kids.[32]

## Key Takeaways

1. Programs that strive to serve those who struggle the most must commit to "welcome the messy"—complex, challenging, and complicated children and families.

2. To provide felt safety to children living in fear, the adults in charge need to modify their behavioral responses and focus on building relationships with those they hope to reach.

3. For kids to feel safe, they need an environment that accommodates their situation. This includes healthy snacks, managing transitions, celebrating positive character traits, staying calm in the moment, consistent staff, a plan to respond to challenges, and checking for connection.

## Discussion Questions

1. This chapter explains that both children with complicated histories *and* their parents need more than what is typically available in many programs. Discuss whether this is true in your program and what obstacles you've seen to "welcoming the messy."

2. If you were a child with "messy" behavior, how might you have viewed yourself differently if the adults in charge saw you as a diamond in the rough? What kind of actions and words would help demonstrate that belief in you?

3. Have you ever considered that the children in your program might be fearful in that environment? What are some behaviors you have noticed that might indicate fear in a child's heart?

4. If you were to implement some of the strategies presented in this chapter, where would you start?

5. The self-connection check described in principle seven can help keep us accountable and ensure that we don't overlook any of the kids we encounter. What does your program need to be able to connect with each child? More staff or volunteers? A shift in perspective? What would be personally helpful for you?

## Application Strategies

1. Dr. Ford says that her first recommended strategy is to
   pray. When we don't know what to do, when we fear the
   unknown, when we encounter frustrating or confusing
   behavior, we ask God for wisdom. He delights in giving us
   just that (James 1:5).

2. "What kids don't talk out, they act out," says youth expert
   Josh Shipp.[33] Incorporate ways for kids to talk about their
   feelings safely and not be afraid that others will judge them.

3. Change happens one step at a time. Start this week by
   implementing the self-check regularly. If you didn't connect
   with each child you encountered, don't get down on yourself.
   Instead, determine to get a little closer to your goal next time.
   Notice any shifts in you and the kids you work with as you
   make progress in this area.

# 5

# "BRING ME THE FOOTBALL"

*Building Resilience through Connection, Part One*

When you connect to the heart of a child,
everything is possible.

KARYN PURVIS

An unfamiliar man sat in the back row of the classroom, and I (Jayne) wondered if he actually wanted to be there. We were leading an early-morning session on how to engage children with a history of trauma. Midway through the class, I noticed the man typing on his phone, and I was convinced that he was marking time until the one-hour class was over. When class was over, the man waited until the room cleared and came up to me. He introduced himself as Ryan, a volunteer teacher with early-elementary children.

I thought I had learned not to make assumptions, but I had done it again, and I was so wrong. It turned out that Ryan was *very* interested in the material. "In just one hour, this class has transformed me," he said. Ryan told me about an eight-year-old boy named Matt who comes into his classroom almost every Sunday. Regretfully, he admitted, "I am relieved when he doesn't show up, because he isn't in the room for very long when his behavior mushrooms out of control. When that happens, I have him removed to sit in the hall.

"I know this little fellow's background," Ryan continued. "He lives in a chaotic home environment and has been in and out of foster care." What Matt needed so desperately, Ryan discovered, was *connection*.

Here's what Ryan learned in our session that day:

> This young man needs me to connect with him when he comes into the class. I now know how. And even more, when he becomes dysregulated [unable to control his emotional responses], I know he needs me even more to connect. I know he loves sports, so while you were talking, I was texting my wife to have her bring me a football. If Matt begins to become dysregulated today, instead of having him sit in the hall, Matt and I will go outside and throw the football. Instead of disconnecting with him, I will connect.[1]

I love Ryan's story because it relates to how so many of us feel and respond to disruptive children. What Ryan and the other teachers learned that day was the transforming power of connection. In this chapter, we will discuss some connection principles and strategies that have been life-changing for us. But first, we need to address a foundational question:

Why is connection so powerful and so necessary?

## The Greatest Needs: Attachment and Orientation

We earlier introduced Dr. Gordon Neufeld and his work on understanding the impact of trauma on children and teens. From the beginning of life until the end, we all have two significant needs: *attachment* and *orientation*. Attachment is who we belong to, who we are connected to, and answers the question *Who are my people?* Orientation, meanwhile, answers the questions *What am I supposed to be doing?* and *How am I to act?*

## Children and Teens' Greatest Needs[2]

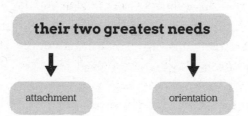

As modern families continue to fracture, attachment issues abound. When children and teens have no safe adults to connect with, they will look elsewhere to meet that need. Therefore, many behavioral issues, especially with detached adolescents, are rooted in the absence of a parental/adult emotional connection and the resulting reliance on peer relationships.[3]

It seems like more children than ever live with grandparents or other relatives due to family breakdown within their own homes. Many of them never experience feelings of deep attachment and connection, which are a vital part of a healthy childhood. Likewise, without involved parents to provide orientation, these same kids grow up lacking direction on how to live.

Family breakdown is certainly a major cause of attachment interruption, but there is another factor that must be addressed: distracted and inattentive adults.

Today's parents and teachers are certainly members of the distracted generation: overworked at our jobs, overscheduled with our kids, and exceedingly overstimulated by our electronic devices—our computers, our TVs, and especially our phones. This issue is so significant that researchers are now studying the generation of children raised by distracted parents. This generation, they've found, lacks the parental interactions that are key to healthy emotional and spiritual growth, a situation that Dr. Bruce Perry calls "relational poverty."[4] Those of us who work with children need to understand the significance of this trend. After all, almost all of us have smartphones and use them regularly. If we aren't careful, these small devices have the power to distract us from what matters most: building relational connections.

So what are the dangers of distracted adults?

### Distractions Create Unpredictable Care[5]

Katrina's mom anticipated a long wait in the doctor's office. With that in mind, she thought it might be a good time to catch up on work emails. While Mom was busy on her phone, seven-year-old Katrina wandered over to the waiting room's book table, thinking this would be a great opportunity for them to read a book together. Glancing over to where her mother was sitting, Katrina hesitated even to pick up a book. Lately, it had been "Katrina, we will do that later," but *later* never arrived. Katrina decided to look at the books alone.

"When seeking parental attention or care, children cannot predict what response or reaction their parents will have," says Dr. Dan Siegal. "Predictable care creates a sense of felt safety. Unpredictable care does not. Emotional safety is the core of . . . attachment experience. It allows kids to feel connected and protected."[6]

### Distractions Send a Message: The Child's Needs or Accomplishments Are Not Important

When a child enjoys success but no adult is there to acknowledge it, does it really make a difference? For example, take eleven-year-old

Carson, who had just hit a fantastic double. His parents are always too busy to attend his baseball games, so Carson was excited that two adult leaders from the children's-ministry group came to watch him play. But when Carson glanced over to the stands to see their reaction, there was no response. They never cheered Carson's success because they were busy looking at their phones. The next time he came up to bat, he didn't even bother to look over. Carson was silent on the way home, angry inside. What he accomplished didn't matter to those two adults. They were physically present but emotionally absent. They were too distracted to make a difference.

Chronically distracted care can send our kids looking elsewhere for attachment and meaning. Take, for example, the "glue boys" we saw when traveling abroad. Groups of young boys lay sprawled out by the side of the road—some with eyes glazed over, just staring ahead; others fast asleep. I couldn't believe how young many of them were.

We were driving through the streets of Kisumu, Kenya, and had heard the tragic stories about the glue boys—predominantly homeless children who live on the streets of Kenya and are addicted to sniffing glue. Discarded by adults, these kids inhale glue fumes because the high they experience helps them feel good, stay warm, and ward off their never-ending hunger pangs. Moreover, their shared coping mechanism gives them something in common, a shared sense of belonging. They are a peer group out of tragic necessity.

This sort of attachment deficit is extreme, but it isn't limited to faraway countries. Thousands of children and teens in the US lack significant adult connections in their lives. Their parents are disconnected, distracted, or just plain absent. Which of us have actually taken the time to find out how many kids we know and work with have healthy adult attachments? We might be unsettled by the answer.

I recently asked a pastor to teens, "What percentage of the kids in your youth group have disconnected relationships with their parents?" He serves in an upper-middle-class area near Cincinnati, one with good schools and lots of available extracurricular activities. "Probably 40 percent," he replied. His estimate was much higher than I'd imagined, which means it's probably a good idea for anyone who works with kids to consider the same question.

The following graphic[7] helps better illustrate the issue of connection:

## Children and Teens' Greatest Needs

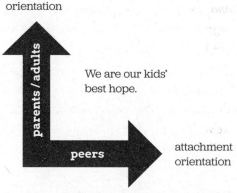

The vertical arrow represents the attachment and orientation children are supposed to get from their parents, teachers, coaches, mentors, and so on. The horizontal arrow represents peer attachments. If kids don't have healthy relationships with safe adults, they will invariably seek attachment and orientation with/from their peers. Children rarely provide mature guidance to one another. They can be impulsive and unsafe. And without positive adult connection, their growth in all areas of development—social, intellectual, emotional, spiritual—will slow or even cease.

Attachment and orientation are needs, not wants. The glue boys are an example of negative peer influence in each other's lives.

Peer attachment and its consequences are a wake-up call for those of us who work with younger children and teens. If the youth pastor's description of his kids' relationships with their parents is correct—if some 40 percent are disconnected—then it's pretty safe to assume that those young people are getting guidance and direction from their peers, who are often equally disconnected and fragmented. The good news is that by reaching these disconnected kids, we can also touch the lives of many additional young people. The bad news: We don't know where in the world to begin.

We begin with the power of connection.

Perhaps you are thinking, *I work with thirty kids or more every week, and I only get them for an hour or so. Most days I can barely get through the lesson. How am I supposed to connect with each one of them?* We know that feeling. We have faced those same challenges ourselves, and we have learned how to better engage with the kids we encounter. We've experienced how to make connecting easier and volunteering more enjoyable. Best of all, the guiding principles we've developed over the years can help change the trajectory of a child's life.

## Connection Principle One: Presence Matters

It was children's day at the church in Ohio where I (David) had previously served for more than a decade. We were just visiting that day, so we didn't know what the pastor was planning to speak about. That Sunday morning, Pastor Bryan made a simple yet profound statement—one that would serve as a rallying cry for connection: "For children, presence matters."

I grabbed on to that statement and considered the depth of its meaning. Yes, *presence matters*.

If I want to deepen my connection with any child, that child needs to know that I enjoy his presence and I am delighted to see him. "I am so glad to see you, Colton. I have missed you. As teachers, parents, and caregivers, there are always more tasks to accomplish, but no task is more important than being fully present for our children. We can implement this principle by slowing down, getting down to the children's level, and engaging with them face-to-face.

For children, presence matters.

### "You Changed My Life"

We were having lunch at a restaurant in Branson, Missouri—a city where I (David) had pastored some twenty years earlier—when a young lady approached us. "Are you Pastor Schooler?" she asked.

Then this young lady said something I will never forget.

"You probably don't remember me, but I want you to know that you changed my life."

"How did that happen?" I asked.

"When I was five years old, I came to your church with my grandmother. When we walked up the steps, you were standing at the front door. You got down on your knees and noticed my new shoes and socks and remarked that they were so cute. The next time I came, you remembered my name. After that, every time I came back, *you remembered my name*."

That was it. The simple act of engaging with this little girl—of being *present* in her life—made a tremendous difference. We had no idea at the time, so it was great to hear from this woman years later.

### Eye Contact and a Smile

Much of what we communicate is nonverbal. Our body language and facial expressions alone convey countless feelings. Understanding the power of body language is essential for anyone who works with children and teens, especially those with CUTS (chronic unpredictable toxic stress; see chapter 1). These kids are typically hypervigilant, constantly evaluating whether they are safe or not. They closely observe body language and facial expressions for any indication that a particular place or person is trustworthy.

The pattern of hypervigilance taught us a valuable truth: Maintaining eye contact, sharing a smile, or even giving a gentle nod can help reduce fear and foster connection.

Think about your own experiences. What is it like when you encounter someone with a positive, engaging expression? I don't know about you, but I feel it all over—a sense of warmth and welcome. The other person is *inviting* you into his or her presence. Proverbs 15:30 describes it well: "The light of the eyes rejoices the heart, and good news refreshes the bones."

It's no surprise that modern science validates this scriptural principle. Each one of us has what is called a vagus nerve. It is the longest nerve in the body, extending from the brain stem to the body's major organs, including the heart, liver, lungs, and intestines. As such, the nerve is sometimes referred to as the "key to well-being." The vagus nerve plays an important role in feelings such as stress, anxiety, and depression. For example, when a person experiences a positive interaction (eye contact and a smile), it stimulates the vagus nerve and calms the body, reducing stress and fear. It opens the brain up to new possibilities.[8]

Indeed, the power of a positive interaction can impact another person's life.

## Connection Principle Two: Connection before Correction[9]

"Before I understood the correction principles, my 'go-to' working with the kids in my ministry was to jump right to behavior,"

Shelly, a children's pastor, shared. "That's the model under which I grew up. Unfortunately, what I found was, with some of the kids whose behavior was so challenging, I found myself in a chronic cycle of only responding to behavior."

But, of course, that was not successful, Shelly discovered. The following graphic[10] explains that cycle.

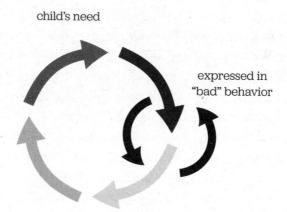

child's need

expressed in "bad" behavior

adult's reaction to "bad" behavior

Here is the cycle of negative reaction:

- The child has a need (hunger, tiredness, sensory overload, frustration).
- He or she expresses that need with negative, dysregulated behavior.
- The adult reacts with a disciplinary reaction.
- The negative reaction cycle repeats itself.

According to Dr. Gordon Neufeld, "There is a correlation between my emotional connection to a child and my tolerance of his or her behavior."[11]

What does this mean? If I feel a real connection to Chrissie and she misbehaves in my classroom, I can tolerate that and stay regulated. If I don't feel a real connection to a child and don't enjoy her presence, I react when misbehavior happens because my tolerance level is much smaller.

A few years ago, a local foster care agency called me (Jayne) with what was a very unusual request: "We have a foster family parenting two children who are now available for adoption. They want to adopt the nine-year-old boy but not his seven-year-old sister. Will you meet with them and talk them into adopting her?"

"Of course I will meet with them," I said, "but I don't talk anyone into doing anything."

It was a snowy December night when I met with the parents at a local restaurant. For over an hour I listened to their story and the reasons why they didn't want to adopt the little girl. I heard over and over again about her behavior. The foster mother said nothing positive about her. I took a napkin and sketched a diagram of the negative reaction cycle. "It sounds like you are stuck in this pattern," I said.

"That's it," the mom told me. "I am. She cannot even drink a glass of milk without my commenting on the slurping or something. How do I break this cycle?"

We spent the rest of the time together discussing how this mother might better connect with her foster daughter, even when she didn't want to. I shared a lot of the concepts featured in this chapter and the next. I agreed to mentor her using these principles. Over time, the mother's emotional connection to her foster daughter improved, and so did Mom's tolerance of her behavior. About six months later I received an email from the foster care agency: "We wanted you to know that the Harrison family's adoption day for both children is next week."

What does "connection before correction" look like with the

kids we work with? Sammy Summerlin, a friend of ours and a trauma expert and trainer with Back2Back Ministries, offers some examples. Keep in mind that we can all apply her ideas, much like the Harrison family did, whether we are parents, teachers, youth workers, coaches, or mentors.

- Connecting before correcting can be as simple as making eye contact. It's a moment to stop and truly *see* the child in front of you rather than simply noticing his or her behavior. Before correcting, offer a gentle "Can I see your eyes?" Once you establish eye contact, breathe deeply and then gently redirect the negative behavior.
- Using playfulness is a great way to connect with kids in challenging situations. While serving as a full-time caregiver to ten boys in a children's home, I (Sammy) often encountered lots of resistance at bedtime. One night, one of the boys refused to get in bed and instead sat on the couch in silence—unmovable. Once the rest of the kids were in bed, I sat next to him on the sofa. "Oh no, it looks like Antonio is frozen," I said aloud. "He's probably a popsicle. If he is, I wonder what flavor he would be, and I hope he's orange, because that's my favorite. I sure hope he isn't grape." At that moment, his frozen demeanor finally cracked, and he smiled and said, "I'm grape." It was just the opening I needed to reconnect *before* correcting his disobedience.
- Connecting before correcting often works better when we first let a child know that his or her desires are seen and heard. When a child says something like "I don't want to come inside!" we can connect first by saying, "I understand," "I know it's more fun to play outside," or "I like playing outside too." Leading with empathy

and understanding about what the child wants will help establish a foundation before effective correction can happen.

• Taking time to validate a child's feelings and ask meaningful questions—questions about what happened from his or her perspective—can help build a connection in which both children and teens feel safe to open up and share.[12]

## Connection Principle Three: Connect, Don't Disconnect

When the two brothers ran into the Sunday school classroom, loudly announcing their presence, I had a feeling it was going to be a challenging morning. They were semi-regular attendees, so I knew this wasn't typical behavior for Nick and Justin. Then again, I was only subbing for another children's-ministry volunteer, and I wasn't in charge of the class.

Moreover, I didn't know then what I know now.

As the hour progressed, the boys became less cooperative and more agitated. Finally, in a moment of frustration, the main teacher told Nick and Justin to go outside the room and stand in the hallway. The teacher then asked me to escort them to the sanctuary and back to the adult who had brought them, a neighbor who picked them up for church most Sundays. I later learned that the police had been at the boys' house after midnight because of a domestic violence report. As a result, the boys were operating on little sleep. I now understood why they arrived in our classroom in a totally dysregulated state.

Whether or not children come from a traumatic background, when they move into misbehavior or dysregulation, they need safe adults to help them connect, not disconnect.

What are some ways that adults can unwittingly disconnect

from children who are experiencing behavioral episodes like Nick and Justin were?

- putting the child in time-out
- sending the child to her room
- dismissing the child from the classroom
- using harsh disciplinary language
- using physical discipline—particularly with a child who might have a history of suffering abuse

And what are some ways adults can help create connection with kids who are experiencing behavioral episodes?

- Remaining with a child during a "time-in" communicates, *No matter what, I want to be with you.*
- Sitting quietly next to a child on the floor during a meltdown says, *I am in this with you.*
- Getting down to the child's level and making eye contact (if the child isn't too dysregulated) communicates, *I see you.*
- A gentle touch on a hand or shoulder says, *I am here.*
- Kind words reassure a child, indicating, *I want you to feel safe.*

Once a child is calm, a parent or teacher can talk with the youngster to work on his behavioral needs.

In that children's-ministry incident with Nick and Justin, what could I have done differently? First, I could have tried to establish a connection. The boys already knew me, so I would have sat down with them and quietly spoken some reassuring words. Sometimes just standing or sitting next to a dysregulated child without saying a word can be calming.

"Allowing a child emotional space to safely dissipate this energy will then allow him to calm down," advises Heather Forbes, LCSW and author. "As we provide reassurance, unconditional love, and emotional presence for our children, the need to act out will disappear. . . . Staying present and reassuring a child that you really are listening to him can sometimes be enough to help him begin to regulate. The life lesson that the bad behavior is inappropriate does indeed need to be taught and reinforced. However, this life lesson can only happen once the child is fully regulated (when the child is calm) and his cognitive thinking is intact."[13]

∞

Learning to *connect* with a child before *correcting* takes practice. Approaching it in this way doesn't always mean we are dealing with disruptive behavior, but with attitudes as well. A friend of ours shared the following story about connecting with her daughter, who was home from college for the summer. Applying some basic connection principles changed the entire trajectory of their summer together:

> When my daughter, Corinna, came home from college after her junior year, she arrived at the house in an intense manner. I can be intense too, so I knew I had to work on connecting with her. I didn't want to experience a huge disconnection between us.
>
> The next morning, when I came downstairs, my daughter still had her basket of clothes from college just sitting in the living room. Apparently she was waiting for them to miraculously make their way up to her room.
>
> I looked over at the couch, and next to the pile of clothes was a pile of her dishes. And next to the dishes was a huge pile of library books. So . . . she made it home

from college, didn't have time to put anything away, but still had time to go to the library in her first twelve hours back. And she brought home a huge stack of books.

After thinking about it for a moment, I decided exactly what I was going to do. "We are going to do a reading club together," I said. I let her pick the books, and we read and discussed them together.

Corinna was so excited when I told her. Truth is, we were only able to meet a few times that whole summer due to our work schedules, but here's what really struck me: After intentionally connecting with her over something she loved, we had a great summer—no behavioral issues, no ridiculous arguments. It really was like we were both on the same team for the rest of our summer together.

Remember Ryan, the teacher introduced at the beginning of this chapter? I watched him walk out of that classroom with more compassion and understanding than when he'd first arrived. I was confident that his interactions with Matt and other children would be different. He learned a valuable lesson: There is almost always a deeper meaning behind a child's behavior. Ryan hadn't been texting out of boredom. He'd been texting to change a life. We can all have an impact on a child's life when we consider the power of connection.

Now that we've learned the importance of cultivating connection with children and teens, we'll next dive into the resilience it ignites within them.

## Key Takeaways

1. Attachment and orientation are among the biggest needs in a child's life. When those needs are not met by their parents,

kids will try to meet those needs for themselves—most often through other kids.

2. Connection is a key to reaching kids from hard places. When we witness behavioral issues, what these children typically need is for a safe adult to connect with them.

3. When it comes to hurting children, our *presence* matters. Presence often requires more than just physical proximity; it actually requires that we—adults—pay attention to and respond with kindness to the children in our care.

## Discussion Questions

1. Think about what this chapter said about the importance of children being *seen*. When you were a child, who really saw you? What did they say or do to let you know that you were seen?

2. How easy or difficult is it for you to be present with the children in your life? What gets in the way of your ability to be present?

3. Imagine a children's program in which connection is prioritized. What kinds of things would you see? What would you hear?

4. Now imagine a children's program that lacks connection. How would the sights and sounds be different?

5. Remember Ryan's story about young Matt and the football? Think of a child you know who needs to feel connected. Think of a strategy you might try the next time you're with that particular boy or girl.

## Application Strategies

1. It's not always easy to shift the way we think about the more challenging kids in our programs. Ask God to help you see every child with eyes of compassion.

2. Give yourself permission to step away when necessary. When you feel overwhelmed by a child's behavior, take a moment to step away, breathe, and pray. Try treating the situation like a puzzle: What is it that this child might need? Once you think you might have an answer, reengage with the child and see if you can meet the need.

6

# GETTING ON THE SAME PAGE

*Building Resilience through Connection, Part Two*

The key to healing and building resilience
is connecting with others who can validate,
empathize, and understand our feelings
and experiences.

HELGA LUEST

We could tell that the woman was in intense thought. She was a foster mom, probably in her early forties. She sat in the back of the large room at a table with two other individuals. Like most of the other folks in this Canadian training session, she was an Indigenous person.

Indigenous people in Canada for decades had a history of being marginalized and traumatized by government programs. For example, Indigenous people represented the highest number of children in the nation's foster care system.[1] Their experiences with abuse, family separation, and even torture devastated the population and set into motion an ongoing pattern of trauma.

The history of this woman's people was an integral part of her life and experience.

We noticed her looking intently at the ACEs (adverse childhood experiences) survey.[2] When it was time for a break in the session, she indicated that she would like to talk with us.

"I have ten ACEs on my survey," she said. "I had no idea how my early growing up had so much to do with my adult issues. But I am doing very well now. My husband and I have four children, we are foster parents to two more, and most importantly, I feel emotionally and physically healthy."

Our immediate response was "Why do you think you are doing so well?"

She told us her story of early-childhood abuse and abandonment that had left her in a very broken foster care system for Indigenous people in Canada. By age fourteen, she had already been in a dozen different homes. But that's when things began to change for her.

"I could tell that my twelfth home was different," she said. "My foster mom, who is my mom today, worked at connecting with me. She was kind, patient, and encouraging. We did things together as a family that I had never experienced. I learned to cook. I learned how to keep a budget. I learned how to have healthier relationships. She is the most important person in my life, and I credit her with helping me heal."

I wanted to shout: *That's it. Resilience comes from connection!* But I didn't, of course. Instead, we asked her to share her experience with the entire group after the break. As I suspected, her story had a tremendous impact on the others.

## What Is Resilience?

By definition, *resilience* is the "psychological strength to deal with stress, setbacks, crises, and an array of hardships that confront us in life."[3] It is the ability to create the life I want to make instead of allowing things from my past to control me. We often think of resilience as individual hardiness or toughness, but it is not. Resilience is a learned skill. The foundation to cultivating resilience is *connection* with others who can listen to my story, validate what I say, empathize with my pain, and understand my feelings and experiences.

Grasping the healing power of connection is so vital that we have dedicated two chapters to this topic. God created us for relationships. He created us to desire social and emotional support. Engaging in supportive relationships is a critical skill *and* an excellent opportunity for those who encounter wounded children, teens, and adults.

In the previous chapter, we talked about these tools and strategies:

- attachment and orientation
- presence matters
- connection before correction
- connect, don't disconnect

Now let's add to our list of tools and strategies for cultivating resilience through connection.

## Use the Skill of *Yes, When* or *Yes, Instead*[4]

Let's say you're leading a Sunday school class. Seven-year-old Kayla asks, "May I go to the toy table?"

"Not now, Kayla," you respond. "It's time to do our Bible story."

Kayla explodes in anger. She is on the floor, near a complete meltdown. You don't know her history of chronic unpredictability, broken relationships, and emotional abuse. From the time she was a toddler, Kayla has been a playing card in her parents' split. When with either parent, the only thing she hears all day is no. *No, you can't call your mom. No, we are not going there; your dad will be there.* Her parents use the word as a weapon toward the other parent, and Kayla doesn't understand. No one at the church knows much about Kayla's family history. They only know that her grandparents pick her up every other Sunday and bring her to the children's program.

Think of all the nos Kayla hears every single day. *No, you cannot go there. No, I won't listen to you. No, you can't have a snack. No, you cannot sit on my lap.* Children like Kayla live in a world of no, no, no.

Do we ever really consider why we so often respond to children with a no?

- We're preoccupied with another task.
- The child's timing is inconvenient.
- We prioritize a lesson/project over our relationship with the child.
- We don't want to take the extra steps that a yes might require.

We've learned that when children live in CUTS (chronic unpredictable toxic stress), their brains are often incapable of receiving the word *no.* The chronic nature of living in a helpless, hopeless, and powerless environment typically means that the part of the brain that processes *no* has become impaired due to toxic stress chemicals.[5] When a child like Kayla is caught in a powerless situation, she is stuck in the present. She sees no future to speak of. She's trapped in survival mode.

You might have a child or youth in your program who's experienced chronic sexual abuse yet has no one who knows because the child remains silent. She is trapped. In her mind, she doesn't know if she is going to live or die. She doesn't know if she will ever come back to see her favorite teacher again. The part of the child's brain that considers the future has failed.

To children with this sort of history, it sounds like the adult saying no simply doesn't care about what they need or want. According to child psychologist Mary Vicario, when children like this are told no, what they hear is *never*.[6]

So what is the solution? One answer is to look for ways to offer a yes while still retaining our position of authority as a safe adult. This is what we mean by *Yes, when* or *Yes, instead*. Unlike how we typically address other adults, we reverse the order of our words.

What would this mean for our example with Kayla?

Kayla asks, "May I go to the toy table?"

Our previous response: "Not now, Kayla. It's time to do our Bible story."

Our new, *Yes, when* response: "Yes, Kayla, you can go to the toy table when we finish our Bible story."

Here's another example:

Garrett asks, "Can I sit in the tent with Robbie and Thomas?"

Our no response: "No, Garrett, we are going to have our worship time right now."

Our *Yes, instead* response: "Yes you can, Garrett, but instead we are going to have worship first. The three of you can sit in the tent for five minutes with Mr. Josh at 10:30."

Here's a *Yes, when* example to use when managing transitions, especially when children are enjoying the present activity but it is time to move on:

Teacher: "Garrett, it's time to move to our Bible-story time."
Garrett: "But I want to stay here."
Teacher: "Yes, Garrett, I hear you. You can come back and finish when we're done with our Bible story."

When a child (or anyone) hears "Yes, when" or "Yes, instead," his brain can begin to heal. He can start to anticipate the future. His emotional growth is supported and his spiritual growth encouraged. He can begin to approach life in a far more positive way. A yes response indicates being heard. It indicates being seen.

> A yes response indicates being heard. It indicates being seen.

We're going to continue looking at ways to cultivate connection, knowing that out of healthy relationships comes resilience.

## Give a Child a Voice

Twelve-year-old Liam is a pouter. He comes to the after-school program only because he has to. His single mother works until six, and no one else is home to watch him. The volunteers basically ignore him when he shows up acting moody, which is usually every day. If they understood that Liam's pouting is an essential part of his vocabulary, they might approach him differently.

**"Behavior is the language of children who have lost their voice."**[7] This statement, from the late child-development expert Dr. Karyn Purvis, is one of the most powerful ones we have encountered in our journey to understand the impact of trauma on children. When a child or teen encounters abuse, the child often learns to keep silent. When a child or teen experiences neglect, that child learns that it does no good to express a need. In other words, *behavior* becomes the child's vocabulary.

A simple yet profound response signals to a child that it is safe to talk—that it is safe to express a need. That response, spoken in a reassuring tone, is **"Use your words, not your behavior. What do you need?"**[8] It may take repeated uses of this phrase for the child to start actually using his or her words to express a need. But once children learn to use their words, they can express their needs to anyone, anytime and anywhere.

## Look for Intentional Times of Connection

In chapter 4, we discussed the essential need to create a ministry environment where children feel safe. This same safe environment also needs to be a place where children are *seen*.[9] Being seen sends the message *I see you, and I care about you.* I (Jayne) have been guilty myself of hurrying through a lesson in order to cover everything, thus leaving the class not connecting well with any youngster.

So how does one create intentional connection times?

### When They Arrive

Many children line up outside the door before Sunday school starts or an after-school program begins. If they've attended before, the children likely know who the instructor is that day and already anticipate doing something enjoyable before they enter. For children who are new, it helps to post the teacher's picture on the door, as well as some of the ways that students can choose to greet the teacher:

- fist bump
- high five
- pinky shake
- hug

In every case, the teacher can also greet each child by name.

"We have worked hard to create an environment of intentional connection," says Tony, a youth pastor who works primarily with middle schoolers. "It has become part of the DNA of our ministry.

Each child is connected with *by name* multiple times during our time together. When it becomes part of who you are, it isn't hard. It just happens."

We have long understood the connection that happens when you call a person by name. One of the first things I (Jayne) work at when training adults is to make sure I can see everyone's name, whether it's a tag on their shirt or a cardboard name tent on the table. I try to always use names when calling on people. And if this simple connection point works with adults, imagine how much more powerful it is for children and teens.

Using a child's name reinforces *I see you. I care enough about you to call you by name.* It's a simple connection, and yet so easy to make. When a child raises his or her hand, instead of saying "Yes?" or pointing, call him or her by name.

### Start with Welcoming Circles

"We used to jump right into the scheduled activity but realized we hadn't heard from the children yet," says Joy, a children's volunteer. "So each Sunday, we now start with connection huddles, and the kids know that.

"Each youngster is encouraged to share something fun or different that happened during the week. Next, we pray together and then start the lesson. So now we have heard from the children and are modeling the importance of praying together."

### Watch for Struggling Children

Once every few weeks, it is my (Jayne's) turn to take part in children's church. I look forward to this very much. After we started teaching our church about trauma-informed care, it was interesting to observe what happened when a new family arrived to test our newly developed skills.

It was evident to all that this was an overwhelmed family with five chaotic kids. Five-year-old Annabel was in my classroom, and from the moment I met her, I could tell that she had some developmental delays. She would need a lot of assistance and encouragement with the activities we were doing. When I first entered the room, Annabel was already running around in circles. I connected with her immediately and remained with her throughout our time together. We did a coloring page together. I helped with her craft activity. I stayed by her side during worship time. We even enjoyed our snack together. Annabel left calm and happy that day, with a sense (I hope) of being seen, heard, and loved.

### Use Closing Circles

Heather Forbes, a developmental trauma expert, writes in her book *Classroom180* that using a closing circle at the end of a class or activity can pull children together meaningfully, settle them down, and prepare them for the transition to leave.[10] I use closing circles by gathering the youngsters together and simply asking them something they learned or something that was meaningful or fun.

### End the Day with Character Reinforcement/Praise

One of the things I most look forward to is the end of our time together—not because I am done for the day, but because of what we get to do before they leave. I have children line up at the door when I hear that the adults' church service is over. Then, when their parents arrive to pick them up, I say a word of character praise to each youngster, loud enough that their parents can hear.

"Gunnar, thanks for being so kind today. I saw how you spoke to Josie."

"Thanks, Ruthie, for being so helpful. I noticed how you helped Simone clean up her project."

The looks in the children's eyes when they hear these words is priceless.

## Initiate Positive Interaction

Fifteen-year-old Troy now arrives excitedly each Sunday for youth ministry time, but it wasn't always this way. When Troy's parents separated, he ended up moving to town with his father. They were brand new to the church, and with the trauma of a new environment and an impending divorce, Troy didn't have much emotional energy—or interest in much of anything.

The church's youth pastor, Zack, has a soft spot for kids like Troy. Awhile back, Zack learned a powerful truth about connection, and he learned it from experience: *If I want to connect with kids who are not interested in participating, I need to maintain my positive interactions with them, no matter what response I receive in return.*

Whether you are a parent, teacher, coach, or other mentor, a positive interaction cycle can cultivate connections over time.[11] And those connections, in turn, will cultivate resilience.

> The more positive social interactions children experience, the more likely they will be to open their hearts and connect.

But what does that look like for you, the adult, in this equation? I'll be honest—it isn't easy, especially in the beginning. As the teacher, youth worker, coach, or mentor, it's all on you to pour into a child's life with positive affirmations. Even tougher, you need to expect nothing in return.

It's your task to welcome that disengaged youngster who walks into your after-school program every day: "Wow, Michael, I am so glad you are here. We have missed you! You have so much to offer."

It's your task to affirm a youngster who rarely, if ever, hears the words *I love you.* When that child is coloring a page, let her know, "You are such a great kid, and we love having you here."

It's your task to encourage a teen who thinks no one cares: "Hey, Ava, I heard how well you did in the soccer game last night. You are such an amazing athlete and young woman."

We have learned through experience that the more positive social interactions children experience, the more likely they will be to open their hearts and connect. Kids who might seem hard to appreciate *can* change over time. They *can* become resilient and well regulated. Your personal interactions with them are essential to building self-esteem—the critical factor in resilience.

∽

Thus far we've talked about cultivating relationships by using *Yes, when* and *Yes, instead*; by giving a child a voice; by seeking out intentional connection times; and by using positive interactions. These are just some of the ways we've used to foster stronger relationships with the children we serve. Invite those you work with to come up with others.

## Behavioral Matching

While it's hard to pick a best or favorite technique, behavioral matching is mine. Our friend Sammy Summerlin, a trauma-competent care instructor, says getting to know the kids you work with is essential, but that obviously takes time. "The fun skill of behavioral matching is a great place to start," Summerlin suggests. "And it doesn't seem overwhelming."[12]

Behavioral matching begins with looking for natural points of connection. The good news is that you don't need to know a child's history to do this. For example, if you don't know much (if anything) about a child, simply begin with the most basic connection points.

### Level-One Matching

- "Hey, that's a great superhero T-shirt. I like superheroes too."
- "You're sitting cross-legged on the floor. I can do that too."

### Level-Two Matching

- "I remember that you like soccer. I went to a soccer game on Saturday night. Do you want to see my pictures from the game?"
- "I noticed last week you like to draw, and so do I."

### Level-Three Matching

- "I heard that you like to play [name a game]. You know, I want to learn how to play it too. Maybe we can play it together next week before class starts."

## Playfulness Wins

When I (Jayne) take a turn volunteering in children's church, all my regulars know I have one crucial rule: *No smiling!* That's because children's church is *very* serious business. You can probably guess how this one plays out: The youngsters all look at me and try not to smile, yet it doesn't last long. Usually it's just a matter of seconds before they are all smiling and laughing. I love connecting with them right away through playfulness. They can tell from my tone of voice that I am only kidding, and by the time I have engaged them in laughter, I know they are with me and ready to learn.

Some of you reading this may be thinking, *I'm not very good at playfulness.* Perhaps you didn't grow up in an environment where your parents encouraged fun, imagination, and creativity. But it's never too late to learn—to at least *try*.

I recall delivering our trauma training at an orphanage in Ukraine. One of the house mothers, who looked more like a military commander than a nurturing parent, expressed that same concern. "I don't know how to play," she said, "and I am not going out and playing soccer with the children!"

Yet I had watched her closely while we were there. I saw how she teased her colleagues and laughed with them. I brought that to her attention.

"Being playful doesn't mean you always have to engage in a game," I told her. "But it does involve having a playful attitude with the children. I have watched you these last two days, and that is exactly what I saw in you. You *are* playful."

She was greatly relieved that she didn't have to participate in the next soccer game, but she agreed with my assessment. "I can be playful with my children," she said.

During another overseas training, as we concluded our series on trauma, the director of an orphanage spoke up: "The most important thing I have learned in this workshop is that I am supposed to play with the children. We provide a bed, food, and education, but I didn't know that I was supposed to play with them."

It's one of the most powerful lessons we get to impart.

Why is play so important, even within the context of ministry? Play does many things for a developing child: It improves language skills, it aids in developing self-regulation, it helps foster a sense of self-worth, and it increases creativity—just to name a few.

So how do we integrate play into our church ministries and afterschool programs? Emily Grubbs, a children's pastor in Cincinnati, uses playfulness to help reach and teach the kids in her classrooms.

"I think effective children's ministries tap into play," Grubbs says. "You really have to meet kids where they are at their developmental level. It's really hard for a kid to just sit and listen, like you would as an adult. We lose out on a lot when we don't know where kids are at developmentally and how they learn. I'm really big on engaging kids using all different types of learning styles."[13]

Most of us retain more information when we do things in a familiar environment or, better yet, when we are active participants, even as adults. That's why I try to make my lessons experiential. I'm not just reading a story, for example, but inviting the kids to be a part of it. Having them act out a story is one of my favorite things to do. When telling the biblical story of Jonah and the big fish, I opened a can of sardines and had one of the other adults walk around the room with it. The sights and smells of an open sardine can may be kind of gross, but there was so much laughter among the kids. I could see the happiness and engagement of learning on their faces.

Building connections to young people's hearts is a key aspect of learning, healing, and developing. I trust that these two chapters have inspired a few strategies to help you in relationship building with the students you love and serve.

## Key Takeaways

1. Resilience is the ability to help create the life we want to make instead of allowing circumstances and experiences from the past to control us. Resilience comes, at least in part, from connection with others who empathize with my feelings and experiences.

2. For children who live in a CUTS environment, the word *no* can sound like *never*! Explore creative solutions for being the safe adult in their lives while still giving them boundaries. Using *Yes, when* and *Yes, instead* is one of those ways.

3. Watch for the kids who are struggling, and look for opportunities to come alongside them. You can use a number of tools, such as calling them by name, offering special greetings, welcoming and closing circles, behavioral matching, demonstrating playfulness, and ending the day with character praise.

## Discussion Questions

1. Based on what you learned about resilience in this chapter, how resilient would you say you currently are?

2. You've likely heard the phrase *Children are resilient.* While this may be true for some children, it isn't true for all. What criteria would you use for evaluating whether this phrase is true for the children you interact with?

3. Is using the phrase *Yes, when* somehow letting the child be the boss? Why or why not?

4. As an adult in a room filled with children, it's easy to miss the ones who are struggling. Is this your experience, or are you drawn to the kids who are viewed as challenging? What would it take for an adult to be aware of and proactive with those who are struggling?

5. Review the third key takeaway above and choose one of the connecting tools mentioned. Discuss with a partner an idea for how you might use this tool in your work with children.

## Application Strategies

1. You can help build resilience in children's lives by listening to their stories, validating what they say, empathizing with

their pain, and understanding their feelings and experiences. Write down the name of one child you want to help build resilience. What verb from the list above do you want to focus on initially for this child—*listening, validating, empathizing,* or *understanding?* Write that verb next to the child's name, and keep it where you will see it throughout the week.

2. Begin training yourself to avoid the word *no* whenever possible. Instead, find creative ways to provide the same boundaries (especially if it's for the good of the child) while using words that affirm the child and create a sense of felt safety.

3. Build your connection skills! Choose one of the tools/ strategies from this chapter and start practicing it with the kids you encounter. Once you have developed that skill, choose another to work on. Watch how improved connections help change the way kids see you.

# 7

# ACTIONS SPEAK LOUDER

*Seeing Meaning behind the Behavior*

Behavior is the language of children
who have lost their voice.

KARYN PURVIS

At age seven, Jonathan has already experienced more heartbreak than most adults. He watched his parents' marriage disintegrate into domestic violence. After Jonathan's father died, his mother's mental-health issues left her in no position to raise a child, so Jonathan's grandparents took him in. He is too young to understand adult problems, but that doesn't spare him from his own emotional pain. Jonathan is so withdrawn in his after-school program that his tutors have no idea what to do.

So Jonathan simply comes and sits. He sits, and he stares.

Philip, meanwhile, stopped counting after his tenth foster

care–placement home. At age fifteen, he has learned a critical survival lesson: Trust no one. He does show up at basketball practice, but attempts to engage him usually fail. He either responds with one-word answers or not at all. Philip's lack of trust leads to rejecting behavior toward adults. He literally turns his back when someone corrects him, even covering his ears like a much younger child might do. No one knows quite how to respond. For Philip's coaches, it all feels personal.

## There Is Always Meaning behind the Behavior

When children don't have words to express their needs or feelings, they often use their behavior. The circumstances of life have taught them three survival rules:

- Don't talk.
- Don't trust.
- Don't feel.

As we said in an earlier chapter, the only vocabulary these youngsters have is their behavior. If, as parents, teachers, coaches, or pastors, we rely solely on their conduct, we typically miss their needs.

In chapter 5, we examined the cycle of negative reaction:

- The child has a need (hunger, tiredness, sensory overload, frustration).
- He or she expresses that need with negative, dysregulated behavior.
- The adult reacts with a disciplinary reaction.
- The negative reaction cycle repeats itself.[1]

child's need

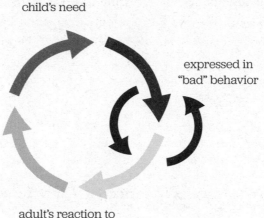

expressed in "bad" behavior

adult's reaction to "bad" behavior

As we learned earlier from Dr. Gordon Neufeld, there is a correlation between an adult's emotional connection to a child and tolerance of the child's behavior. If I feel a real connection to young Chrissie and she misbehaves in my classroom, I can better tolerate her behavior and remain regulated. If I don't feel a real connection to Miles and don't enjoy his presence, I'm more likely to react when misbehavior happens. My toleration level is much smaller, and I probably won't meet the child's needs.

The same thing is also often true of our relationships with adults. If I've worked to build a healthy connection with a colleague and there is a rupture along the way, I'll move quickly to repair it. But if an unfamiliar person at work (or church) rubs me the wrong way, I have little tolerance and no desire to work on any relationship.

What behaviors do we attempt to manage at home or in a school/ministry setting? The following chart is just a sampling of typical behaviors and possible meanings behind those behaviors.[2]

| Behavior | Potential Meaning |
| --- | --- |
| meltdowns | sensory or emotional overload |
| anger, crying | physical needs: hunger, thirst, tiredness |
| hitting | frustration or too much noise or visual stimulation |
| arguing about every instruction | need to control, defensiveness |
| defiance/challenging authority | loss of trust in adults |
| slamming doors/throwing chairs | need to be heard |
| laziness/withdrawal | survival through shutting down |
| pushing boundaries | need to be seen and heard |

In the pages ahead, we'll explore additional issues that explain the meaning behind the behavior.

We'll look at the *window of tolerance*.

We'll examine *indications of detachment*.

We'll walk through the *frustration box*.

## Understanding the Window of Tolerance[3]

Two boys, both eight years old, have grown up in two completely different home environments. For the most part, Andy's home is calm, nurturing, and structured. Andy is securely attached to both his parents, and because of that attachment he has developed good self-regulation skills.

Billy's home life is very different. As an infant he experienced neglect. His parents failed to meet his basic needs during his first three years. Due to living in a CUTS (chronic unpredictable toxic stress) environment, Billy never formed a healthy attachment with his parents. By the time Billy was four, his parents were divorced and he was shuffled between his single mother and his grandparents. Billy never learned any self-regulation skills. His window of tolerance is small. His actions are often disruptive and look to the untrained eye like typical bad behavior.

Every training we conduct on trauma-informed care includes an overview of Heather Forbes's window of tolerance. When participants see this graphic,[4] I often see them recognize some of the children or teens in their homes or classrooms.

### Window of Stress Tolerance

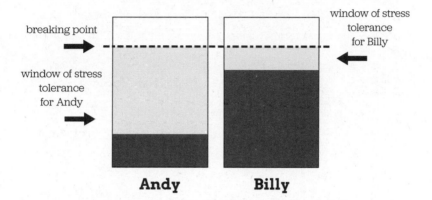

breaking point

window of stress tolerance for Billy

window of stress tolerance for Andy

**Andy**      **Billy**

The window on the left represents Andy. He has a larger window of tolerance because his parents coached him as he grew up. So when someone tells Andy, "No, not right now," he can regulate himself and put off the request he made until later.

On the right, Billy's window of tolerance is very small. When he hears, "No, not now," he might respond by throwing a toy or turning over a chair. It absolutely looks like bad behavior unless and until we understand how small Billy's stress window is. If we could see inside his body and brain, we would have a better idea what is going on within him. Billy's brain is essentially stuck in fear and survival mode, and his body is flooded with stress chemicals. When we better understand the factors that are influencing his behavior, we can respond differently.

"Our responsibility and calling are really to help Billy increase his window of tolerance," says Heather Forbes. "It doesn't mean that we accept his negative behavior, but we see it not as simply bad behavior. We see him as a child who needs help getting regulated and increasing his window of tolerance. This perspective leads to healing.

"We can help children heal—give them the long-term ability to regulate and expand that window of tolerance. They can start thinking clearly, and when they are held accountable, they can process what that means versus always being angry."[5]

## The Engine Plate: A Self-Regulation Tool[6]

Every day after school, about twenty youngsters show up for the after-school program at a local church. First, they get their engine plate out of their cubby holes. Then, once every child is seated, they do an engine self-check.

What is an engine plate?

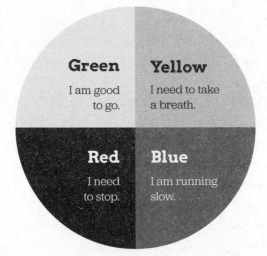

An *engine plate* is a simple tool used to help children become more aware of their thoughts and feelings. As children develop this self-awareness, they can better regulate themselves and remain calm. Engine plates are helpful in teaching children about *self-regulation*. We say a child has developed self-regulation skills when she has learned to control her behavior, emotions, and thoughts to the point that, when something negative or unexpected happens, she doesn't explode into destructive behavior. Self-regulation is a valuable life skill for anyone in any environment, especially those that involve working with children and teens.

## Making Your Own Engine Plate

*What You Need*

- a paper plate
- black construction paper for the arrow or clothespins to move around the plate
- a hole punch and a paper fastener/brad for attaching the arrow
- a ruler
- crayons or colored pencils (blue, green, yellow, and red)

1. Draw a horizontal line through the middle of a paper plate, dividing it into two halves.
2. Divide the top half into four equal pie-shaped sections.
3. Color the four sections (from left to right) blue, green, yellow, and red.
4. If using the arrow, punch a hole in the middle for the brad, or use a clothespin to select the appropriate colored section.
5. Finally, write the child's name on the bottom half of the plate.

### *"How Is Your Engine Running?"*

This question is a simple way to help children assess how they are doing/feeling on the inside.

- When their internal engine is running in the blue, children probably have low energy and are tired, hungry, or sad.
- When their internal engine is running in the green, children feel they have the right energy and generally feel good.
- When their internal engine is running in the yellow, children might feel on edge—anxious, stressed, excited, silly, or nervous.
- When their internal engine is running in the red, children are experiencing abundant energy—perhaps too much. They might be upset or angry about something that happened during the day and have brought those emotions with them into the classroom.

### *Moving Children toward the Green*

We recently began using engine plates in our children's-ministry program on Sunday mornings. The children love it, since one of the powerful things about an engine plate check-in is that it gives kids a voice. They feel seen and heard. The check-ins also help the teacher gauge the emotional temperature of the class. Again, the children are seen and heard.

Here's an example of how the engine plates work for me (Jayne):

Good morning, children. So glad you are here. Go to your cubby and get your engine plates. Let's do an engine check and see how you are all doing this morning!

How many of you are in the green today? That's great! Tell me why you are in the green.

How many of you are in the blue today? Are you tired, hungry, or sad today? What can we do to get you back into the green? *(Children can usually tell you if they have been doing this for a while.)* We will have our worship music time in a few moments, which might help you move into the green. *(A healthy snack and some type of body movement can help children regain energy, plus take care of any nutritional needs.)*

How many of you are in the yellow today? What can we do to get you back into the green? *(Children might say things like "I can pick one of my self-regulation activities [see examples below]. I can color, I can listen to quiet music, or I can take a walk around the room." Body movement can also help children who are in the yellow.)* After worship/snack time, we will listen to our Bible story and then color.

How many of you are in the red today? What can we do to get you back into the green? *(Children might say things like "I can do my deep-breathing activity. I can ask to go to the quiet corner in the room. I can use my words to tell you why I am mad." Body movement can also help children who are in the red.)* After we do our deep-breathing games, we will then go to worship time and snacks.

You might be saying to yourself, *I don't have time to do all this.* But you do. It doesn't take more than five minutes to begin your teaching sessions with an engine check. We always want our children to be in the best mood possible for the lessons and activities ahead.

Learning to regulate one's own physical and emotional state is a helpful skill at any age. It helps people make good friends, share thoughts and emotions, and better connect with others in healthy ways.

## Self-Regulation Activities

**Alerting activities** may help children who are running slow. They are also great to use after a lengthy time sitting in order to get their juices flowing again. Keep in mind that more energetic kids might also need a calming activity after an alerting activity before they sit back down to learn and work again.[7]

Alerting activities might include drinking water, going for a walk, organizing books or stacking chairs, lining up for a snack, listening to upbeat music, or finding ways to laugh, such as watching a funny video.

**Physical activities** are helpful for kids who tend to be quieter or more lethargic. These include jumping jacks, bouncing on a therapy ball, playing outside on a playground, jumping on a small trampoline, spinning, skipping, or running a relay race.[8]

**Calming activities** help children who are anxious or running too fast. These include turning off the lights, listening to soft music, light touch, such as running a feather over the arms, using manipulation objects (like Play-Doh or TheraPutty), or taking multiple deep breaths.[9]

## Recognizing the Meaning behind the Behavior: Indications of Detachment[10]

As we have learned in previous chapters, one of our greatest needs in life is attachment. God created us with the desire for connection and relationships. Think about what it feels like to go into a new situation where you know no one. What do you do? Most of us quickly begin to look for someone with whom we can connect.

If one of our greatest needs in life is attachment and connection with others, then one of our greatest fears is losing those relationships. Unfortunately, many children from a CUTS environment have experienced a (short) lifetime of loss and separation. As a result, they are incredibly fragile and can lose control at the slightest hint of another separation.

According to Dr. Neufeld, these children rarely have the skills to cope with the fear that occurs when facing a separation that is too much to bear. This fear can manifest whether the separation is physical or emotional.

> If one of our greatest needs in life is attachment and connection with others, then one of our greatest fears is losing those relationships.

There are three primary defensive responses to a fear of separation. All three can be triggered by fear of disapproval or disappointment or by the anticipation of separation, isolation, or loss.[11]

## Defensive Detachment

When children fear separation from someone, one possible response is that they might preemptively pull away to distance themselves from the pain.

Defensive detachment sounds like this: "I don't care! It doesn't matter. I don't like it here anyway."

Defensive detachment looks like this: We want a child to be with us, but he shies away. We want him to listen to us, but he ignores us. We want to provide good things for him to do, but he ruins every attempt.

Do any particular youngsters come to mind? Does defensive detachment explain their behavior?

### Defensive Reattachment

Carrie's main interest is talking to her friends. They are, after all, the most important people in her life. At age sixteen Carrie has learned that her parents are simply too distracted by their own problems and have little emotional time for her. To protect herself from ongoing rejection, she has attached to an unhealthy group of friends. Carrie knows her parents love her at some level, but they act as though they do not like her.

Carrie is engaging in defensive reattachment—a survival strategy for when the pain of separation and rejection becomes too much. Kids will instead attach to a peer group, often an unhealthy one, or to things like video games or social media. The kids in our programs who have adopted this survival strategy are often hesitant to connect with the adults who want to help them. These are typically the kids who gravitate to the back of the room and take refuge in their phone screens and earbuds.

Do any particular youngsters come to mind? Does defensive reattachment explain their behavior?

### Defensive Dominance

When Josh entered the gymnasium, the look on his face said it all: *I am angry, so don't come near me. I am in charge of myself, and I won't listen to anyone else.*

Josh was exhibiting defensive dominance—a survival strategy youth use in order to control their emotional environment. Trouble is, kids like Josh think they are in control, but they're not. What they are is demanding and bossy. They resist accepting guidance, direction, or rules. These kids are often the easiest to spot in our programs because their behavior stands out, and we usually call it "bad" behavior.

Once again, do any particular youngsters come to mind? Does defensive dominance explain their behavior?

∞

We explain these defensive strategies in an effort to increase understanding, yet to some it probably sounds overwhelming, depressing, and defeating. Where's the hope? Well, the hope comes with the realization that we actually *can* give each one of these kids what they need—a safe adult who's willing to work through their defensive walls. What it takes is an adult who is committed to building trust. According to youth expert Josh Shipp, hurting kids equate *trust* with *time*.[12] It takes time for an adult to gain a wounded child's trust. How long does it take? Well, it takes as long as it takes. It takes long enough for *you* to become the answer a child needs to feel seen, heard, and loved.

We have examined the window of tolerance as a way to explain the meaning behind the behavior. We have looked at three common defensive strategies youth use to protect their wounded hearts. Yet there is one more way to explain the meaning behind the behavior.

## The Frustration Box: Things We Do Not Like and Cannot Change

Natalia was adopted at age five from an Eastern European country. By the time she was a teenager, Natalia's behavior was unmanageable. Her parents contacted me (David), but when they scheduled an appointment, they told me, "We will bring her, but she won't talk."

They were mostly correct. Now fourteen years old, Natalia was decidedly resistant and barely answered my initial questions.

I worked at connecting with her, searching for any interests we might discuss. It took time, but slowly her defensive walls began to come down. Things changed dramatically when I asked her two questions: "What was life like in the orphanage? Did things happen there that you did not like and can't change?"

A flood of words and tears came forth as Natalia told me about the horrific things that had happened to her. Almost nightly, the older boys would visit the little girls' wing of the orphanage with only one purpose—to molest the little ones. After all, there were no adults on duty.

With Natalia's permission, I shared what she told me with her parents. They had never heard this before.

Whether it is moderately chaotic or severely abusive, a CUTS environment will subject kids to things they do not like and cannot change—sometimes on a daily basis. They can't change the fact that their parents are emotionally or physically absent. They can't change the reality that their father or mother (or both) has a drug-dependency problem that no one wants to acknowledge. They can't undo the years they spent in an orphanage where they experienced sexual abuse. They can't change the fact that they now live with distant relatives or foster parents due to the breakdown of their biological family.

The following graphic, adapted from Dr. Neufeld's work, is a helpful visual for understanding what behavior results from chronically encountering things we, especially children, do not like and cannot change. Those things are represented by the black box—the *frustration box*. If we don't learn how to adapt—to go around the box—we will end up feeling frustrated with, and maybe aggressive toward, ourselves or others. We use this graphic all the time, whether we're teaching a large group or are meeting one-on-one with a frustrated parent or teacher.[13]

### The Frustration Box

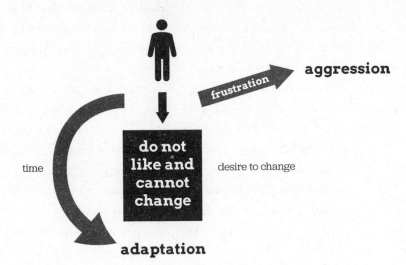

What we often see in kids who identify with this visual is high levels of frustration—deep disappointment with a society full of people who have failed them. This frustration often turns into aggressive behavior toward themselves or others. Using this frustration-box graphic when teaching young people is extremely helpful for several reasons: it stimulates discussion, it prompts teens to use their voices and be heard, and it helps pave the way for future one-on-one conversations.

As in Natalia's case, the frustration box represents things she does not like and could not change. A wounded child becomes deeply frustrated or angry when she can't change what she doesn't like. This is true not only for children but also for many of us as adults. Our past or current struggles, disappointments, and heartaches can all put us into the frustration box.

It's true that we all have frustrations in our lives. It might be as simple as not getting something we wanted for Christmas or as complex as childhood abuse or the divorce or death of loved ones. All these can fall into the realm of things we do not like but cannot change. When we experience these disappointments and traumas, we have essentially two choices—get stuck and suffer the consequences of being stuck or move around the issue (i.e., adapt) through grieving, learning, and continuing to pursue growth, maturity, and health.

You can help children go around the things they don't like and cannot change and thus *adapt* to the realities that face them. Adaptation begins with grieving the things that have been lost. As we talk with kids about their losses and allow them to grieve (tears are encouraged), healing can happen. Once grieving and healing take place, you will begin to see behavioral changes over time.

### Fallout from the Frustration Box

If one does not accept and grieve the reality of what is in their frustration box, the following outcomes may occur:

- **Toxic emotions.** The most dominant emotions among these are frustration, anger, depression, bitterness, and aggression.
- **Negative beliefs.** These might include feeling trapped, powerless, victimized, immobilized, or stuck.
- **Detrimental "pain management."** When the contents of a frustration box are not processed in a healthy way, some people try to *medicate* their emotional pain with addictive substances such as drugs or alcohol. Others might choose to *marinate* in the events and emotions of their past. One way of marinating involves constantly revisiting those painful events and memories. Still others choose to engage in a never-ending *marathon* of activities and distractions in an attempt to forget or block out the past.

- **Personal consequences.** *Neurological chaos* is a term used by Dr. Caroline Leaf, a communication pathologist and clinical neuroscientist, to describe what goes on in the brain when we wallow in anger, bitterness, resentment, and other harmful emotions. Living in this chaotic neurological state can negatively affect our mental and physical health as well as our emotional, relational, and spiritual well-being.[14]
- **Object focus.** When we are unable or unwilling to have healthy personal relationships, an object focus can distract us from a topic that we don't want to talk about. Instead, one might overly focus on non-relational things like homes, cars, or hobbies. As a result:
  - Maturity and development slow in those who are object focused because the brain is distracted, as Dr. Leaf says, like a kid who is overwhelmed by fear.[15]
  - The personal presence of someone who is stuck in their past pain can become both toxic and contagious. One's emotional state, whether sadness or joy, has the power to impact others.

### *"Moving Around" and Adapting to the Frustration Box*

The good news is that there are ways to work around the frustration box. We can learn to accept—and help the children we work with accept—the realities of life that we do not like but cannot change. Once we accept those realities, we can start to move around and adapt to them.

This is sometimes a difficult choice, and it is the beginning of a challenging journey. Paul, for example, faced many things he did not like and could not change. He speaks of these beginning in 2 Corinthians 11:16 and continuing into the next chapter. Paul's sufferings could have caused him to halt his journeys.

Instead, in Philippians 4:10-13, he reveals the secret of how he kept going in every situation—by relying on the strength that God provides.

The following are a few ways that we—and those we work with—can move around the frustration box toward healing:

- **Develop a relationship with Christ.** It is within an authentic, grace-based relationship with Jesus that the broken pieces of one's life can best heal.
- **Recognize that you have a choice.** Whether we remain stuck where we are or decide to move forward, we always have options in life. Jesus would often ask questions such as "What would you have me do for you?" or "Do you want to be made well?" Jesus is there to help us, but He doesn't make our choices for us. I know of a woman who described many things in her life that she did not like and could not change. Someone finally asked her, "What are you going to do about it?" It was the first time she realized she had a choice. Don't let the victim mentality of a stuck person overpower your ability to make more positive choices.
- **Find a safe, present, positive adult.** Scripture, social research, and experience all teach us that one of the essentials for a healthier, more productive life is the presence of a safe, mindful person who will make the journey with you.
- **Embrace mindfulness.** Remaining stuck in regret over the past and fearful of the future is a very stressful mindset that leads to mental, emotional, and physical problems—not to mention missing out on the joys and challenges of the moment. In Matthew 6:34, Jesus speaks of mindfulness in terms of avoiding anxiety and worry. Mindfulness is about paying attention to what is happening both *to* you and *in*

you. Mindfulness can be difficult for some to achieve for several reasons:

- Those raised in an environment where the caregivers were not mindful of the children's needs can come to believe that their needs were not important.
- They have come to believe that being *present* means they won't be able to avoid painful feelings.
- For whatever reason, they never learned the principles of self-awareness that are essential to growth and maturity.

• **Accept undeniable reality.** This happens when one can no longer deny the facts and circumstances in front of him and thus realizes that *he* must do something to change course.

• **Process your abuses.** Those wounds from the past that we do not like and cannot change are the issues we have to face if we want to heal. But how does one go about processing traumatic experiences and moving toward forgiveness?

- Identify the events that took place.
- Allow yourself to *feel* what you feel.
- Name the people involved—not simply to place blame but to help in coming to grips with the past.
- Share your story with a safe, trusted person.
- Be aware of how your experiences and belief system might influence your interpretation of past events.
- Emotionally, verbally, and visually release the past to God as an act of faith.

• **Grieve your losses.** When a person's journey is marked with the loss of relationships and opportunities, with failures, and even with unpleasant transitions (kids leaving home, retirement), these need to be identified, processed, and grieved. Grieving one's losses and transitions is essential to emotional and spiritual health.

- **Seek internal understanding and external wisdom.** Overcoming the difficulties of life and finding genuine healing rarely happens by someone solving our problems for us and telling us what to do. The Lord can certainly help us overcome the past, but we have to look inside ourselves and do the work. As Proverbs 20:5 suggests, we should seek to become people of *understanding*.

- **Recognize and work on inappropriate behaviors.** When we were in our "stuck" environment, we probably adopted maladaptive behaviors in order to survive and retain some sort of control. Those behaviors will likely continue long after our adverse experiences have ended. That's why it's so vital to identify and correct those negative survival strategies—or to at least replace them with healthier behaviors as we move toward healing.

> Working with or living with youngsters from traumatic backgrounds requires us to view the world from their perspective. Their behavior is actually their vocabulary.

- **Walk in the power of being content.** As we mentioned previously, Paul described how he went through many things he did not like and could not change. We read in Philippians 4 that he endured by learning how to be content in all circumstances.

∞

Remember that working with or living with youngsters from traumatic backgrounds requires us to view the world from their perspective. Their behavior—as complicated as it can get—is actually their vocabulary. It's their way to express the needs in their lives. When we consider that *all behavior has meaning*, it changes how we respond to those around us.

## Key Takeaways

1. Every individual, young or old, has a window of tolerance. The window of tolerance is almost always smaller for children who have experienced significant stress and trauma.

2. There are three typical responses to the fear of separation: defensive detachment, defensive reattachment, and defensive dominance.

3. The frustration box represents those things we do not like and cannot change. There are specific ways we can adapt to these realities in order to heal.

## Discussion Questions

1. What observations have you made about the windows of tolerance among different children in your program?

2. In this chapter we learned that understanding the window of tolerance concept can help us remain under control when children reach their breaking point. Think of a child who often melts down or gets angry. How can understanding their window of tolerance influence your response?

3. Consider having the kids in your program do an engine check as the first activity when you're all together. Do you think it's worth the extra five minutes it usually takes before the other activities begin? Share your thoughts with others in your program.

4. When you think about defensive detachment, defensive reattachment, and defensive dominance, do any particular children come to mind? Does thinking about these responses in terms of survival skills help you view the children you thought of in a different light?

5. Without mentioning names or identifying details, share some of the frustration-box hardships and stresses that the children you serve have experienced.

## Application Strategies

1. Think for a moment about three specific kids in your program—kids with varying skills and abilities. For each one of them, draw a box that represents their window of tolerance. Who has the largest window of tolerance? Who has the smallest?

2. Create an engine plate. Practice using it yourself first, and then use it as a tool with the kids in your program.

3. Consider how what you learned about the frustration box might help you bring some of the children in your program one step closer to healing.

# 8

# THE HEALING POWER OF STORY

*Preparing Yourself to Hear What Kids Have to Say*

There is no agony like bearing an
untold story inside of you.

ZORA NEALE HURSTON

"You know I was adopted," said ten-year-old Heather in front of
the children's small group. "Do you know why I was adopted? My
daddy did awful things to me."

"Like what?" the other kids called out.

Brittany, a volunteer group leader, was caught off guard. She
wasn't prepared to manage this sudden revelation in front of a
group of children. She quickly and quietly responded to Heather,
"Let's just you and I talk about that ourselves."

Brittany later took Heather aside and suggested that they have
this particular conversation with her parents. She didn't want to
step into a child's highly personal life story without them knowing.

We need to be prepared to hear painful, tragic stories from
the children we work with. In this chapter, we discuss some of the

We need to be prepared to hear painful, tragic stories from the children we work with.

things you might hear from the children in your program. How can you prepare for some of the stories that might arise? What should you do with what you hear? What are some boundaries you should implement? And how do you help these kids process the stories they share with you?

## What You Might Hear

Childhood trauma is in many ways a silent epidemic. We hope we have made that point clear throughout this book. Some statistics show that the vast majority of children today have experienced at least one significant adverse event. Traumatized kids and adults are all around us—in our classes, our after-school programs, and our sports teams—and multiple traumas are common, with an average of somewhere between six and eight traumatic events.[1]

As prominent author and Christian therapist Dan Allender writes, "Everyone's life is a story."[2] And many of those stories are filled with pain.

That was the case for Heather. Brittany tried to hold back her tears as she sat down with Heather and her adoptive parents and listened to Heather's story. Rather stoically for such a young child, Heather shared that as far back as she could remember, her father had sexually abused her.

"I know my mom knew, but she didn't stop him," Heather said. "I think I was around two when he started doing things to me. As I got a little older, I knew that if he came home drunk, it meant an awful evening for me."

Heather's adoptive parents sat quietly as she continued sharing her story with Brittany. It was the first time she had truly opened up to anyone about the details. Heather felt safe with Brittany and had a level of attachment to her. Heather explained that her father had demanded secrecy. "If you tell anyone, it will break up the family," he told her.

After sexually abusing Heather, he would often beat her, claiming, "You made me do this to you." She wondered why her mother, the one person available to protect her, failed to do so. (Childhood abuse victims like Heather often harbor more deep-seated anger toward the non-protective parent than the actual abuser.)

One day at school, when Heather was eight, her gym teacher noticed her extensive bruises and notified the school counselor. That counselor contacted authorities, who removed Heather from her home. She entered the foster care system. There was no way Heather could return to her family—her father was sentenced to prison and her mother was unstable. Fortunately, her foster parents loved her and adopted her when she was nine.

Unfortunately, there are many, many children with stories like Heather's. Behind those kids' smiles, there often resides deep pain—pain that needs to be shared, processed, and eventually healed. And what could be a better way to help process that pain than with safe adults who have learned how to respond? Wounded children may not open up to an unknown professional therapist at first, but they might open up to a teacher, tutor, coach, or classroom volunteer like you, mainly because you've already established a trusted connection.

What you hear from these hurting kids might shock you at first, probably because their world is not the same world in which you grew up. On the other hand, what you hear might remind you of your own unresolved childhood trauma. (The next chapter focuses on adults and their trauma history. If this sounds like you, it is an important chapter to read.)

To better grasp the vast number of children who've experienced abuse or neglect, think of your favorite college football team and the size of that team's stadium. The number of children who are abused and neglected in this country *every year* would fill ten of these stadiums.[3] It's thus highly likely that some of these more than seven hundred thousand children are in your program and have stories to tell.

What might some of these stories include?

### You Might Hear about Domestic Violence

For several years, Calvin, age ten, only *witnessed* domestic abuse at home. That was bad enough, but eventually his father's rage turned on him. Concerned for his younger siblings, Calvin told the school counselor. A children's protection services worker removed all the children and placed them in separate foster homes. Calvin now deals with guilt for telling on his father and the grief of losing his sisters. When he comes to his after-school program, Calvin isn't motivated to do his schoolwork and is very slow to connect with others. He wonders, *Is it safe to talk to my tutor about what is happening in my life?*

Calvin desperately needs to speak to someone. His behavior demonstrates what many foster parents, adoptive parents, and therapists already know: *What we don't talk out, we act out.*[4]

### You Might Hear about Ill Parents or Grandparents

Oliva, thirteen, appeared in a daze when she entered the Wednesday-night middle-school meeting at church. Her mother's cancer had returned, and the prognosis was grim. Oliva had received that news the day before, and it had sent shock waves through her entire family. Oliva's relationship with Randee, her youth leader, has always been excellent. Randee connected with Oliva as she always did, but she was still broadsided by the news. Randee certainly wasn't expecting to hear this about Oliva's mother.

Randee has never had to help a child facing this kind of crisis. She isn't sure how to respond, but she knows that Oliva needs her.

*You Might Hear about an Alcoholic Parent—*
*One You Didn't Suspect*

Fifteen-year-old Benjamin and his family have been regular church-goers for years. His mother misses a lot, however, and when asked, Ben usually says she is feeling sick. The truth is that Ben's mother has had a severe drinking problem for years. Ben doesn't understand why this is happening, but his father does. Ben's mother was sexually abused and has long used alcohol as an unhealthy remedy for her emotional trauma. To make matters worse, she refuses to seek counseling or any other form of treatment.

As a result, Ben, along with his two younger brothers, have been neglected at times by their emotionally absent parents. Their mother is neglectful because of her addiction. Their father, meanwhile, has emotionally shut out almost everyone and everything. Ben knows that his parents want to keep their issues secret, but he can't hold it together much longer.

Ben needs a safe adult in whom to confide, but he's not sure who that could be.

We could fill the next several pages with tragic story after story of what the children in our programs are carrying. (The COVID-19 pandemic prompted even more of those children to hide what was happening in their homes and families.)

More than ever, we need to be prepared to hear stories we never imagined possible.

## How to Prepare Yourself

We need to be there for the children we work with and their painful stories. That requires carefully managing our own emotions and responses. In Eric's first year of ministry, right out of seminary, he took a role as a youth pastor and joined a church team that was dedicated to becoming trauma informed.

"What I learned in my first months on the job were things that they didn't teach me about in seminary," Eric said. "Learning how to hear children's stories began with spending several months reading, studying, and participating in workshops focused on trauma. That was foundational."

With this understanding and knowledge now in his trauma-informed toolbox, Eric took even more steps to prepare for hearing stories from the wounded and hurting. Like many others in this type of role, he learned to implement the following principles.

### Become Self-Aware

April sat in the pastor's office. "I don't know what happened to me today," said the classroom worker, "but I shut down when Lynn started telling me about her father's physical abuse. It is hard to hear what happened to a seven-year-old child. I couldn't stay focused. I thanked her for talking to me and asked her to play with the others. Pastor, what is going on with me?"

What was going on with April is that Lynn's story tapped into memories of her own childhood abuse. April had never discussed it with anyone before. As a result, she lacked self-awareness regarding her own story.

Self-awareness begins with asking and answering two questions: *What has happened to me?* and *What have I done to pursue healing in my life?* These are essential questions to consider. Not only should we ask them, but we also need to think long and hard about the answers.

### Practice Mindfulness

Aaron regularly works on being aware of his thoughts and emotions.

"When sitting with a youngster I am mentoring and hearing his story," says the camp volunteer, "I try to pay real attention to how I feel, what I am thinking, and how my body is reacting. I quietly take deep breaths if I sense myself becoming dysregulated because of what I hear. It helps me remain calm and focused."

Beth Bench, a clinical family counselor, says, "When your physiology gets in the way of your ability to be fully present and actively engaged, you have reached a critical point of personal responsibility."[5]

Aaron has a healthy perspective on mindfulness. He tries to maintain an awareness of his thoughts, his emotions, what's happening in his body, and his own alertness to the surrounding environment.

*Find a Confidential Debriefing Partner*

Finding someone in your program to debrief with is vital to remaining emotionally healthy. We'll go into more detail about this later, but finding such an individual is the first step.

∞

We've spent the last several pages discussing *how* to listen to a hurting child's story. Now it's time to discuss *what to do* based on what you hear.

## When You Hear a Story

Eric waited until all the other youth-group kids had left. One teen had lingered behind, and Eric could tell that he wanted to talk.

"I need help," Michael said. "After what you taught us tonight—about social media and pornography—I know I need help. I've been watching pornography on my phone for the last two years. But, please, this is confidential. No one knows, especially my parents."

Eric took a deep breath and replied, "Michael, you can count on my being a safe person with this. I do have some questions. Do you think we could meet for dinner tomorrow night and talk about it?"

"Sure," Michael said.

After Michael left, Eric took another deep breath. Because he had researched quite a bit in preparation for tonight's lesson, he knew the sobering truth—that plenty of children today are viewing pornography.[6]

Perhaps naïvely, Eric didn't think that any of the kids in his ministry were watching pornography. His conversation with Michael quickly changed his perspective. (A quick note: This section isn't about dealing with pornography in particular; that would be a whole chapter—or an entire book—on its own. This section is about how to respond emotionally to what we've heard.)

No matter what we hear from a hurting child, there are essential steps involved in the debriefing process. Many people who work with these kids just stuff down their own feelings and never take the time to consider how the experience affected *them*. A debriefing session can definitely be confidential regarding the identities of the children involved, but sharing one's feelings about the interaction is critical to staying emotionally healthy.

> It's crucial to debrief after tough conversations in order to remain emotionally and spiritually healthy.

Eric, for example, was upset by his conversation with Michael. He wasn't upset *at* Michael but rather at the trap of pornography that Michael and so many others have fallen prey to.[7] Eric felt like he had failed Michael and perhaps other kids in the youth group. He needed to talk to someone about his feelings. Eric recognized that and made an appointment to meet with his church's pastor.

What does the debriefing process look like for someone like Eric?

One of the first things Eric's pastor addressed during their meeting was what the conversation looked like. He wanted Eric to set the stage in order to better understand the situation. He then asked Eric, "What was the hardest part of all this for you? What was your reaction to the situation in the moment, and what is your reaction now?"

After about an hour of conversation, Eric's pastor encouraged him to stay attuned to his feelings. In other words, to practice mindfulness. They also discussed how Eric could be better aware of what had triggered his anger or sense of failure and how to manage those feelings. Together they agreed to make a follow-up appointment for the next week in order to continue their conversation.

You don't have to consult with a pastor for your debriefing process. You can meet with an experienced counselor, therapist, or even a safe, trusted colleague if no one with specific training is available, but it's crucial to debrief after tough conversations in order to remain emotionally and spiritually healthy.

## Helping Kids Process Their Stories

Preparing yourself is obviously only part of what's involved in engaging with the tough stories you'll likely hear. There are several additional skills involved if you want to make a difference with the wounded kids you encounter.

### Listen, Value, and Validate

One of the critical listening skills that Eric, the youth pastor, learned was how to be truly *present* with the kids he talked to. That meant not looking at his watch or his phone as well as minimizing potential distractions. It also involved making good eye contact and being aware of his facial expressions. Eric made sure to demonstrate interest and concern during these conversations and to convey his attention through frequent nods of affirmation.

"I've learned," Eric says, "that it's important to express to a youngster his value to God and others—and for me to validate his story."

### Learn to Ask Good Questions

Questions are like doorknobs. They grant us access to another person's life and story. I (David) have a reputation for asking questions. When our grandchildren bring friends to our home for dinner, they often alert them: "Get ready; my granddad will ask you many questions."

Your questions don't all need to be deep and probing, but they should be ones that help you tap into a child's interests. Recently, one of our friends asked me to meet with his grandson. Thomas was belligerent and full of anger. He was in a new and unfamiliar situation—living with his grandparents in a new town, with a new school and a new church. It didn't take long to figure out that Thomas didn't want to be there.

I knew one thing about Thomas—that he loved to play video games. I have very little interest in video games myself, but asking Thomas questions about this passion would help me engage in conversation. Connecting with a child begins with asking him questions, not by telling him all the things he needs to do or think.

I spent the next two or three meetings asking Thomas questions about video games while weaving in additional questions about his story. It worked: Thomas soon opened up, and his anger and frustration decreased. Long story short, Thomas is doing much better today. He learned to connect with his grandparents (who were also willing to learn new parenting techniques), and they now have a positive relationship. Thomas is currently completing his college degree, and his grandparents visit him at his university.

Success stories like this are known as *therapeutic moments*.[8] Those critical moments of establishing a trusted connection can help open up a child's heart for future healing.

### Know Your Boundaries

Jen helps run a weekly program for inner-city kids. More than fifty kids pour into the church gym every Wednesday night for games, Bible study, and mentoring time. One of the kids Jen works with, Candice, is a twelve-year-old girl from a tough place. Jen spent three consecutive Wednesday nights talking with Candice, and their fourth night turned out to be a significant turning point.

"Jen, can I talk to you about something?" Candice asked. "I've wanted to talk to someone about this but have been afraid."

Jen waited for her to continue.

"Did you know that I'm in foster care?" Candice asked. "I'm in foster care because of what my daddy did to me, but what I have never told anyone is what my brother did to me. He did the same things my dad did."

Jen knew she had to be very careful regarding such a sensitive conversation. She kept in mind her boundaries: Candice had brought up not only a deep personal wound but also a legal issue.

Jen didn't feel like she had the skills and experience to go any deeper with such a delicate discussion. She also knew that she had to speak with someone in authority.

"Candice, I care very much for you," Jen said. "I want you to know how important it is to get you the best possible help. And you should know already that we need to talk to your caseworker. Would you let me go with you to tell him?"

### Understand Their Perspective

We've already shared a few experiences from Eric, the youth pastor, but we'd like to mention one more. Eric was sitting with Bekah, age fourteen, as she went on and on about her life in the foster care system. Her story seemed unlikely, but Eric had learned the importance of listening.

"I have lived in fourteen different homes," she told Eric. "The last one before this one was awesome. We went almost every weekend to a festival or theme park. They let me do whatever I wanted."

Eric, however, knew differently. Because of her trauma-filled history, Bekah never lasted in any single foster situation. She was known as a frequent runaway. The home she was most recently removed from—the "awesome" one she'd described—was her fifth foster home, not her fourteenth. There were few fun weekends, just everyday living. Her previous foster parents were an older couple who had asked Bekah's caseworker to remove her because they couldn't cope with her running away.

Kids who've lived as foster children or in orphanages overseas often don't accurately understand—or describe—their life stories. They have no coherent narrative to tell—certainly not one that follows a logical sequence. They have gaps in their memories. Many have lived in multiple foster homes, like Bekah, or moved from one orphanage to another. There are too many changes in their young lives to keep track of, and everything gets mixed up.

The stories you hear might sound too good to be true or too difficult to believe. Focus instead on listening, and try to understand the perspective of this hurting child. Ask questions about how a particular experience they describe made them feel. They might come up with a false feeling if the experience didn't happen, but that's okay. It's rarely our role to correct every story. Our role is to listen and understand, not to react.

∞

When we are given the privilege of listening to a hurting person's story, we in turn give them the gift of being seen, being heard, and being known. It might not feel like a blessing in the moment, but both parties benefit when we give of ourselves to others.

## Key Takeaways

1. You might hear hard stories of childhood trauma and abuse. Your boundaries and your response are critical in these moments, and you need to be intentional about both.

2. There are several aspects involved in hearing a wounded child's story: being self-aware, practicing mindfulness, valuing and validating as you listen, asking good questions, setting up healthy boundaries, and understanding the other person's perspective.

3. When we have an emotional response to what we hear, it's important to discuss how that experience affected us with someone we can trust.

## Discussion Questions

1. How aware are you of the difficult chapters in your own story? How would better understanding your own story help you as you listen to someone who is hurting?

2. Has someone ever shared a story with you that you weren't ready for? How did it make you feel? What did you do?

3. We presented several foundational skills in this chapter. Discuss which skill(s) you find the easiest, and which ones

sound most difficult. (Those skills include being self-aware, practicing mindfulness, valuing and validating as you listen, asking good questions, setting up healthy boundaries, and understanding the other person's perspective.)

4. Take a moment to practice mindfulness right now. Where do you notice tension in your body? Are you feeling sluggish or full of anxious energy? Are you able to focus, or is your mind wandering? Answering these questions is a way to practice mindfulness.

5. What are some things to be careful of when debriefing after listening to a hard story?

## Application Strategies

1. Make time to sit down with someone you trust, and share a difficult part of your story with them.

2. Be aware of asking good questions in your normal conversations. Practice this skill and pay attention to how it becomes more natural to ask good questions the more you work on it.

3. Pay attention to how engaging with other people's stories affects you. Does it impact you emotionally? If you are ever not okay, find someone you trust to explore those feelings.

**9**

# CARING FOR ADULTS WITH
# A HISTORY OF TRAUMA

*Everyone Has a Story That Needs to Be Heard*

The simple act of caring is heroic.

EDWARD ALBERT

To outsiders, Darlene's life appeared ideal. She was a nurse practitioner with a growing list of patients. She grew up in a Christian home, attended a Christian college, and had been active in ministry for decades. Her husband owned a successful computer company. They had two adult children, both of whom were married.

Yet nobody knew what was going on behind that picture-perfect façade.

There was no domestic violence; their home was a safe place. The hidden agony in Darlene's life stemmed from the horrific sexual abuse she'd experienced as a child. She carried those memories into her marriage, and they even affected her parenting.

Darlene had told no one about her past. Even her husband had no clue.

Because Darlene grew up with no control over the terrible things she'd endured as a child, she became extremely controlling as an adult. Her husband, Steve, had learned to adapt to Darlene's nature, as had their children—until they became adults. When Darlene's demands for control spilled over into the relationships with her three sons-in-law and grandchildren, her daughters eventually confronted her.

"If you don't get help and figure out what is wrong with you," her children told her one afternoon, "we are done."

It took several decades and the threat of losing her relationships with her children, but Darlene finally broke the silence about her past. She finally reached out to a counselor and began the long journey toward healing.

The key takeaway from this story is that Darlene had long been and continued to be part of a church that never addressed, never considered, the deep wounds that many people carry. She could keep it all hidden for years because no one talked about such things, especially in church. If a traumatic event is not discussed with a safe, caring adult within a day or two after the trauma occurs, it can become embedded in one's emotional circuitry, where it often remains for life. Those memories and feelings are essentially "buried alive,"

> **If a traumatic event is not discussed with a safe, caring adult within a day or two after the trauma occurs, it can become embedded in one's emotional circuitry, where it often remains for life. Those memories and feelings are essentially "buried alive," and they can show up later in life expressed as anger, depression, relational problems, and other negative behaviors.**

and they can show up later in life expressed as anger, depression, relational problems, and other negative behaviors.

## The Long Road to Freedom

Robin called me (David) one day to discuss her ongoing issues with anger, depression, and a fear of relationships. I'd met with many individuals over the years with similar concerns, and Robin's story was not unlike those of many others sitting in our pews and participating in our programs.

The phone call that day was not our first introduction. In fact, I've known Robin since she was a junior in high school. She attended our church's school, and her family was part of our congregation. I saw her almost every day of the school week as well as most Sundays. I thought I knew her well. We'd had plenty of conversations over the years. I officiated at her marriage ceremony and dedicated her three children in church.

What I didn't know, nor did she know at the time, was what she would eventually share with me. The horror of what had happened to her was buried deep in her past and even deeper in her mind. Robin represents countless believers who know the love and saving grace of God yet have also experienced unbelievable trauma.

My traumatic story began even before I was born.
When my mom found out she was pregnant with me,
my father decided that he was too young to be a dad,
so she became a single mom. We lived with her parents,
my grandparents. My grandfather was many things—a
husband, a father of three, a hard worker, and a Sunday
school teacher. And we were very close. I remember him
singing silly songs with me, taking me out for ice cream,

bringing me to church every week, and always buying me special gifts. I loved him.

But that's not all he was. He was also an abuser and a predator.

As far back as I can remember, my grandfather sexually abused me. As you might imagine, that messed up my perceptions of who God is. I figured I was alone; that no one was coming to save me; and that if anyone was going to help me, it would have to be me. *I'd better learn to take care of myself.* I believed God was out there *somewhere* and that He loved me, but He must have been too busy to think about me and what I needed.

Fortunately for me, our brains are wired to help us survive trauma. I learned to tuck that abuse away in a tiny space in my brain, someplace where I didn't have to feel it. I learned how to check out and be numb—an ability I used in my adult life to avoid feeling sadness, grief, anger, shame, or even good things like excitement and happiness. It was just easier this way. Even though I could tuck away the abuse and trauma and pretend it hadn't happened, what I didn't know and understand was that I still carried its effects with me.

I married at seventeen and had a baby just a few months later. After I finished college, my husband and I built a business and had two more babies by the time I was thirty. I carried all of the pain with me into my marriage and my parenting. To deal with life, I became an emotionally closed, walled-off person. I didn't let anybody get too close because that might result in more pain.

In my efforts to insulate myself from feeling, I isolated myself from the same emotional connections that could bring me healing. Whenever something painful happened,

I pretended like it wasn't real and stuffed it away in that tiny space. I didn't realize what I was doing; it's just how I survived.

Then, in my mid-thirties, I became very depressed and couldn't figure out why. I was in a safe place, with a good husband, three great kids, and a thriving business. I should have been happy, yet I was in a very dark place.

Picture a closet in your house—well, at least in my house—that's full of junk. You open the door to stuff one more thing in, then close it quickly before everything else falls out. Eventually you have to lean on it in order to get it closed. Then, before you know it, the junk starts pouring out the sides and the bottom, at which point you're afraid to open it again. That closet overstuffed with junk was what my life felt like.

All the pain from my childhood that I had refused to deal with was now overflowing from the past and into my present, and I didn't know what to do about it. I experienced deep sadness, overwhelming grief, and lots of hidden anger. Then, one beautiful fall day, I found myself driving around in my minivan, wondering if I could simply go off the road and end my life. I could make it look like an accident so my family wouldn't think I didn't want to be with them.

I eventually pulled the car over and just sat there. I cried—no, I *sobbed*. I was desperate. And in those next few moments, I felt God speak to me. I don't know that it was an audible voice, but it was clear: *I don't want you to live this way. Call David.*

David Schooler had been our pastor. He was also a family counselor. Right away I began to reason with God about what a bad idea that was, how embarrassed I'd be, and how he'd think I was crazy. I mean, I hadn't talked to him in ten years! But I couldn't escape those words: *Call David.*

So I did. David didn't seem shocked, and he didn't think I was crazy. We made an appointment for counseling and prayer. That simple call was the first step on an incredible journey of healing and restoration for me.

That day in the car, let's imagine I'd felt God say, *Call David, make an appointment, show up for the appointment, then make about a hundred more appointments. We're going to pull out a bunch of that ugly junk from your past and dig through it. Then I'm going to ask you to feel it and process it, I'm going to ask you to forgive the people who hurt you, and I'm going to ask you to forgive your grandfather. And then I'm going to ask you to talk about it publicly!*

If that had happened, I'm confident that I would've responded *No, thanks. It's too much. It is not happening.* But that's not what God did. He simply said, *Call David.* God knows we don't need a long to-do list when we're barely hanging on. He simply gave me the next thing to do, and that next thing brought me one step closer to finding healing.

I wish I could tell you that my life was sunshine and lollipops after that moment in the car, but it wouldn't be true. Working through my brokenness required a long-term commitment. I had to want the truth about who I am and who God is.

I believe God doesn't want just to help us manage the *symptoms* of our pain. He wants to heal us at the very point of our loss and brokenness—where we were hurt the deepest. Yes, managing symptoms requires work. But true healing brings freedom. I know this because

I'm experiencing it. God is allowing me to feel again. He is rebuilding what was broken and restoring what was taken.

I now have healthy relationships with boundaries to protect me instead of walls. Sure, I now have conversations when I'm bothered, but that's better than hiding. I've learned how to give and receive affection with my kids, and I truly enjoy my marriage.

At one point, my husband told me, "You need to get some help, or we won't be married in five years." Well, we just celebrated our thirty-fifth wedding anniversary! Our lives are forever changed.[1]

## "Follow Me"

When Jesus called Matthew the tax collector to follow Him, we know Matthew did so immediately (see Matthew 9:9). Had I been Matthew, I probably would have asked Jesus some questions, such as where we would be going, what we would be doing, how much the job paid, and so on. Scripture doesn't indicate that Matthew asked any such questions. Yet later, while having dinner at Matthew's house, Jesus does help explain His approach. He says to those at Matthew's home and those of us who follow Him today that He came for those who need Him most: the sick, the sinners, and the outcasts (see Matthew 9:10-13).

Those of us who have responded to the radical, life-changing invitation to follow Jesus have learned that He will lead us to the same people—sinners, the sick, and outcasts, including the abused and neglected like Darlene and Robin. These people come to our programs, sit beside us in the church pews, work alongside us, and maybe even live next door to us. They need salvation, healing, and community too. Our task in following Jesus is to help the poor and the prisoners, the blind and the brokenhearted, and to proclaim God's Good News (see Isaiah 61:1-3 and Luke 4:17-18).

In the rest of this chapter, we are going to discuss how to best minister to the needs of those Jesus sets in front of us. A couple of things we need to know going forward: First, everyone has experienced trauma on some level. Second, becoming trauma competent will help us better understand what happened to people in the past, how it has influenced their lives to this point, and how to help them today.

## What I've Learned in Fifty Years of Ministry

For many years I (David) have shared what I refer to as the Five *C*s of ministry. They are based on the words of Psalm 78:70-72:

> He chose David his servant
> and took him from the sheepfolds;
> from following the nursing ewes he brought him
> to shepherd Jacob his people,
> Israel his inheritance.
> With upright heart he shepherded them
> and guided them with his skillful hand.

These are the Five *C*s:

- *called*: David was chosen by God to serve.
- *compassionate*: He took care of the ewes with nursing lambs.
- *character*: He shepherded them according to the integrity of his heart.
- *commitment*: He guided them . . .
- *competent*: . . . with his skillful hands.

Of these Five *C*s, which one do you think is most important? When I ask this question, I typically get a variety of responses. Some say compassion. Others say character. Still others say commitment. All these are important, of course, but I believe competence is the most essential.

We can be strong in the first four *C*s, but it will limit our effectiveness if we are not competent. Here's a personal analogy: You might ask me to set up an IT system in your church or sing a special song in your music program. However strong I might be in the first four characteristics, I am *not* competent in technology or singing.

Too often, we find ourselves (or place others) in positions where we are not competent, which doesn't work out well. I have personal experience with incompetence. My first position in ministry was as a youth pastor. I did not understand that role, nor did I understand much about working with young people. To be honest, I didn't really know what they needed. I could go on, but you can probably fill in the blanks. I meant well but didn't know how to do the job. I moved on from that role feeling like a failure.

I'm convinced that *competency is key to ministry*. That's why we feel so strongly that ministry—or any program wherein we work with hurting people—needs to be trauma informed. Robin's and Darlene's stories should alert us to that need. The statistics for sexual abuse alone are staggering: About one in five girls has experienced some form of molestation, along with one in twenty boys.[2] Many types of abuse and neglect discussed throughout this book have affected children who are now adults—adults who've never had anyone to help them process what happened. Many of them, if not most, manifest the effects of their abusive past in their behavior today. Even as adults, *their behavior is their vocabulary*.

How do we minister to those who come from such a history? We begin with our own story.

## First, Understand Your Own Story

As a senior pastor for many years, I had the privilege of leading four different churches. All four were unhealthy and emotionally and spiritually unsafe when we arrived. They all had experienced church splits and conflicts. The common denominator in all four situations was a failure of leadership to recognize and deal with their unresolved issues. It takes a healthy leader to lead a healthy congregation.

To help others who come from hard places, we must first make sense of our own story. We need to know what happened to us, how those events impacted us, and how our past influences us now. We need a coherent narrative of our life.[3] This journey of self-awareness needs to be intentional, open, and honest. It radically enriched my life, relationships, and ministry when I began this process, and I am still on this journey today. It's been said that self-awareness is the doorway to freedom, and I could not agree more.

I've counseled many leaders who've suffered personal, professional, and pastoral conflicts wherever they have served. In my experience, they tend to blame someone or something else for these conflicts. I often suggest they look instead at their own story to see if they have contributed to the conflict. "A person gets to be a grown-up when they take responsibility for their life," writes pastor, professor, and author Rob Reimer.[4] Reimer describes three compelling truths about becoming emotionally and spiritually healthy:

- We cannot rise above the level of our self-awareness.
- We cannot rise above the level of our secrets.
- We cannot rise above the level of shame we carry.[5]

We must make our spiritual and emotional health a priority. We must ask ourselves, *What potentially traumatic events have happened to me?* It doesn't sound like a fun process, but trust me—it will be the beginning of a healing journey.

When I first started in ministry, I had lots of people coming to me with stories of depression, trauma, anger, bitterness, and other toxic emotions. As I listened to each of them, I realized two things: First, as far as I knew, they were all devoted Christians with varying degrees of discipleship training. Second, I had no clue how to help them. What I did know was that simplistic, pat answers wouldn't help.

I decided then to learn how to help people who are going through difficult times, mostly due to early-childhood experiences that were never processed and healed. I knew that they needed to seek emotional and spiritual healing. For example, Peter Scazzero, pastor and cofounder of the ministry Emotionally Healthy Discipleship, says it's essentially impossible to be *spiritually mature* if we are *emotionally immature.*[6]

As I started learning how to help those hurting people, my own wounds were exposed. A former pastor had contacted me in the first year of my ministry at a small church in the Ozark Mountains of Missouri. I thought he was calling to help encourage me, but I was wrong. He had called to tell me things that would remain embedded in my mind and soul for years to come:

- *You are incompetent.*
- *You are going to ruin the church.*
- *Your theology is all wrong.*

This man went on and on and on about all the areas where I was incompetent or unqualified. His words stuck in my brain for a long time. Even as the church began to grow and develop, I never forgot what this older pastor had told me about how it was just a matter of time before I failed and the church failed as a result.

(It didn't help that I was already struggling with my own fears of failure stemming from unresolved issues in my past.)

Good thing I know now what I did not know then—that this man's verbal attacks on me were coming from a place of woundedness in his own life. And thankfully, all four of the churches I pastored did well as I overcame my fear-based beliefs and those words spoken out of woundedness. I've since learned that fear is a toxin that must be exposed, removed, and overwhelmed by the Word and Spirit of God.

Negative words have the power to profoundly impact our thinking. Our belief systems are altered when we believe lies. These lies not only affect the way we feel and behave; they also weaken the foundations of our lives and our faith.

Our beliefs are formed by the words we hear and the experiences we have. My behavior and emotional state are based on what I believe to be true. Therefore, a belief system can be altered by encountering (and believing) new words and experiences. An excellent illustration of this is found in Acts 26:9-11. There, Paul talks about what he used to believe—that believers in Christ were a threat—and how he had despised and persecuted them.

Notice the progression: What Paul felt and did was based on what he thought was true. Beginning in verse 12, we read about how Paul had had a new experience and was later given new words. That's when his life and mission changed dramatically.

### Second, Understand the Lasting Impact of Trauma

Whenever we're trying to help wounded individuals in any capacity, we need to keep in mind that much of the behavior and words we see and hear are nothing more than an unresolved manifestation of what happened to them in the past. Without that perspective, we might spend all our time wondering what is going on in their minds. We might question why they are acting in such an unhealthy manner. We might waste time reacting rather than responding.

We tend to develop false perceptions about others' behavior because something is missing—the truth. Unless and until we understand the meaning behind the behavior, we won't know how to respond to the person.

An excellent illustration of this is a story recounted by pastor and author Jimmy Evans. Evans describes Chad, a man he encountered in his church during the early years of his ministry. Chad wanted to remove Evans from the pastorate, so he tried to start trouble that would cause Evans to lose his position. Chad did everything he could to destroy Evans's ministry. It got so bad that Evans says he began to use the word *hate* to describe his feelings toward Chad. He was furious at Chad and wanted to return evil for evil. These emotions were intense and very toxic.

Jimmy later discovered the truth about Chad. When Chad had been a young boy, a man he trusted had abused him. In other words, Chad was acting out of his unresolved trauma history. Although Jimmy never established a close relationship with Chad, his anger and hatred dissolved.[7]

When we are troubled by another person's actions, we need to remind ourselves that there is always meaning behind the behavior. As we often say, instead of asking, "What's wrong with you?" ask, "What happened to you?"

Many people with a traumatic history have no safe, mature adult to help them process what happened. They have buried the trauma alive, yet it still manifests in their adult lives in various ways. When they come to our programs and churches, we need to help them face the unresolved issues lodged deep in their brains.

Riley was an angry eighty-year-old man in our congregation. When he contacted me, his anger toward his children—even into their adulthood—was already well-known. I was convinced that he wanted to complain about something at church, or about me, but I agreed to meet with him anyway.

When I began asking Riley questions, out poured his story of the severe abuse he'd experienced as a child. He had never told anyone about it. Over many visits, we processed the pain Riley had buried so long ago, and he emerged from those sessions a different man.

The tragedy of this story is that Riley waited *decades* to reach out for help. He spent most of his life as an angry man; his losses were legion and his presence was toxic. He died just a couple of years after our conversations but by then had made heartfelt peace with his family. Riley is a prime example that there is meaning behind behavior and that healing happens in the context of a safe, nurturing relationship.

These principles work. Transformation can and does happen.

### Third, Practice Mindfulness

After more than fifty years of ministry, I've learned that mindfulness is a fundamental skill that applies to *all* relationships, not just those that involve working with hurting youth and other traumatized individuals.

> Being mindful of ourselves *and* the needs of others is critical to healing. We can never rise above the level of our self-awareness.

*Mindfulness* means that I am aware of what's happening inside me, around me, and in the lives of those I am helping.

Mindfulness has two main aspects: The first is being mindful of *ourselves*. This goes back to self-awareness, which we also mentioned in the previous chapter. We want to know what we are doing, how we are feeling, and why. Second, being mindful of *the needs of others* is critical to healing. We can never rise above the level of our self-awareness.

Finally, we want to be mindful of how others respond to what we say and do. Ask yourself, *Is my presence peaceful and reassuring?* Your presence is powerful. Never estimate that.

### Fourth, Speak Life-Giving Words

I've already referred to the Five *Cs* of ministry, but I also have what I call the Three *Is*. I first read about the principles that inspired these in Dan Allender's book *The Healing Path*.[8] The Three *Is* are *interest, imagining the future*, and *investment*, which I have adapted in my own counseling.

*Interest* refers to showing interest in and being intrigued by the lives and stories of others. Allender writes, "The heart of every human being is an unexplored continent, dark and foreboding, beautiful and compelling."[9]

I think of Proverbs 20:5 when demonstrating interest in someone. "The purpose in a man's heart is like deep water, but a man of understanding will draw it out." Helping wounded people begins by having and showing interest in them. Sadly, many are not interested in one another. As we read about Jesus throughout the Gospels, we see that He showed incredible interest in the people He engaged with, and that interest drew many people to Him. Showing interest in someone is a great connector. And in order to help someone, we must first connect with them.

*Imagining the future* (or *imagining the unseen*) refers to looking beyond an individual's present flaws, mistakes, dysfunction, or history and seeing something of beauty and worth. The disciples Jesus called to follow Him—those who would ultimately take the gospel to distant lands—were less qualified (at least on paper) than many others He might have chosen. But Jesus saw something in them. He spoke not of what they *were* but of what they would *become*, and together they ended up changing the world.

When I pastored in the Ozarks, Mary Lou and her parents

attended our church. Mary Lou was a teenage girl from a dysfunctional family who knew nothing but generational welfare dependence. I noticed that Mary Lou demonstrated great potential, so one day I suggested she consider attending college in Springfield, about thirty-five miles north of where she lived. Her immediate response: "Oh, no, I couldn't do that. They wouldn't give us welfare."

For the rest of my time at that church, I demonstrated interest in Mary Lou, imagining what she could become and speaking words of encouragement. Several years later, I received a letter from Mary Lou. She had heard my encouragement to get an education and had acted on it. The signature on Mary Lou's thank-you letter indicated that she is now a registered nurse!

*Investment* involves walking alongside someone and being a predictable and dependable presence in his or her life. Jesus, the Son of God, left His heavenly home to enter the human story and suffer what He endured to establish a relationship with us, and in doing so He provided an excellent example of investment. John 1:17 tells us that Jesus came to us with grace and truth. Now He walks with us, promising never to leave nor forsake us (Hebrews 13:5) and to finish the work that He began in us (Philippians 1:6).

I often think of foster and adoptive parents when I consider investment. Sometimes it takes many years of commitment before they see the fruit of their investment manifested in the life of a wounded child or teen.

Allender sums up the three principles like this:

- "[*Interest*] takes us into the complex web of story and the deep purposes of the heart.
- "*Imagination* moves us to glimpse what a human heart and life is meant to become.
- "[*Investment*] takes on the suffering of others to bear the cost (or a portion) of their plight."[10]

I think this is what Paul meant when he wrote, "Bear one another's burdens, and so fulfill the law of Christ" (Galatians 6:2).

## My Two-Chair University

I refer to my time working with people individually as my TCU—Two-Chair University. I believe that preaching and teaching are essential aspects of any church, but hurting people usually need one-on-one conversation. They need to talk with someone who will listen and who will pray with them and for them. That is the role of my TCU. Research shows us that when people have a two-way, "serve and return" conversation, the brain architecture actually begins to heal.[11] (I've learned as much about my own journey from these times as those I have helped have learned about theirs.)

We who serve others need to be mindful of the messages we convey, whether in the classroom, on the sports field, at church, or in our homes. How can you do this? First, get out from behind the desk. I prefer to pull up two chairs. Second, give your time and attention to those in front of you. Whatever you do, make sure they feel seen and heard.

These are a few practices I usually follow while in session at TCU. You might also find them helpful when working in your own program. Before anyone else arrives, I pray that God's Spirit will be present during our time together. After all, the Lord already knows who we are, what our needs are, and how to best proceed.

### Connect

Connection is critical to the healing process. It bears repeating: Before we can *correct*, we must first *connect*.[12] So when I speak with someone one-on-one, my first task is to make them feel welcome, comfortable, safe, and connected. I thank them for coming and tell them that they honor me by wanting to talk to me. This is a common connecting principle.

I try to sit so we're facing one another, neither too close nor too far away. I don't want to create any discomfort or disconnection. Once, I had a woman come to my office, and I mistakenly pulled my chair up too close for her comfort. She immediately pulled back. I later learned that she was a sexual abuse victim, having been abused by an older man. When I got too close, it triggered her traumatic memories. I apologized for getting too close and let her know that she was safe.

This reinforces our earlier discussion of the need to be mindful of the actions and reactions of those who have experienced trauma. It might take several conversations to ensure the other person feels both safe and connected. Connecting takes as long as it takes. You can't rush it.

### Ask Questions

You've likely picked up by now that I like to ask lots of questions. As I said earlier, I liken questions to doorknobs. They allow us to enter the lives and stories of others. So when someone comes to see me, I ask them questions. My questions are fairly general at first, asking about family, work, and other nonthreatening topics. It's all part of the connecting process.

Questions are indeed powerful, yet we want to ask them at appropriate times and in the correct order. My goal is to eventually move past the generic questions. I often make the transition to deeper questions by asking about the person's childhood. I want to understand *their* story. Keep in mind that what's happening in a person's life *now* has its roots in what happened to them *before*.

## Listen

Healing can begin in a person's life when we listen to their answers. Listening to them enables us to honor them and validate their stories. Some say listening is becoming a lost art, yet it is a powerful tool in helping others heal. Too often, when we are listening to someone, we give the impression that we can't wait for them to stop talking so that we can tell them *our* story.

I'm going to be blunt: You can tell your own story another time, but not now—not in the context of listening to someone else's story. Do not interrupt them. Do not sermonize. Do not correct them. Let them tell their story the way they tell it. Because as they do so, and as you listen, something else is happening.

Once again, research shows that brain architecture is affected when we share our story with an empathetic listener. Through a simple yet thoughtful conversation, our brains change. That's powerful. Perhaps this is why James urges us, "Know this, my beloved brothers: let every person be quick to hear, slow to speak, slow to anger" (James 1:19).

Never force anyone to talk, since that can quickly shut them down, and don't push anyone to keep going if they seem tired. Sharing one's past, especially if it is a troubled past, is hard work. It can be very exhausting, so be mindful of the other person's cues about their energy level. While you listen to the other person's story, additional questions will probably come to mind. You might want to clarify something you don't understand. But be sensitive about where you are in the conversation and whether further questions at the moment might be helpful or potentially harmful.

As the process continues, if the other person feels safe and comfortable with you, they will likely consider telling you their most profound stories. These stories might involve abuse, neglect, cutting, eating disorders, pornography, or a host of other concerns.

Refrain from reacting in shock or disbelief. Such a response could shut them down, and they might never seek help again.

Keep in mind that many situations might require another level of skill. Don't hesitate to suggest finding someone with more training and expertise. You can help out by referring them to a professional counselor.

### Offer Words of Blessing

Most people have had very few, if any, words of blessing spoken for them or to them. A special blessing, spoken at the appropriate time, can be life-changing for them. Speak words that give them hope to believe that there is freedom and healing for them. The words of that blessing can be whatever you choose, but if you're not sure what to say, a profound example is found in Numbers 6:24-26 (NASB):

The LORD bless you, and keep you;

The LORD cause His face to shine on you,
And be gracious to you;

The LORD lift up His face to you,
And give you peace.

I spent many hours with a woman in our church who suffered from severe depression. After her health had greatly improved, I asked what had meant the most to her during her healing journey.

"It was the day you told me, 'Catherine, you are going to get well,'" she said.

Those words of life penetrated her darkness and gave her hope. "Death and life are in the power of the tongue" (Proverbs 18:21, NASB).

*Before They Leave, Seek Closure and Pray with Them*

Before you end your conversation, be sure to affirm the other person. Let them know what an important thing they've done in seeking help. Consider once again thanking them for coming and allowing you to hear their story. They might need to be reassured that you can be trusted with the information they've shared. Betraying their confidence would be a profound wound and can be highly damaging to a person who might still be evaluating whether you are trustworthy.

Other than a special blessing, a simple prayer is the best way to end your conversation. The prayer can incorporate elements of your conversation, but it certainly doesn't have to. Be open to how God's Spirit might lead.

We work with and meet many hurting people because we live in challenging times. Countless kids today grow up in what psychiatrist and author Bruce Perry calls "relational poverty."[13] Families are fragmented and broken. There are, for many children, no safe adults on duty, which leaves them vulnerable to abuse and neglect. If no one intervenes for these children, they will grow up with significant emotional and mental wounds. Having a TCU-like model available for them can go a long way toward bringing healing and hope.

In the words of professor and theologian Rob Reimer:

I believe soul care will be the gateway to evangelism in this generation. I think people will come to faith in Christ today more because they know they are broken and need a healer than because they know they are sinners in need of a Savior.[14]

I wholeheartedly agree. So pull up two chairs and get ready to listen.

## Key Takeaways

1. Helping others requires that we first look at ourselves and make sense of our own story.

2. The next step involves recognizing the lifelong impact of trauma and how we can carry it with us into adulthood.

3. Finally, we need to practice mindfulness, which includes the concepts of showing interest, imagining the future, and investing in those we're trying to help.

## Discussion Questions

1. It's easy to assume that, as adults, we are okay. Robin, for example, seemed like a functioning adult, yet the walls she'd built to protect herself eventually came crashing down. Discuss your thoughts about her story. Did it make you think of anyone else? Did it make you wonder if there are parts of your own story you still need to explore?

2. We believe that the essential characteristic of a healthy program is *competency*. How can you improve your competency? What are some ideas for how your program might help the staff and volunteers enhance their competency?

3. What went through your mind when you read that the starting point for helping others is to begin with your own story? Did you embrace that idea, or did you become defensive? Why do you think you reacted that way?

4. When you think about creating a welcoming environment, whose responsibility do you think that is?

5. Have you ever experienced anything like the Two-Chair University? What aspects did you find helpful? What aspects made you want to disengage?

## Application Strategies

1. Begin the process of getting to know your own story. This might involve a conversation with a safe friend or a trusted pastor, or it might begin with journaling about stories you remember from when you were young.

2. It's sometimes easier to give up hope that someone can change instead of *imagining the future* or *imagining the unseen* in them. Do you find yourself lacking hope as you think about a wounded person you know? Pray that God will awaken hope in your heart (and theirs!) again.

3. Write down three ways you can demonstrate to others that you are approachable. Be specific about how and with whom you would use these methods. Choose one and put it into practice this week.

# 10

# THE SOUL TAKES THE HIT

*Caring for Our Own Souls*

After many years of walking this ancient
path, I have come to know this one truth
most certainly: The world within you will
create the world around you.

ERWIN RAPHAEL McMANUS, *THE WAY OF THE WARRIOR*

When you take a drive outside the city and away from main thoroughfares, you often notice that some of the road signs have endured some wear and tear—from flying rocks or even the occasional gunshot. The signs have taken hits, and they show it.

The image of a beat-up road sign is a useful analogy when we discuss caring for the soul. The soul, just like so many roadside reminders, takes the hit of our troubles—our dysfunctional relationships, unhealthy family patterns, emotional hurts, spiritual pain, hidden abuse, and more. If these hits are not dealt with in a timely manner, they often become internal, invisible wounds that can lead to all sorts of physical and mental problems.

The analogy applies to troubled children *and* adults, since the two are often related. I (David) hear similar words all the time, around the world and in many different cultures: "I have a history of trauma too," they tell me. "How can I heal so that I can help my children?"

It's a reasonable question, and merely asking it reveals a profound truth: *You cannot pour from an empty cup.*

If we tend to the needs of every child but fail to meet the needs of the adults who care for them, then our work will have little impact. It's an essential principle of any trauma-informed approach that those who work with children with a history of trauma must also deal with their own trauma history. If we do not help the helpers, then the work can easily become overwhelming. The result? Burnout, or worse.

I will always remember the first time Jayne and I taught a course on soul care. We were in a Central American country with an audience of government social workers and various ministry staff. One government official in particular appeared quite stern and precise, but midway through the morning session, I glanced over to see her silently weeping. At last she raised her hand to speak, something I later learned she'd never done.

"Everything you are saying speaks to me," she said. "I had a painful childhood, and I've never before heard that there is help for someone like me."

This woman, like so many others, had a battered soul. She wanted to change—to get better—but she didn't know it was even possible. The first step for her, and for all of us, is to recognize that we are created beings who depend on the One who gave us life. The One who gave us eternal souls.

"No one can change without facing the harm that has come from living in a fallen world and his own disastrous attempts to make life work without God," explains author and Christian therapist Dan Allender.[1]

After spending thousands of hours with thousands of people over more than fifty years, I have learned that same lesson—that the soul takes the hits in this fallen world.

## Neglecting Our Souls

In the last few years, I expanded my ministry to include offering workshops on self-care. Yet it wasn't long before I realized that self-care training wasn't touching the deepest of hurts. Why was that?

A study cited by the *Journal of the American Medical Association* revealed that in the twentieth century, people in any generation are three times more likely to experience depression than those who came before them. Despite a vast expansion of mental-health providers, it feels like more people than ever are dealing with depression.[2]

Noted psychologist Martin Seligman has a theory that John Ortberg relates in his book *Soul Keeping*. "We have replaced church, faith, and community with a tiny little unit that cannot bear the weight of meaning," Seligman says. "That's the *self*. We're all about the self. We revolve our lives around ourselves."[3]

Ortberg concurs: "Ironically, the more obsessed we are with ourselves, the more we neglect our souls"[4]—our mind, will, and emotions.

In my work as a minister, especially early on, I struggled with several questions: *What about the needs of those around me? If I take any time for soul care, won't I be neglecting others? Don't they come first? As a pastor, don't I always have to be available?* Unfortunately, I'd bought into the notion that I had to be ever present, ever available. I eventually came across the work of author and educator Parker Palmer, who said, "Self-care [soul care] is never a selfish act—it is simply good stewardship of the only gift I have, the gift I was put on the earth to offer others."[5]

Once again, we cannot give what we do not have. Our role model in this regard is Jesus Himself. When Jesus needed food, He asked for it. When He needed support from His friends, He did not hide it. Jesus wept openly and unashamedly. Jesus took care of Himself physically, emotionally, and spiritually. Do not believe the lie that you are somehow acting selfishly by taking care of yourself.

## The Journey of Soul Care

Every soul is different in that every individual has experienced painful events and heard hurtful words that are unique to each one of us. Every soul has been wounded, some more than others, and those wounds impact us in different ways.

What has happened to you might not have been your fault, but it is your responsibility to pursue healing—to do the necessary work. This is actually wonderful news: We do not need to remain stuck in our woundedness, nor do we have to wait for someone else to do the work and rescue us. There is a way out, and soul care is an essential part of the process.

Humans alone among God's creation were given eternal souls. In Genesis 2:7, we read: "The LORD God formed man of the dust of the ground, and breathed into his nostrils the breath of life; and man became a living soul" (KJV).

I use the following graphic to teach about the body, soul, and spirit, including the functions and needs of each one. The graphic is not comprehensive, but it does summarize the three aspects of our created selves.

## Understanding Ourselves

Soul care involves body, soul & spirit.

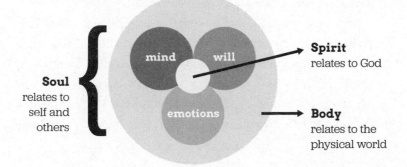

Your *body* relates you to the physical world around you using your senses—sight, sound, taste, touch, and smell.

Your *spirit* connects you to God in a personal, relational way.

Your *soul* relates you to yourself and others through your mind, emotions, and will.

The body needs to be *recognized* as a temple of the Holy Spirit (see 1 Corinthians 6:19), yet strangely—and often tragically—the body is regularly overlooked when it comes to soul care. We need to remember that Christ is in us, indwelling our bodies so that He can minister through us. If your soul is in distress due to worry, anger, or fear, then that distress often shows up in physical symptoms in your body. When your body is overwhelmed, it greatly diminishes your effectiveness in helping and serving others.

The spirit, meanwhile, needs to be *reborn*. The spirit is the part of us that died when sin entered human history in the Garden. Jesus says in John 3:3 that we must be "born again" in order to gain eternal life. This happens the moment we receive Christ by faith. The Bible says we are "made complete" (i.e., reborn) through our union with Him (Colossians 2:10, NASB). It is from our position in Christ, through knowing Him, that we grow in grace and peace (see 2 Peter 1:2-4).

The soul, like the body, needs to be *renewed*. Even after you discover new life in Christ, your soul still carries wounds and needs to be renewed, restored, and healed. Renewal happens over time, and the process needs to be intentional. As I've said, the soul takes the hits from life's abuses and disappointments. This is critical: If you experience inner turmoil after conversion (and you will), you might assume that it is a spiritual problem instead of a soul problem. You might think that your salvation isn't working, leading to the mistaken belief that you need to be converted all over again. I actually struggled with this issue myself for a time.

Now that we have a clear picture of the soul—our mind, will, and emotions—let's consider that the soul itself has needs.

## The Soul Needs to Detoxify

Walk into any drug store or health-food store, and you will likely notice displays urging you to detox your body from environmental and food toxins. The products in question are designed to purge physical toxins, but other toxins are often overlooked or ignored. I am talking about *soul toxins*. These particular toxins cause problems at an emotional, spiritual, and yes, a physical level too. As author and minister Mark Rutland writes in *Courage to Be Healed*: "You can be saved. You can be filled with the Spirit. You can love Jesus. You can read the Scriptures. You can experience God's grace in a thousand areas of your life. It is still possible, though, with all of this being true, that you might have toxins in your soul, ruining your life."[6]

Early on in my ministry, people asked to meet with me privately. I heard about struggles with pornography, anger, depression, panic attacks, hatred, and a host of other concerns. I added counseling to my pastoral duties and have continued to develop those skills for almost fifty years. (As I mentioned in chapter 9, I call this practice my TCU, or Two-Chair University.)

In Psalm 32, David writes openly and honestly about the devastation he suffered by holding in and denying what was going on in his soul. He remained silent about his sin and kept everything inside. His body wasted away, and he suffered in anguish. He tried to hide his guilt, even as the weight of it sapped away his strength.

These are common symptoms and complaints of a soul that has not detoxed. We see in Psalm 32:5 that when David finally confessed his sins (the source of his toxins), his guilt faded and his pain disappeared. In essence, David detoxed his soul. A toxic soul can and will hamper and hinder our faith walk with Jesus and others, not to mention our physical health.

> "You can be saved. You can be filled with the Spirit. You can love Jesus. You can read the Scriptures. You can experience God's grace in a thousand areas of your life. It is still possible, though, with all of this being true, that you might have toxins in your soul, ruining your life."
>
> MARK RUTLAND

There are five deadly toxins that I encounter almost every day in my counseling practice. According to Mark Rutland, these particular toxins have contaminated many souls and destroyed many lives.[7]

1. *Shame*: The lie behind shame is that there is something deeply wrong with me—I am dirty, unlovable, and unworthy. This false belief often stems from a traumatic event in

the past. If this trauma is not processed at the time with a safe, engaged adult, that's when shame takes root. Shame-based conduct ranges from living in isolation to hyperaggressive behavior.

2. *Unforgiveness*: At the root of unforgiveness is the belief that someone must pay for wrongs committed. Mistakes—whether mine or others—demand justice. Wounds of unforgiveness typically arise in one of two ways—they are based either on bad things done to us or on good things that should have happened to us but didn't. The pain of these wounds leads to anger, hurt, and resentment. *Someone* needs to pay. Unforgiveness also leads to other toxins, like bitterness, hatred, and a desire for revenge, among others. Research also suggests that unforgiveness is a major contributor to health-related issues.[8]

3. *Rejection*: We've already mentioned (in chapter 2) that children—and adults, for that matter—have two essential needs: attachment (relationship) and orientation (guidance and direction). Because these are significant needs, to lose (or never have) them is a great wound indeed. The toxin of rejection can manifest in everything from not being chosen for a sports team to witnessing the breakup of one's family through divorce or abandonment.

4. *Condemnation*: The lie behind this toxin is the belief that nothing and no one can help me. I am hopeless. I am condemned. The belief often arises based on the wrong things I have done, the bad things that were done to me, or the problems in my toxic, dysfunctional family of origin. How can an individual even imagine a life of faith, hope, and love when living with a sense of condemnation?

5. *Fear*: Perhaps the most potent toxin of all is fear. It has the power to completely overwhelm. To paralyze. To make life virtually unlivable. Fear comes from the belief that I am not safe, competent, equipped, or powerful. Not feeling safe causes my brain to go on high alert, which leads to a host of mental and emotional problems. This is why it's vital for children to have a safe, present adult to help them process their fear and to protect them from further harm.

Carolyn, a thirty-five-year-old woman, came to see me about her deep anger, bitterness, and suicidal thoughts. She'd grown up in a Christian home, gone to a Christian school, and attended church all her life. Yet Carolyn's negative emotions had gone unaddressed for all those years and were now ruining her life. Her traumatic memories were coming to the surface and infecting her soul. It took a lot of time and work for Carolyn to overcome a past filled with toxic beliefs related to deep shame, condemnation, and unforgiveness, but she now helps other young women who have experienced similar trauma.

Not only are these toxins harmful, but they can also become addictive. In counseling many individuals through the detoxing process, I've seen some realize that they can't imagine a life free from these controlling emotions. As a result, they actually choose to hold on to them.

A young woman named Becky had been abused by her mother's boyfriends many times. The mother knew about the abuse but did nothing to protect her child. Becky was very angry—both at the men who had abused her and at her mother for not intervening.

One day I said to her, "Becky, we need to talk about your anger." She immediately stood up, put on her coat, and never came back. Becky's anger actually empowered her, and she could not imagine life without it.

So how does one detox the soul? It begins with an awareness that soul toxins often manifest as negative emotions or behavior. I agree with the counselor who said, "Self-awareness is the gateway to freedom."[9] Once you accept their presence, you need to identify which toxins you struggle with and begin the emotional journey of healing. A trained, competent counselor can be extremely helpful.

## The Soul Needs Renewal

On my wall is a statement that I have repeated many times during my teaching and counseling conversations: "The things we struggle with the most are tied back to the lies we are believing." Some friends of ours heard me say it and had it printed and framed. The statement speaks about the chaos in the soul if our belief system is based on lies and false beliefs.

The Bible indicates that wrong thinking has consequences, which can range from a simple inconvenience to an outright catastrophe. Genesis 3:13, for example, illustrates what can happen when someone believes a lie and then acts on that belief: "Then the LORD God said to the woman, 'What is this that you have done?' The woman said, 'The serpent deceived me, and I ate.'"

> The things we struggle with the most are tied back to the lies we are believing.

Before Eve did the wrong thing (eat the forbidden fruit), she believed the wrong thing (the serpent's lie). A wrong belief preceded a wrong action.

When teaching on this subject, I often ask my students how the lies they've believed have proved to be problematic. I hear a lot of stories about how their lives have been negatively impacted by false beliefs. Again, in Acts 26, Paul says that when he believed that followers of Jesus were evil, he felt rage, and he took action by persecuting them. Like Paul, we act based on what we believe to be true. (Paul later describes in Galatians 1 how his belief system changed after his conversion.)

In his book *Live No Lies*, pastor and teacher John Mark Comer discusses the twofold power of lies: Lies first move us away from God; then they redefine what's true.[10]

It's helpful to understand how belief systems form and how to change them. I often use this visual:

## Our Belief System

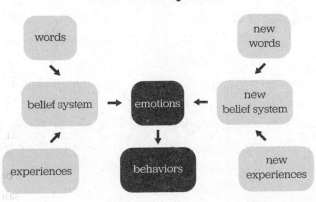

Since our belief systems are formed through words/teaching and our experiences, the most effective way to change false beliefs is with demonstrably true words and experiences. Understanding this method is critical for those of us who work with wounded people. Jesus Himself said that "the truth will set you free" (John 8:32).

The only source of absolute truth is the Word of God, which

reveals who we are and who God is. Writing in *The Cure*, author and pastor John Lynch and his coauthors ask a foundational question: "What if God isn't who you think He is and neither are you?"[11] This question emphasizes our need for accurate, biblically based beliefs about God and ourselves.

James was a sixty-year-old man who came to me with a lifelong struggle. Despite his pastoral training, James struggled with who God is, what God required of him, and how he could be sure of his salvation. Why would a credentialed pastor, who was raised in a Christian home and graduated from a Christian college, struggle with these questions? It all came down to his inaccurate understanding of God.

How we view God will, in turn, determine how we think God views us. And those perceptions influence how we live our lives. If, for instance, we think God evaluates us based on our performance, then we inevitably conclude that He is constantly evaluating us and is almost always disappointed. If our theology is performance based, then the soul can never fully rest in Him. A mixture of grace and performance can be equally confusing. Years ago I said something from the pulpit that I thought was true but was actually dead wrong: "We are saved by grace, but we have to work to keep it." I unknowingly presented a toxic mixture of law and grace.

There are countless passages that define how God relates to us through His Son, Jesus Christ—through *grace alone*. Ephesians 2 in particular makes it clear: "For by grace you have been saved through faith. And this is not your own doing; it is the gift of God, not a result of works, so that no one may boast" (Ephesians 2:8-9).

What I should have said from the pulpit: "We are saved by grace, and we *don't* have to perform to keep it."

The following graphic shows what the soul needs by illustrating how to develop a healthy view of God *and* ourselves.

## How do I develop a healthy view of God and myself?

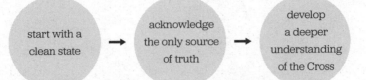

The first step is to begin with a clean slate, like when we start writing a letter with a blank sheet of paper. We all have an understanding of God based on things we've heard and experienced throughout our life. Soon after becoming a believer, I (David) spoke with several different denominational leaders seeking answers about who God is and what He requires of me. I got as many different answers as the number of conversations I had. So I determined to learn for myself who God is and who I am.

The second step is to acknowledge the Word of God as the only source of truth. Some years ago I studied why some Old Testament leaders failed and others did not. The common denominator of those who were successful was they had an accurate view and understanding of God and of themselves based on Scripture.

The third step is to develop a healthy view of God and oneself in order to comprehend what Jesus did at the Cross, why He did it, and what His sacrifice means for believers. The Cross reveals the heart of God and His deep love for each of us.

In summary, one develops an accurate view and understanding of God by starting with a clean slate, acknowledging God's Word as the only source of spiritual truth, and looking to the Cross, where Jesus demonstrated who God is and who we are.

## The Soul Needs Stress Relief

When I am teaching on soul care, I often ask the question "What is the leading cause of premature death in the United States?" I usually hear the same responses—unhealthy lifestyles, smoking, drug use, poor diet, lack of exercise, and so on. And while all those choices can contribute to premature death, the leading cause is stress.

There are several different ways to define *stress*:

• Stress is the feeling of being overwhelmed or unable to cope with physical, mental, or emotional pressure.
• Stress is any type of change that causes physical, emotional, or psychological strain.
• Stress is the body's natural reaction to a real or perceived threat.[12]

When a threat is perceived, the body reflexively releases hormones in preparation to fight, flee, or freeze. Ideally, after the threat passes, the body returns to a normal state called *homeostasis*. This stress reaction is natural and might happen multiple times throughout a day.

Yet if one's stress is chronic, the hormones that were intended to help keep us safe can now become harmful and cause emotional and physical damage. We've already examined how children raised in a CUTS (chronic unpredictable toxic stress) environment experience harm to their brains, bodies, biology, behavior, and beliefs. Chronic stress can also be damaging to the soul.

When I was in college, I worked for the Green Giant company harvesting their green bean crop. My role was to visit the fields and grade the beans to see if they were ready to be picked. One day as I was preparing to evaluate some samples, one of the farmers told me to watch out for copperhead snakes that had been seen in the fields. My internal response system immediately spiked, and my top priorities became vigilance and survival. After I got my samples with no snake sightings, my internal response system returned to normal.

Think for a moment what your stress level would be like if you lived in constant fear of encountering poisonous snakes. You'd likely experience chronic emotional exhaustion, which would eventually wear you down physically. Your soul, likewise, would not escape unscathed.

It's true that we can't avoid all stress. Stress is a natural part of life, but too much is known to be harmful. It's our job to monitor our stress level and work to keep it under control. I like what psychologist Bruce Perry says about stress—that it needs to be "predictable, controllable, and moderate."[13] If your life is filled with chronic stress, then it might be time to investigate what's causing it.

## The Soul Needs Rest

Gene is a bivocational pastor. He works full-time as a counselor in a rehab center while also pastoring a growing church. Telling Gene that he needs to find rest might not go over well. *Rest? What's that?* Gene rarely gets to bed before midnight and is up again by six thirty. Rushing out the door most mornings, he tells his wife and three kids that he'll try to be home by nine if he has a board meeting after work. Gene will discover—likely by default, when he collapses in utter exhaustion—that rest isn't a luxury. It's an absolute necessity.

I (Jayne) once led a life like Gene's. I was a full-time social worker, served alongside David at the churches he pastored (I loved being a pastor's wife, by the way), raised our biological daughter, and served as a foster parent to several children. I also wrote or cowrote several books. Then, one morning, while preparing to lead an out-of-town workshop, I stood up and almost fainted. I slumped into a chair, trying to catch my breath.

The next thing I knew, some first responders arrived and whisked me to the emergency room. It was a big wake-up call about the importance of rest. That's when I began making a concerted effort to manage my body, soul, and spirit in a new and better way.

I learned that there are several aspects when considering what it means to rest:

- physical rest
- mental rest
- emotional rest
- spiritual rest
- sensory rest

## Physical Rest

I didn't know until I needed to know that there are two types of physical rest: *passive rest* and *active rest.*[14]

Sleep is the type of rest that most often comes to mind. It falls in the category of passive rest. Since I began paying attention to rest, folks now know me as a "professional napper." I allow myself to sleep or just be quiet for reflective moments during the day. Passive rest is *not* wasted time.

Researchers at the Brain and Creativity Institute at the University of Southern California found that these reflective moments—free from external stimulation—let your brain access what is known as a "default mode of neural processing." This mode helps you develop a greater sense of self-awareness, recall personal memories, and make moral judgments, and it can give your life meaningful context.[15] Unfortunately for many of us, with our jam-packed schedules, finding time for passive rest is a challenge. It's on each of us to make it a priority.

I was pleased to learn that another type of physical rest is *active rest*. It simply means that I make time to involve myself in stimulating activities—ones that give me joy. Such activities might include physical hobbies like golf, bike riding, or walking. Active rest can boost your mood, help you control stress, and give you a healthier and longer life. For example, researchers at Massachusetts General Hospital have reported that people who work at something they enjoy, whether it's mental or physical, are more likely to function as "super-agers"—the kind of folks who maintain cognitive functions comparable to those much younger.[16]

As my knowledge of active rest evolved, I eventually returned to the tennis court. I grew up playing tennis but had given it up because I was too busy. My two newest active rest hobbies are playing the piano and making homemade cards for folks. I love both and make time for them each week as a part of my regular routine.

### Mental Rest[17]

Every morning when Kathy got ready for the day, her mind began to fill up with noiseless chatter. *I have so much to do today, I will never get it done. I am not smart enough to be doing this job—what if they let me go?* On and on it went, to the point that Kathy was mentally exhausted by the time she arrived at work. She allowed her thoughts to drain her energy and her focus.

Author and physician Saundra Dalton-Smith, in her book *Sacred Rest*, refers to *mental rest* as taking note of the ongoing chatter going on inside one's mind. Like Kathy, many of us might be bombarded with what Dalton-Smith refers to as "cerebral background noise."[18] From the moment we wake up, our minds begin chattering. Some of that chatter is positive—ideas, thoughts, future dreams. But for many of us that chatter is negative and filled with stress, worry, and anger.

Mental rest involves learning not to fixate on this constant stream of thoughts and to quiet one's mind. One of the best ways to do that is to set aside time—preferably in the morning—to silently focus on the Lord. We can use that time to elevate His Word above everything else, including the negative chatter within.

## Emotional Rest

I can say with confidence that many of the families you meet— whether in church on Sunday or at school on Monday—are not doing as well as they appear to be on the surface. Whenever they leave the house, these folks put on their "everything is fine" masks, but on the inside they are emotionally exhausted. And the masks they wear are heavy and often getting heavier.

Emotional exhaustion results from not allowing ourselves to experience or reveal authentic feelings. Emotional exhaustion comes from forcing ourselves to live up to the expectations of others, including those in church. The church can actually be one of the most emotionally exhausting environments we spend time in if the people who gather there refuse to reveal their authentic selves.

Emotional rest, according to Dalton-Smith, occurs when we remove the emotional masks that keep us from processing authentic feelings. Emotional rest results when we acknowledge and deal with the issues that caused us to bottle up our emotions. Emotional rest comes with living *genuinely*—a life that's consistent with our values, desires, strengths, and weaknesses.[19]

## Spiritual Rest

*The soul takes the hit.* Painful things happen to us that leave us emotionally wounded. Those wounds, in turn, impact our faith and ability to trust God. We run from life. We retreat to a valley that Dalton-Smith calls the "valley of the wounded."[20] What we need is another place where we can go—a place we can call our *sanctuary*. A sanctuary is a safe place, a quiet place. It is a place of rest where we stop fighting the things that have wounded us and learn to lay them down and rest in our spirit. In other words, a sanctuary is not just a place of rest but a *time*.

Our overwhelmed lives make it seem like finding such a time and place is nearly impossible. Yet even busy families can make it happen. We have friends who have just such a sanctuary. It's called the Sabbath.

For twenty-four hours, from Saturday evening at five to Sunday evening at five, everything work related, social media related—everything not rest related—stops. Other than doing things like attending church or eating meals, no one works, and no one plays on computers, phones, or tablets. Our friends enjoy meals together. They read books. They engage in conversation. It is restorative for everyone.

We have learned from these friends, and you can too. You don't have to do things exactly the same way, but if you don't make time for spiritual rest, your soul will take the hit.

## Sensory Rest

Think about the last several days. Where have you gone? What environments have you experienced? A noisy workplace? Noisy homes? Noisy restaurants? I've never understood why so many establishments think that blasting loud music, to the point that people can barely hear one another, is a good idea. That's why we look for quiet places where we don't have to yell to be heard above the noise.

Our senses—seeing and hearing in particular—need a respite from overstimulation. We need periods in our busy days and weeks that are free from external distractions and sensory chaos. We need these times in order to restore our senses from the overload they otherwise endure.

Sensory rest is a deliberate choice. It's vital not only for adults but for children as well. Have you ever established any guidelines for yourself and your family regarding sensory overload? If you don't have any, you might consider sitting down together and planning sensory breaks for everyone.

∽

In our new, post-pandemic world, we're learning just how critical self-care—and soul care—is, not just for the kids we work with but for all of us. We need to be ready and able to help others recognize and overcome the issues that the pandemic has left in its wake.

Understanding the soul and its needs should compel us to meet those needs in the children we encounter, beginning as soon as possible. In so doing, we can potentially change their life trajectory. If parents, teachers, coaches, and caregivers can help meet these soul needs early on, these children might not look to meet their needs in all the wrong places and in all the wrong ways.

Every soul, whether a child's or an adult's, has critically important needs. The soul needs to detoxify. The soul needs (mind) renewal. The soul needs stress relief. The soul needs rest. We've specifically covered these four in this chapter, but there are more that we've touched on elsewhere in this book—things like community, blessings, to be seen and heard, and to feel safe. We all need these things, and perhaps no one needs them more than the hurting children we encounter in our classrooms and our programs.

They are the kids from hard places, and they need our help.

## Key Takeaways

1. Every soul has been wounded, and whether or not those wounds are your fault, it is your responsibility to pursue healing.

2. The soul still needs healing and detoxing, even after one's spirit has been reborn in Christ.

3. We need both passive and active rest for our souls.

## Discussion Questions

1. What did this chapter help make sense of for you? Did it help connect some things in your life and heart that might have felt confusing before?

2. Did any of the five deadly toxins surprise you? Did any of them feel familiar?

3. "The things we struggle with the most are tied back to the lies we are believing." Discuss whether you have found this to be true in your own life and in the lives of those around you.

4. In your own words, define each type of rest discussed in this chapter (physical, mental, emotional, spiritual, and sensory). Feel free to refer back to these sections as needed.

5. Brainstorm ideas for how to find rest in each of the areas listed above. Be specific and write down the ideas that you find most helpful—and restful!

## Application Strategies

1. If you have not prioritized caring for your soul, acknowledge that truth to God and commit to do things differently moving forward.

2. Consider an area in which you are struggling. Carve out some time to talk to the Lord about what the struggle is and what lie(s) it might be tied to. (It sometimes helps us stay on track if we write down our prayers and thoughts as we go.)

3. Prioritize your soul care: Choose one or two of the five areas of rest to work on this week. Be specific about what you'll do and when you'll do it. Put it on your calendar.

# Afterword

*Speaking to the Heart and Equipping for the Journey*

More than ten years ago, I (Jayne) wrote in the afterword of *Wounded Children, Healing Homes* that more ministries are paying attention to the world of troubled children and hurting families— that they are approaching this reality with a heart of new compassion. Since that book was published, we have continued to promote the need for even more trauma-informed practices. It is our goal to equip as many people as possible—especially those living with and working with children and teens with a traumatic past.

God's Word is full of trauma-informed principles, and *Caring for Kids from Hard Places* strives to connect those principles and practices with scientific, evidence-based answers. It has been exciting and life-changing to see how social science and medicine are catching up with what Scripture has told us all along.

We have many hopes as you finish this book. Our first hope is that you have experienced in these pages how faith and science have something to say about helping the children and teens in your life and in your program heal from the harms they have experienced. The content might have also spoken to your own need for healing. As we've presented this material in more than twenty-two countries, we've had long discussions with caregivers who have identified their own woundedness and need for restoration.

Another hope for this book is that you will continue to refer to it as you develop your trauma-informed practices, whether you are a youth mentor, a teacher, a volunteer, a coach, a ministry leader, or a foster/adoptive parent. No matter whom you work or live with, we want to provide practical ideas for helping wounded individuals of all ages. Let this be a starting point for building a ministry, a team, a program, or even just a household that is known as safe and restorative for those with a traumatic history. *If you build it, people will come.* You will be known as a healing place.

Our final hope is that you will see those you work with quite differently than you did before. This will inevitably happen as you better understand the challenges of helping those with adverse childhood experiences (ACEs). Speaking from our own experience, we have seen our heavenly Father accomplish wonderful things, and it is our prayer that you experience for yourself His compassion for the vulnerable and hurting.

*David and Jayne Schooler*

## Appendix 1

# BEING A SENSORY SMART PARENT OR TEACHER

*Lindsey Biel*

Your child learns about the world through his senses, with all the sounds, sights, touches, movement, tastes, and smells working together to provide an accurate picture of the world. For most kids, sensory integration (SI) develops automatically.

Kids with sensory problems experience the world differently. Sensory input can come in too loud or too quiet. A child may be terrified by the vacuum cleaner—and yet not seem to hear you when you call his name. A gentle touch on a child's arm can feel like coarse sandpaper.

Sensory problems can range from mild "quirks" to intense reactions to everyday sensations. The behaviors are a problem when they are way out of proportion with the actual experience. Being afraid of a bleating goat at the petting zoo is not unusual for a toddler, but having a meltdown every time you put him in the bathtub or take him to the supermarket is a warning sign.

Sensory problems can cause distressing behaviors and developmental delays. If the noise of other children on the playground alarms a child, it's no wonder he'll only play in the sandbox in the corner rather than learn to climb the chain ladder. And if a school-age child is distracted by every sight and sound in the classroom, he won't be available for learning.

## Common Signs of Sensory Problems

- being over- or undersensitive to touch, movement, sounds, sights, tastes, or smells
- disliking getting messy (especially on hands or face)— or seeming oblivious to it
- being bothered by particular clothing, fabrics, tags, and so on
- avoiding or excessively craving intense movement
- squinting, blinking, or rubbing eyes frequently
- resisting grooming activities
- avoiding foods most children enjoy
- getting dizzy easily or never at all
- seeming clumsy or careless
- being uncomfortable in group settings
- always being on the go or never sitting still
- having poor attention and focus

## The Seven Senses

*Touch*

There are tactile receptors not only on the outer skin but also lining the mouth, throat, the inside of the ears, and so on. Light touch is often upsetting to a child with sensory problems. He may be distressed by diaper changes or clothing fabrics, by the feel of lotion or sticky substances, and by grooming activities such as hair washing. Firm touches such as bear hugs are often more tolerable.

Vibration from a toy or an appliance such as a refrigerator can be disturbing for some children. On the other hand, a child might think that sitting on the washing machine or using a vibrating toothbrush is marvelous!

Feeling pain and high and low temperatures are also tactile experiences. Some children crave freezing cold ice cream while others want to gobble up pizza while the cheese is still bubbling. Some children refuse to eat any food that isn't their exact favorite temperature. Some children with tactile problems are very sensitive to small scrapes while others can be unaware of broken bones.

A child with a sensory problem can show a confusing mix of both hypersensitivity and undersensitivity, such as refusing to walk barefoot but not reacting when banging his head.

### Auditory

Listening involves both hearing *and* processing sounds. Sound has many dimensions: loudness, frequency/pitch, duration, and localization (where it's coming from). A child with sensory problems may have trouble putting all these qualities together.

A child with hypersensitive hearing picks up on things others don't hear. With so much input, it's hard to filter out irrelevant sounds and attend to what's important. Most of us get uncomfortable when sound volume exceeds a certain level, but an oversensitive child may become miserable when sound is at a much quieter level. Some children are sensitive to higher sound frequencies (like ringing phones) or to lower frequencies (like trucks rumbling outside). If a child tells you that a sound hurts, believe him.

### Vision

Poor visual acuity and impaired ocular motor and other visual-processing skills are common and can make tasks like playing ball, reading, and writing difficult. A child may be hypersensitive to color, patterns, lights, movement, and contrast—and even see and hear the flicker of fluorescent lights.

Some children are visually distractible. With so much to see, they have problems attending to what's important. A child might compensate by hyperfocusing. A child engrossed in rolling a toy car back and forth may be taking a break from an overwhelming world by tuning it out.

### Taste and Smell

We only taste four things: sweet, salty, bitter, and sour. Everything else is smell. For some children, life literally stinks—from that minty toothpaste to the smell of their own diaper, clothing detergent, and so on.

Kids with sensory issues are notoriously picky eaters. Food issues can be about taste and smell but more commonly revolve around texture and temperature as well as neuromuscular issues inside and around the mouth.

### Proprioception

*Proprioception* is the perception of external stimuli. It relies on receptors in joints, muscles, and connective tissue to tell you where your body parts are without looking. A child who lacks a trustworthy internal body map may be clumsy, move slowly, and have trouble with fine motor tasks such as handwriting.

Some kids crave proprioceptive input; they crash into walls or bang and throw toys and roughhouse to get stronger sensory messages. Other children avoid it, preferring to slump on the couch or floor like wet noodles.

### Vestibular Sense

Anytime a child moves his head, vestibular receptors inside the ear signal a change in relation to gravity. He uses this information when he bends over to pick up a ball, making postural adjustments to avoid losing his balance.

Children with vestibular issues often respond to movement with exaggerated reactions that are way out of proportion with the possibility of falling. Going on playground swings or down the slide may feel like bungee jumping. These children may quickly get dizzy or nauseous on carousels or riding in the car. They may have low muscle tone and difficulty moving gracefully.

## Where to Get Help

Fortunately, much can be done to help a child with sensory issues. The first step is to get an occupational therapy (OT) evaluation. If your child is under age three and living in the US, he is eligible for a multidisciplinary evaluation and (usually free) services through each state's early intervention (EI) program. Find a local EI agency by looking online or visiting SensorySmarts.com to find your statewide program's contact information. Children older than three can get a free evaluation through the local school district. You can also obtain an OT private evaluation, which is covered by most insurance.

If your child has sensory issues, an OT will work with you, your child, and your child's school to strengthen his sensory skills and may also suggest environmental and activity modifications to make them more comfortable for your child. The OT should also provide your child with an individualized "sensory diet" of daily activities that satisfy your child's sensory needs.

∽

Lindsey Biel is an occupational therapist with a private practice in New York City. She is the author of *Sensory Processing Challenges: Effective Clinical Work with Kids and Teens* and the coauthor of *Raising a Sensory Smart Child*. For more information on sensory issues, visit SensorySmarts.com or search "Sensory Digest" on YouTube. This article originally appeared at: https://parentguidenews.com/articles/sensory -smart-parenting. Used by permission. All rights reserved.

## Appendix 2

# SENSORY SMART CLASSROOMS ON A BUDGET

*Erin Arant*

Interested in creating a sensory smart ministry room on a budget? The following suggestions can serve as a guide to create a safe and conducive environment for kids from hard places.

## Plan Your Room Colors

Use calming, neutral colors for the walls. Primary colors can be overstimulating and can even promote hyperactivity. Greens, grays, blues, whites, and muted colors are calming and can help children focus.

## Provide Calm, Safe Places

Provide designated areas where children can opt out of activities. Consider nonthreatening spaces such as teepees, tents, or quiet corners. Outfit those places with books to read, fidget toys, soft stuffed animals, coloring books, self-regulation tools, and headphones to help cancel noise.

## Pay Attention to All the Senses

When planning a school or ministry room, keep all the senses in mind. Both learning and self-regulation can be influenced by the state of our sensory systems. The following is a list of our senses and some ideas for items or practices you can use to help nourish—or soothe—these senses.

### Tactile
*Through Our Skin/What We Touch*

- Play-Doh
- kinetic sand
- soft carpet
- Velcro strips (with grip on both sides)
- feathers

### Audio
*Through Our Ears/What We Hear*

- soft music
- earplugs or noise-canceling headphones for children who don't like loud noises
- times of quiet or silence
- speaking times with limited background noise (because some individuals can't filter out one noise from another)

### Visual
*Through Our Eyes/What We See*

Visual stimulation in the room decor should be minimal. (Less on walls = less distraction = less overstimulation.)

- bright lights for alert times and lower lights for calm times
- disco balls and lava lamps
- mirrors

## Gustatory
*Through Our Mouths/What We Taste*

- healthy snacks (mix of crunchy and chewy, soft and mushy, thick and thin, cold and warm, etc.)
- gum (it's great, but it can also be abused; use with caution and parent permission!)
- chewy tubes (be careful about sanitation)

## Olfactory
*Through Our Nose/What We Smell*

This is a great sense to stimulate when working one-on-one. Be careful, however, when working with multiple children. Scents that are calming to one child can be triggering to another. Some scents can also trigger past trauma.

- no strong scents or odors
- unscented cleaners

## Proprioceptive
*Through Our Muscles and Joints/Where Our Bodies Are in Space and Where Our Limbs Are in Relation to Our Bodies*

- appropriate bear hugs and deep pressure input
- halves of tennis balls glued to the seats of chairs (to provide calming input)
- wall push-ups
- elastic material like Lycra

## Vestibular
*Through Our Inner Ears/If We Are in Motion*

- using spinning toys, such as a Sit 'n Spin
- turning upside down
- swinging on swings at a playground

### Interoceptive

*Through Our Internal Organs/What Our Bodies Are Telling Us*

Children with issues interpreting interoceptive input typically don't realize it when they are hungry or thirsty. They also often have accidents because they don't recognize their need to use the toilet. Make sure you are prepared for these issues in inconspicuous ways. (This applies to teens, too. You might be surprised by how many teens struggle with this.)

Have new, clean underwear in several different sizes along with leggings or pants at the ready just in case. Consider asking for donations, as well as speaking with a child's parents/caregiver in order to have a change of clothes on hand for a particular child.

∽

Erin Arant is a licensed occupational therapist and Trust-Based Relational Intervention (TBRI®) practitioner specializing in complex developmental trauma and sensory processing. Article used by permission. All rights reserved.

# Acknowledgments

Writing together for the first time has been a joy for us. We shared the idea with Sharen Ford when we first considered this project, and she caught the vision and need for this book. Sharen, thank you for supporting us and our work.

We also want to thank our editor, Jeff, whose guidance and expertise brought this book to life. Your patience and kindness continue to be so appreciated. Thank you.

So many folks gave of their time for interviews and callbacks. The list is too long to share here, but we are grateful to all of you, our friends, for what you gave to this book—your knowledge, expertise, and time!

We want to thank specifically two people who served us throughout this process:

Katie Leonard—Thank you for reading through every chapter and assisting us with the discussion questions.

Pam Ross—Without your administrative help, keeping track of so many people and so many interviews would have been overwhelming.

We believe that God's hand directed this book to Focus on the Family. Thank you, Focus, for accepting this project.

We also thank You, our heavenly Father, for helping us in every way as we finished this book. It is now in Your hands to use as a healing agent in the lives of children, teens, and adults with a traumatic past.

# Notes

## INTRODUCTION | HELPING CHILDREN AND TEENS WITH A TRAUMATIC PAST

1. "Adverse Childhood Experiences (ACEs)," Centers for Disease Control and Prevention, https://www.cdc.gov/violenceprevention/aces/index.html.
2. David and Jayne Schooler et al., *Intro to Trauma-Informed Care* (Mason, OH: Trauma Free World, 2023).
3. Kim Botto (board member, Found Village), interview with the authors, October 2020. Kim led kids' and student ministries in the local church for decades before moving to lead training and programming at a nonprofit, Found Village, in Cincinnati.

## CHAPTER 1 | "WHAT HAPPENED TO YOU?"

1. David and Jayne Schooler et al., *Intro to Trauma-Informed Care* (Mason, OH: Trauma Free World, 2023), module 1.
2. Ibid.
3. Ibid.
4. Jane Ellen Stevens, "The Largest, Most Important Public Health Study," ACEs Too High, October 3, 2012, https://acestoohigh.com/2012/10/03/the-adverse-childhood-experiences-study-the-largest-most-important-public-health-study-you-never-heard-of-began-in-an-obesity-clinic.
5. Ibid.
6. Ibid.
7. Donna Jackson Nakazawa, *Childhood Disrupted: How Your Biography Becomes Your Biology, and How You Can Heal* (New York: Atria, 2015), 67.
8. Ibid.
9. The CDC-Kaiser Permanente ACE Study, accessed May 26, 2023, https://www.traumainformedcare.chcs.org/resource/original-ace-questionnaire.
10. "About the CDC-Kaiser ACE Study," Centers for Disease Control and

Prevention, https://www.cdc.gov/violenceprevention/aces/about.html. Graphic can be found under the "Open All" link.

11. Nadine Burke Harris, *The Deepest Well: Healing the Long-Term Effects of Childhood Adversity* (Boston: Houghton Mifflin Harcourt, 2018), 54.

12. Amanda Merck, "Four Ways Childhood Trauma Changes a Child's Brain and Body," Salud America, February 6, 2018, https://salud-america.org/4-ways-childhood-trauma-changes-childs-brain-body.

13. Anne Murphy Paul, "Anne Murphy Paul: What We Learn before We're Born," TED Talks, November 29, 2011, YouTube video, https://youtu.be/stngBN4hp14.

14. Michael D. De Bellis and Abigail Zisk, "The Biological Effects of Childhood Trauma," National Library of Medicine, February 2014, https://www.ncbi.nlm.nih.gov/pmc/articles/PMC3968319.

15. "Forms of Abuse," National Network to End Domestic Violence, accessed March 6, 2023, https://nnedv.org/content/forms-of-abuse.

## CHAPTER 2 | THE POWER AND NECESSITY OF THE MIDDLE CIRCLE

1. Pastor Raphael, interview with the authors, February 2021.

2. David Schooler, *Visualizing Principles: 20 Drawings and 20 Conversations* (Cincinnati, OH: Back2Back Ministries, 2017), 2.

3. "Neglect," Center on the Developing Child, Harvard University, accessed March 6, 2023, https://developingchild.harvard.edu/science/deep-dives/neglect.

4. Gordon Neufeld and Gabor Maté, *Hold On to Your Kids: Why Parents Need to Matter More Than Peers* (New York: Random House, 2006), 6–7.

5. Ibid, 7.

6. Daniel J. Siegel and Tina Payne Bryson, *The Power of Showing Up: How Parental Presence Shapes Who Our Kids Become and How Their Brains Get Wired* (New York: Random House, 2021), 29.

7. Ibid., xiii.

8. Shirley Garrett and Sean Barrett, interview with the authors, February 2021.

9. First Church of the Nazarene in Dayton, Ohio, held a special service honoring Shirley Garrett's lifelong service dedicated to children and teens. These quotes represent the hundreds of teens impacted by her ministry over the last thirty years.

10. Pam Parish (founder, Connections Homes), interview with the authors, March 2021. To learn more about this amazing ministry to teens aging out of foster care, visit https://connectionshomes.org.

11. Ibid.

12. Brené Brown, "Clear Is Kind. Unclear Is Unkind," *Brené Brown* (blog), October 15, 2018, https://brenebrown.com/articles/2018/10/15/clear-is-kind-unclear-is-unkind.

13. Parish, March 2021.

14. Siegel and Bryson, *The Power of Showing Up*, 29.
15. Bruce Perry, "Bonding and Attachment in Maltreated Children: Consequences of Emotional Neglect in Childhood," The Child Trauma Academy, 2001, https://fosteringandadoption.rip.org.uk/wp-content /uploads/2016/01/bonding-and-attachment-in-maltreated-children.pdf.
16. Aaron Blake (bishop, Greater Faith Community Church; founder, Harvest Family Life Ministry), interview with the authors, January 2021.

## CHAPTER 3 | BOUNDLESS HOPE

1. Nadine Burke Harris, *The Deepest Well: Healing the Long-Term Effects of Childhood Adversity* (Boston: Houghton Mifflin Harcourt, 2018), 158.
2. "Rates of Child Abuse and Child Exposure to Domestic Violence," Resource Center on Domestic Violence: Child Protection and Custody, accessed March 7, 2023, https://www.rcdvcpc.org/rates-of-child-abuse -and-child-exposure-to-domestic-violence.html.
3. Josh Shipp, "The Power of One Caring Adult: Every Kid Is One Caring Adult Away from Being a Success Story," accessed February 12, 2023, https://joshshipp.com/one-caring-adult.
4. "Your Conversation Blueprint," Fight the New Drug, accessed March 7, 2023, https://fightthenewdrug.org/lets-talk-about-porn/blueprint /child-them.
5. "Domestic Violence Statistics," DomesticShelters.org, May 2014, https:// www.domesticshelters.org/articles/statistics/domestic-violence-statistics.
6. Shipp, "One Caring Adult."
7. Ibid.
8. Bruce D. Perry and Oprah Winfrey, *What Happened to You? Conversations on Trauma, Resilience, and Healing* (New York: Flatiron Books, 2021), 17.
9. Ibid., 92.
10. Kim Botto (board member, Found Village), interview with the authors, October 2020.
11. Ibid.
12. Ibid.
13. Leon Ho, "9 Inspiring Growth Mindset Examples to Apply in Your Life," LifeHack.org, accessed March 7, 2023, https://www.lifehack.org/865689 /growth-mindset-examples.
14. Jason Weber (national director, Foster Care Initiatives, Christian Alliance for Orphans), interview with the authors, November 2020.
15. Michael Miller, "Empathy vs. Sympathy," Six Seconds, accessed May 10, 2023, https://www.6seconds.org/2021/01/20/empathy-vs-sympathy-what -the-difference.
16. Dr. Karyn Sue Brand Purvis was "an internationally renowned child development expert, popular speaker, author and passionate advocate for vulnerable children" (https://empoweredtoconnect.org/karyn-purvis).

Dr. Purvis was the Rees-Jones director and cofounder of the Institute of Child Development at Texas Christian University in Fort Worth and the cocreator of Trust-Based Relational Intervention (TBRI®).

17. Karyn B. Purvis, David R. Cross, and Jacquelyn S. Pennings, "Trust-Based Relational Intervention: Interactive Principles for Adopted Children with Special Social-Emotional Needs," *Journal of Humanistic Counseling, Education and Development*, volume 48, issue 1 (Spring 2009): 3–22.

18. Donna Jackson Nakazawa, *Childhood Disrupted: How Your Biography Becomes Your Biology, and How You Can Heal* (New York: Atria Books, 2015), 67.

19. Botto, October 2020.

20. Weber, November 2020.

21. Nakazawa, *Childhood Disrupted*, 67.

22. Weber, November 2020.

23. Botto, October 2020.

24. Ibid.

25. Ibid.

CHAPTER 4 | "AM I SAFE HERE?"

1. Sharen Ford (director, foster care and adoption, Focus on the Family), interview with the authors, January 2021.

2. Erin Arant (occupational therapist), interview with the authors, February 2021.

3. Donna Jackson Nakazawa, *Childhood Disrupted: How Your Biography Becomes Your Biology, and How You Can Heal* (New York: Atria Books, 2015), 67.

4. Ibid.

5. Karyn B. Purvis, *Trust-Based Relational Intervention Caregiver Training, Empowering Principles* (Fort Worth Texas: TCU Institute of Child Development, 2013).

6. Ford, January 2021.

7. Kayla Pray (clinical counselor), interview with the authors, February 2021.

8. Ford, January 2021.

9. Cindy Lee (LCSW; cofounder, Halo Project), interview with the authors, March 2021. Halo Project is a ministry dedicated to encouraging hope for every family and child to experience healing through connection. https://haloprojectokc.com.

10. Ibid.

11. Daniel J. Siegel and Tina Payne Bryson, *The Power of Showing Up: How Parental Presence Shapes Who Our Kids Become and How Their Brains Get Wired* (New York: Random House, 2021), 78.

12. Karyn B. Purvis, David R. Cross, and Wendy Lyons Sunshine, *The Connected Child* (New York: McGraw Hill, 2007), 48.

13. Ibid.
14. Pray, February 2021.
15. Ibid.
16. Josh Shipp, "The Power of One Caring Adult: Every Kid Is One Caring Adult Away from Being a Success Story," accessed February 12, 2023, https://joshshipp.com/one-caring-adult.
17. Pray, February 2021.
18. Erin Arant (occupational therapist), interview with the authors, February 2021.
19. Lee, March 2021.
20. Sandi Schwartz, "How Dehydration Affects Your Child's Brain Function and Mood," Very Well Family, March 6, 2022, https://www.verywellfamily.com/water-to-soothe-childs-anxiety-4098581.
21. Purvis, *Empowering Principles*, chapter 5.
22. Barbara Sorrels, *Reaching and Teaching Children Exposed to Trauma* (Lewisville, NC: Gryphon House, 2015), 163.
23. Lee, March 2021.
24. Ibid.
25. Ibid.
26. Amanda Morin, "The Difference between Tantrums and Meltdowns," Understood, https://www.understood.org/articles/the-difference-between-tantrums-and-meltdowns.
27. Lee, March 2021.
28. Ibid.
29. Ibid.
30. Ibid.
31. Ibid.
32. Ibid.
33. Shipp, "One Caring Adult."

## CHAPTER 5 | "BRING ME THE FOOTBALL"

1. Jayne Schooler, "'Bring Me the Football': The Power of Healing Connections," Focus on the Family, July 1, 2020, https://www.focusonthefamily.com/pro-life/power-of-healing-connections.
2. Gordon Neufeld and Gabor Maté, *Hold On to Your Kids: Why Parents Need to Matter More Than Peers* (New York: Random House, 2006), 8.
3. Ibid., 37–38.
4. Bruce D. Perry and Oprah Winfrey, *What Happened to You? Conversations on Trauma, Resilience, and Healing* (New York: Flatiron Books, 2021), 201.
5. Erika Christakis, "The Dangers of Distracted Parenting," *The Atlantic*, July/August 2018, https://www.theatlantic.com/magazine/archive/2018/07/the-dangers-of-distracted-parenting/561752.
6. Daniel J. Siegel and Tina Payne Bryson, *The Power of Showing Up: How*

*Parental Presence Shapes Who Our Kids Become and How Their Brains Get Wired* (New York: Random House, 2021), 80.

7. Neufeld and Maté, *Hold On*, 119–25.

8. Jodi Clarke, "Polyvagal Theory and How It Relates to Social Cues," Very Well Mind, August 5, 2019, https://www.verywellmind.com/polyvagal -theory-4588049.

9. Karyn B. Purvis, *Trust-Based Relational Intervention Caregiver Training, Connecting Principles* (Fort Worth Texas: TCU Institute of Child Development, 2013), module 3.

10. Adapted from the work of Ruby Johnston and Trauma Competent Caregiving, Trauma Free World.

11. Gordon Neufeld (developmental psychologist), interview with the authors, July 2021.

12. Samantha Summerlin (trauma-competent trainer, Trauma Free World), interview with the authors, June 2021.

13. Heather T. Forbes, "Beyond Consequences 101—A Guide for Your Relatives," *Love Never Fails* (blog), June 10, 2014, http://heather-forbes .blogspot.com/2014/06/beyond-consequences-101-guide-for-your.html.

## CHAPTER 6 | GETTING ON THE SAME PAGE

1. "Interrupted Childhoods: Over-Representation of Indigenous and Black Children in Ontario Child Welfare," Ontario Human Rights Commission, January 12, 2018, https://www.ohrc.on.ca/en/interrupted-childhoods.

2. "ACEs & Trauma," The Pinetree Institute, accessed May 27, 2023, https://pinetreeinstitute.org/aces.

3. Katherine Clark, "Building Resilience in 6 Steps," *Essential Life Skills* (blog), January 3, 2019, https://www.essentiallifeskills.org/essential-life -skills-blog/building-resilience-in-6-steps.

4. Mary Vicario (child psychologist), interview with the authors, July 2022.

5. Ibid.

6. Ibid.

7. Karyn B. Purvis, *Trust-Based Relational Intervention Caregiver Training, Empowering Principles* (Fort Worth Texas: TCU Institute of Child Development, 2013).

8. Ibid.

9. Heather T. Forbes, *Classroom180: A Framework for Creating, Sustaining, and Assessing the Trauma-Informed Classroom* (Boulder, CO: Beyond Consequences), 37.

10. Ibid.

11. "Positive Interaction Cycle for Children," *LAMb International* (blog), May 28, 2013, http://lambinternational.blogspot.com/2013/05/positive -interaction-cycle-for-children.html.

12. Samantha Summerlin (trauma-competent trainer, Trauma Free World), interview with the authors, June 2021.
13. Emily Grubbs (children's pastor, West Chester Nazarene Church), interview with the authors, March 2021.

## CHAPTER 7 | ACTIONS SPEAK LOUDER

1. Adapted from the work of Ruby Johnston and Trauma Competent Caregiving, Trauma Free World.
2. Adapted from the works of Karyn Purvis (Trust-Based Relational Intervention Caregiver Training curriculum) and Heather Forbes (beyondconsequences.com).
3. Heather Forbes (owner, Beyond Consequences Institute), interview with the authors, July 2021.
4. Used with permission from Beyond Consequences.
5. Forbes, July 2021.
6. The Alert Program of the Theraplay Institute created the engine plate to teach children about self-regulation. Visit theraplay.org.
7. David and Jayne Schooler et al., *Intro to Trauma-Informed Care* (Mason, OH: Trauma Free World, 2023), module 6.
8. Ibid.
9. Ibid.
10. Gordon Neufeld (developmental psychologist), interview with the authors, July 2021. These strategies are adapted from Neufeld's work.
11. Ibid.
12. Josh Shipp, "The Power of One Caring Adult: Every Kid Is One Caring Adult Away from Being a Success Story," accessed February 12, 2023, https://joshshipp.com/one-caring-adult.
13. Neufeld, July 2021.
14. Caroline Leaf, *Switch On Your Brain Every Day: 365 Readings for Peak Happiness, Thinking, and Health* (Grand Rapids, MI: Baker, 2018), 83.
15. Ibid., 62.

## CHAPTER 8 | THE HEALING POWER OF STORY

1. Jeremy Loudenback, "The 'Silent Epidemic' of Child Trauma," *The Imprint*, March 24, 2016, https://imprintnews.org/los-angeles/child-trauma-as-a-silent-epidemic/16869.
2. Dan B. Allender, *To Be Told: God Invites You to Coauthor Your Future* (Colorado Springs: WaterBrook, 2005), 1.
3. "Child Abuse Statistics," Childhelp, https://www.childhelp.org/child-abuse-statistics.
4. Josh Shipp, "The Power of One Caring Adult: Every Kid Is One Caring Adult Away from Being a Success Story," accessed February 12, 2023, https://joshshipp.com/one-caring-adult.

5. Beth Bench (clinical family counselor), interview with the authors, May 2021.

6. About 50 percent of eleven- to thirteen-year-olds, 65 percent of fourteen-to fifteen-year-olds, and 78 percent of sixteen- to seventeen-year-olds are viewing pornography. The average age a child is first exposed to pornography is eleven. Fifty-three percent of children said they had seen pornography online, yet 75 percent of parents believe their children have not seen pornography online. "Pornography Facts," Sold No More, accessed May 28, 2023, https://soldnomore.org/pornography-faqs.

7. Porn in the church: 14 percent of pastors acknowledge that they currently view porn; 50 percent of pastors view porn regularly; 68 percent of churchgoing men view porn regularly; 76 percent of young Christian adults 18 to 24 years old actively search for porn; 57 percent of pastors say porn addiction is the most damaging issue in their congregation; and 69 percent of pastors say that porn has adversely impacted the church. Only 7 percent of pastors say their church has a program to help people struggling with pornography. Michael Chancellor, "The Ongoing Epidemic of Pornography in the Church," Baptist News Global, January 27, 2021, https://baptistnews.com/article/the-ongoing-epidemic-of-pornography-in-the-church.

8. Bruce D. Perry and Oprah Winfrey, *What Happened to You? Conversations on Trauma, Resilience, and Healing* (New York: Flatiron Books, 2021), 115.

## CHAPTER 9 | CARING FOR ADULTS WITH A HISTORY OF TRAUMA

1. Adapted from Robin Wientge, "Doing the One Next Thing | SPARK 2018," presentation at Crossroads Church, Mason, Ohio, August 5, 2018, YouTube video, https://youtu.be/hxHGlqZ6Fbc.

2. Child Sexual Abuse Statistics, National Center for Victims of Crime, https://victimsofcrime.org/child-sexual-abuse-statistics.

3. Daniel J. Siegel and Tina Payne Bryson, *The Power of Showing Up: How Parental Presence Shapes Who Our Kids Become and How Their Brains Get Wired* (New York: Random House, 2021), 20.

4. Rob Reimer, *Soul Care: 7 Transformational Principles for a Healthy Soul* (Franklin, TN: Carpenter's Son Publishing, 2016), 14.

5. Ibid., 27.

6. Peter Scazzero, *Emotionally Healthy Spirituality: It's Impossible to Be Spiritually Mature While Remaining Emotionally Immature* (Grand Rapids, MI: Zondervan, 2017).

7. Jimmy Evans, *21 Day Inner Healing Journey: A Personal Guide to Healing Past Hurts and Becoming Emotionally Healthy* (Dallas: XO Publishing, 2021), 154–56.

8. Dan B. Allender, *The Healing Path: How the Hurts in Your Past Can Lead You to a More Abundant Life* (Colorado Springs: WaterBrook, 2000), 195.

9. Ibid., 197.

10. Ibid.

11. See: Center on the Developing Child (2013). *The Science of Neglect* (InBrief). Retrieved from developingchild.harvard.edu.

12. Karyn B. Purvis, *Trust-Based Relational Intervention Caregiver Training, Correcting Principles* (Fort Worth Texas: TCU Institute of Child Development, 2013).

13. Bruce D. Perry and Oprah Winfrey, *What Happened to You? Conversations on Trauma, Resilience, and Healing* (New York: Flatiron Books, 2021), 201, 208.

14. Reimer, *Soul Care*, 249.

## CHAPTER 10 | THE SOUL TAKES THE HIT

1. Dan B. Allender, *The Healing Path: How the Hurts in Your Past Can Lead You to a More Abundant Life* (Colorado Springs: WaterBrook, 2000).

2. John Ortberg, *Soul Keeping: Caring for the Most Important Part of You* (Grand Rapids, MI: Zondervan, 2014), 46.

3. Ibid.

4. Ibid.

5. Parker J. Palmer, *Let Your Life Speak: Listening for the Voice of Vocation* (San Francisco: John Wiley & Sons, 2000), 30.

6. Mark Rutland, *Courage to Be Healed: Finding Hope to Restore Your Soul* (Lake Mary, FL: Charisma House, 2019), 10.

7. Ibid.

8. Johns Hopkins Medicine, "Forgiveness: Your Health Depends On It," https://www.hopkinsmedicine.org/health/wellness-and-prevention /forgiveness-your-health-depends-on-it.

9. Rob Reimer, *Soul Care: 7 Transformational Principles for a Healthy Soul* (Franklin, TN: Carpenter's Son Publishing, 2016), *191*.

10. John Mark Comer, *Live No Lies: Recognize and Resist the Three Enemies That Sabotage Your Peace* (New York: WaterBrook, 2021), 66.

11. Bruce McNicol, Bill Thrall, and John Lynch, *The Cure: What if God Isn't Who You Think He Is and Neither Are You?* (Chicago: Trueface Publishers, 2011), 21–35.

12. Don Colbert, *Stress Less* (Lake Mary, FL: Siloam Publishers, 2005), 6–8.

13. Bruce D. Perry and Oprah Winfrey, *What Happened to You? Conversations on Trauma, Resilience, and Healing* (New York: Flatiron Books, 2021), 178.

14. Saundra Dalton-Smith, *Sacred Rest: Recover Your Life, Renew Your Energy, Restore Your Sanity* (Brentwood, TN: FaithWords, 2017), 7.

15. Siobhan Colgan, "Beyond Sleep: The 3 Types of Rest You Need to (Fully) Recover," Spartan Life, https://www.spartan.com/blogs/unbreakable-focus /types-of-rest-you-need-to-fully-recover.

16. Ibid.

17. Dalton-Smith, *Sacred Rest*, 47.
18. Ibid.
19. Ibid., 56–58.
20. Ibid., 67.

# When kids need help, you step up.

You have the heart — now get the resources you need with Focus on the Family's Wait No More program.

**WaitNoMore.org**

# GET GUIDANCE AS YOU GUIDE OTHERS.

Need advice to help kids, or just need some help, yourself?
Give us a call — at no cost to you.

Scan here or call
**1-855-711-HELP (4357)**